Campaigning for Life

Campaigning for Life

Campaigning for Life

A Biography of Dorothy Frances Buxton

Petà Dunstan

L

The Lutterworth Press

The Lutterworth Press
P.O. Box 60
Cambridge
CB1 2NT
United Kingdom

www.lutterworth.com
publishing@lutterworth.com

ISBN: 978 0 7188 9539 6

British Library Cataloguing in Publication Data
A record is available from the British Library

First published by The Lutterworth Press, 2018

This book is dedicated to Dorothy's grandchildren
so that, on reading this book, they may be as proud of her
as their grandfather predicted.

These are historic days, which your children's children will
remember with pride & inspiration.

(Charlie Buxton to Dorothy Buxton, 28 June 1919)

Contents

Illustrations

Acknowledgements

I am immensely grateful to the Buxton and Jebb families for allowing me free and unfettered access to all the material in their possession. Those who could recall Dorothy personally were generous in sharing their memories. Without the family's support and trust, this project could not have been begun, let alone completed. They have allowed me to research and write freely and without interference or imposing any pre-conditions as to how I have portrayed and recorded their ancestor. My warm thanks to them all.

My thanks go to the staff at archives where other Buxton and Jebb papers have been deposited. Although I cannot list them all here by name, I am appreciative of their efforts to help me in my research. Librarians and archivists are the unsung heroes of academic research, without whom writers would find their progress impeded or even halted: my thanks to them all.

My dear mother patiently endured me reading chapters to her and supported me with thoughtful observations. Ben Buxton and James Buxton, two of Dorothy's grandsons, kindly read the manuscript prior to publication and gave valuable feedback and encouragement. Any errors in the book however remain entirely my own responsibility.

I am grateful to Lutterworth Press for publishing the book and for all their work in bringing this to fruition.

Abbreviations

For people in the footnotes

Annelore	Annelore Albers Gerstl *(Dorothy's daughter-in-law)*
Aunt Bun	Louisa Jebb *(Dorothy's aunt)*
Aunt Noney	Emily Gilmore *(Dorothy's aunt)*
Charlie	Charles Roden Buxton *(Dorothy's husband)*
David	David Buxton *(Dorothy's son)*
Eglantyne	Eglantyne Jebb *(Dorothy's third sister)*
Eglantyne junior	Eglantyne Roden Buxton *(Dorothy's daughter)*
Emily	Emily Jebb, later Mrs Ussher *(Dorothy's oldest sister)*
Florence	Florence Hawkins *(Charlie & Dorothy's housekeeper)*
Louisa	Louisa Jebb, later Mrs Wilkins *(Dorothy's second sister)*
Noel	Noel Buxton *(Dorothy's husband's brother)*
Richard	Richard Jebb *(Dorothy's older brother)*
Tye	Eglantyne Louisa Jebb *(Dorothy's mother)*
Uncle James	James Gilmore *(Dorothy's uncle by marriage)*
Victoria	Victoria de Bunsen *(née Buxton, Dorothy's husband's sister)*

For primary sources

BFA	Buxton Family Archive, papers held by the Buxton family
BUA	SCF papers, Birmingham University Archives
Davidson	Papers of Archbishop Randall Davidson, LPL
HP	Hammond Papers, held at the Bodleian Library, Oxford
JFA	Jebb Family Archive, papers held by the Jebb family
LPL	Lambeth Palace Library
LMA	London Metropolitan Archives
SCFL	SCF papers at SCF HQ in London
WL	Women's Library, collection held as part of the London School of Economics Library

Introduction

Dorothy Buxton led an unusual and intense life. After an upbringing untypical for a girl in rural Victorian England, she found her voice and her vocation during the First World War, insisting people should be able to read a variety of voices on the conflict engulfing Europe. After the war ended, when hunger and deprivation were widespread in many countries, she blazed a trial as a campaigner for the underprivileged. She was the instigator of the Save the Children Fund in 1919 and became a tireless campaigner for refugees and the oppressed wherever she saw them during the following decades.

Her life was led during times of social and political upheaval. After the relative calm of the late Victorian and Edwardian periods, she lived through two world wars and the economic depression between them; the rise of communism, fascism and Nazism; the attack on the class divisions in British society; and the change in the status and rights of women. In these momentous times, Dorothy was a radical voice, refusing to be silenced when she saw injustice. Married to a politician, she at first saw her role in the world of Westminster politics, but as she grew in confidence she became a vociferous and effective campaigner in her own right in a wider social sense.

Hers is an exciting story. The archive of her life is rich and varied, although not complete, as at various times material has been destroyed, both by her own decision towards the end of her life and by the decision of family members after her death. Yet a sufficient number of letters and papers have survived so that her story can be told partly using her own words. This biography relates the story of a woman's journey, her family and personal life. Yet it is also a paradigm of the journey many of her contemporaries took.

We see in her story how those fighting for better conditions for the poor moved from Victorian paternalism to socialism, from charity to legislation.

We also see how Dorothy, and her husband Charlie, lost confidence in the power of individual action as a way of achieving change. As it was for many others in the ruling class, that belief melted away as institutional and group violence began to dominate European politics in the twentieth century, made possible by the frightening developments in weaponry.

In matters of faith, Dorothy's spiritual beliefs changed and her path represented that of many contemporaries who side-lined dogmatic religion, embracing psychology and individual belief to enlighten their spiritual development. Dorothy's view of God changed over the decades, although her faith never disappeared, but instead transmuted into a variety of expressions.

She would not consciously have called herself a feminist, but in how she led her life she was one of those who forged a space in public life for the voice of women in the twentieth century.

Of all her achievements, Dorothy's most lasting legacy has been Save the Children, of which she was the instigator in April/May 1919. Her sister, Eglantyne Jebb, became a co-founder and in the early 1920s emerged as the charity's public face and several books have been written about her contribution. For reasons explored in this book, however, Dorothy's crucial part in launching Save the Children has been neglected and so in the time of Save the Children's centenary, it needs to be rediscovered and acknowledged.

Dorothy was a complex and compelling character, somewhat of an enigma even to her family. Her son, David, who I was privileged to call a friend in his last years, once wistfully in conversation wondered aloud if anyone could 'explain' his mother to him. Sadly, he is no longer with us to read this book, but my hope is that many others will find answers here to the questions he asked.

Jebb family tree (selected)

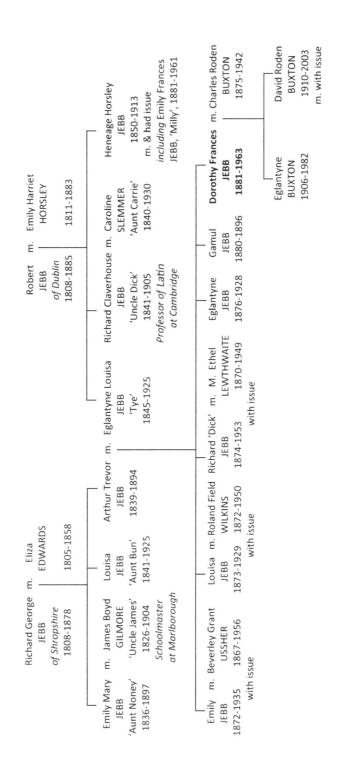

Richard George JEBB of Shropshire 1808-1878 m. Eliza EDWARDS 1805-1858

Robert JEBB of Dublin 1808-1885 m. Emily Harriet HORSLEY 1811-1883

Emily Mary JEBB 'Aunt Noney' 1836-1897 m. James Boyd GILMORE 'Uncle James' 1826-1904 Schoolmaster at Marlborough

Louisa JEBB 'Aunt Bun' 1841-1925

Arthur Trevor JEBB 1839-1894 m. Eglantyne Louisa JEBB 'Tye' 1845-1925

Richard Claverhouse JEBB 'Uncle Dick' 1841-1905 Professor of Latin at Cambridge m. Caroline SLEMMER 'Aunt Carrie' 1840-1930

Heneage Horsley JEBB 1850-1913 m. & had issue including Emily Frances JEBB, 'Milly', 1881-1961

Emily JEBB 1872-1935 m. Beverley Grant USSHER 1867-1956 with issue

Louisa JEBB 1873-1929 m. Roland Field WILKINS 1872-1950 with issue

Richard 'Dick' JEBB 1874-1953 m. M. Ethel LEWTHWAITE 1870-1949 with issue

Eglantyne JEBB 1876-1928

Gamul JEBB 1880-1896

Dorothy Frances JEBB 1881-1963 m. Charles Roden BUXTON 1875-1942

Eglantyne BUXTON 1906-1982

David Roden BUXTON 1910-2003 m. with issue

Buxton family tree (selected)

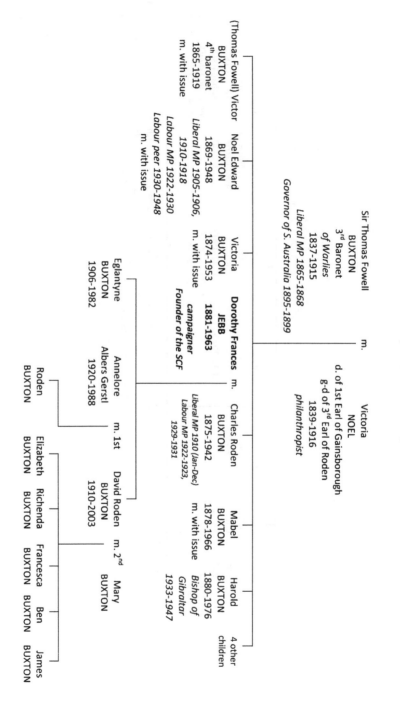

Sir Thomas Fowell
BUXTON
3ʳᵈ Baronet
of Warlies
1837-1915
Liberal MP 1865-1868
Governor of S. Australia 1895-1899

m.

Victoria
NOEL
d. of 1st Earl of Gainsborough
g-d of 3ʳᵈ Earl of Roden
1839-1916
philanthropist

(Thomas Fowell) Victor
BUXTON
4ᵗʰ baronet
1865-1919
m. with issue

Noel Edward
BUXTON
1869-1948
Liberal MP 1905-1906,
1910-1918
Labour MP 1922-1930
Labour peer 1930-1948
m. with issue

Victoria
BUXTON
1874-1953
m. with issue

Dorothy Frances
JEBB
1881-1963
campaigner
Founder of the SCF

m.

Charles Roden
BUXTON
1875-1942
Liberal MP 1910 (Jan-Dec)
Labour MP 1922-1923,
1929-1931
m. with issue

Mabel
BUXTON
1878-1966

Harold
BUXTON
1880-1976
Bishop of
Gibraltar
1933-1947

4 other
children

Eglantyne
BUXTON
1906-1982

Annelore
Albers Gerstl
1920-1988

m. 1st

David Roden
BUXTON
1910-2003

m. 2ⁿᵈ

Mary
BUXTON

Roden
BUXTON

Elizabeth
BUXTON

Richenda
BUXTON

Francesca
BUXTON

Ben
BUXTON

James
BUXTON

Chapter 1
Jebb family life

Dorothy Frances Jebb was born on 3 March 1881 in a house called The Lyth, located in 100 acres of land, near the small town of Ellesmere in Shropshire. By the time that Dorothy was born, the Jebb family had lived at The Lyth for over forty years, Dorothy's grandfather having bought the property in 1838. Richard George Jebb came from a line of Shropshire yeoman farmers, with his mother providing Welsh ancestry and the family's second home, a farmhouse called Tydraw[1], just across the border in Denbighshire, Wales. Dorothy never knew her grandfather, Richard, as he had died in 1878, with her grandmother having long predeceased him. At her birth, the owner of The Lyth was her father, Arthur Trevor Jebb, who had been born in the year after the family purchased the house.[2]

Arthur had been educated at Harrow school and Balliol College, Oxford, but had not distinguished himself academically nor does he seem to have been ambitious. He loved reading and debate, but as an interest rather than a profession. He enjoyed local history and folklore, but he did not pursue them seriously in a literary way and his daughter Emily noted that he never managed to write the books he said he wanted to write.[3] He had trained as a barrister, but seems never to have practised.[4] After his marriage, the arrival of children pushed him to take employment as a civil servant in London to

---

1   This can be translated as 'home over there'.

2   Arthur was not born at The Lyth but at sea, just off the coast at Fleetwood, on a steamboat named Victor. See his census form entries for 1881 and 1891.

3   For this and other points in this chapter, see Emily Ussher (née Jebb), *Notes on our Home and Childhood*, dated 1932, unpublished MS in JFA, as well as other family material. The family background is also covered more chronologically than hereafter in Mahood, chapter 1, pp. 13–33; see also, Mulley, chapter 2, pp. 7–27. Both these books are biographical studies of Dorothy's older sister Eglantyne, but contain much detail about their shared childhood and background.

4   On his 1881 census entry, he described himself as a 'Barrister (on Occasional Practice)'.

provide more income. Yet, as someone who loved home life, he missed his family and they missed him, and after a few years he gave it up to return to The Lyth to manage the estate for his ageing father. Serving his family, the estate and the larger 'family' of Shropshire locals seemed to give him enough to do.

Arthur Trevor Jebb

Although Arthur was a Liberal in politics, he was not a radical, and by instinct was conservative and wary of change. He was also a religious man who took seriously the call to be attentive to the welfare of one's neighbours. He believed in the moral responsibility of those with land and position to be philanthropic with those who were less fortunate. The obligations of class and position were as sacrosanct to him as its privileges and he could not follow those who took a selfish and acquisitive approach to social relations. He was active in charitable causes in Ellesmere, such as the establishment of a local hospital, and he cared for his family's retired servants, as well as those still employed. He did not raise his tenants' rents for his own comfort if they could not afford to pay. He provided his children with a model of self-respect, and showed them how to preserve the inheritance with which they had been blessed, whilst striving to help those who had fewer advantages. Dorothy must have been influenced by her father's outlook as we see it reflected in her life-long struggle to work for the poor and deprived wherever she found them.

Arthur's instincts for philanthropy, however, faced boundaries based on the availability of resources. He could not be generous unless he had accumulated a cushion of wealth to sustain the obligations he felt were his. The prosperity of the Jebbs was not consistently assured or stable as much of the family wealth lay in their land and property holdings, which both provided and absorbed income. There were a dozen servants who worked in the house and on the land who had to be maintained. Agricultural income was unpredictable, with good harvests and bad, that experienced times of both depressed prices and buoyant markets. Inheriting the family estate in

1878, Arthur set out assiduously to save money, going without extras he might have wished to enjoy in order to build up the family's capital. He wanted future generations of Jebbs to feel more secure, as his older son Richard recalled many years later when he noted how the introduction of death duties had hit his father hard. It meant some of what he had so painstakingly saved up would be lost at his death.[1]

The Jebbs were not without income, but the upkeep of the estate and the necessities of local philanthropy dictated by their moral sense of being leaders in their local community meant that they were far less cash-rich than they might have appeared to a casual outsider. Therefore, in recording that Dorothy came from a comfortable background, it must be remembered that, whilst she had many privileges and a given position in local society, hers was not a childhood of untold luxury or opulence. Her later traits of economic and careful budgeting can be traced to the path her family trod of maintaining the essentials of a prosperous life whilst diligently managing expenditure.

Dorothy's mother was also a Jebb, but hailed from the Irish family of that name. Eglantyne Louisa Jebb, always known in the family as 'Tye', was born in 1845 in the Kilkenny area near Dublin. Her ancestors included Irish clerics, barristers and MPs and her father was a judge. They were not a rich family, yet it was said Tye's mother was adept at making others think her household had more money than it actually did. Tye's father and Arthur's father were friends from school days and sharing a surname, they were convinced that they were distant relations, even if no-one ever established the precise genealogical connexion. Having known each other from teenage years, Tye and Arthur married in Dublin in 1871 and Tye moved to Shropshire to her husband's family home. She was not 'the lady of the house' at first, as her father-in-law was still alive and the household was run efficiently by his unmarried daughter, Louisa. Arthur and Tye had a happy marriage, producing six children in their first decade together: Emily (Emm) in 1872, Louisa (Lill) in 1873 and Richard (Dick) in 1874 were the first three; they were followed by Eglantyne in 1876, Gamul in 1879 and Dorothy in 1881. Although Arthur had been based in London for a couple of years, he had been long-established back at The Lyth by the time Dorothy was born. Her parents were both interested

---

1   'You are right in thinking that Father was continually striving to save money for our benefit, and thereby spoiling his own life. I can well understand now the shock it was to him – it seemed so strange at the time – when Harcourt [the then Chancellor of the Exchequer] introduced . . . Death Duties. It meant to him the extinction at once of several years' savings.' Letter from Richard (Dick) Jebb to unknown – probably Emily Ussher, (née Jebb), 24 March 1931, Box 7, 7EJB/B/01/02/06, WL.

in, and affectionate to, their offspring. Tye in particular loved being a mother and she maintained a strong bond with all her children to the end of her life.

One of the qualities that attracted Arthur most about Tye was her intelligence and he ensured she understood how The Lyth and its estate ran. He may have retained the dominant authority as the male in the marriage, but Arthur did regard his wife as a partner and not simply as an ornament or a mere vehicle to fatherhood. Even after Arthur inherited the estate in 1878, Tye's sister-in-law continued to run The Lyth. Tye seems not to have minded this as it allowed her to concentrate on her children, and the two women had an amicable, supportive and understanding relationship. Without the encumbrance of the detailed management of the household, Tye was free to develop other interests and this gave an opportunity for her life to take an unexpected turn.

Tye's own education had included art classes at the Royal Dublin Society's School of Art and she passed on to her children her appreciation of drawing and painting, as well as poetry and literature. She saw the creativity of art in its widest sense as a source of happiness. The early 1880s were a time when, inspired by William Morris and John Ruskin, the idea took hold that the working-class – both urban and rural – could improve their lives by learning handicrafts. For Tye, the idea of helping working-class children experience a more fulfilling life was based on the belief that learning craft skills was not only important, but could also provide an avenue to earning extra income.

In 1882, she founded a charity, which later was named the Home Arts and Industries Association (HAIA), the initial purpose of which was to teach local children crafts. The servant's hall at The Lyth became a classroom, where woodcarving, spinning and weaving, chair-caning and painting were taught. This was not just a practical pursuit for Tye, but a religious one too. It was her way of serving God and living out her Christian faith: to help others to help themselves, to improve their economic circumstances, as well as their self-worth. It sprang from a similar moral imperative that guided her husband's philanthropy. The Association soon spread as other volunteers set up similar schemes, first in Shropshire and then in other counties. Tye wrote articles and began to travel to give talks as she appeared to have found her purpose in a more public domain. By 1887, the Association had become a national one, gaining the support of William Morris[1] and other artists, and it held annual exhibitions in London of work produced in tens of HAIA branches.

However, by that year Tye was no longer at its helm. In the public domain, there is no escaping politics and she over-stepped a boundary when she decided to concentrate on her native Ireland for her own contributions to the cause.

1   William Morris (1834–96).

She was a supporter of Home Rule for Ireland, a controversial opinion for someone in her position and one not shared by her husband, and her initiative in her native land soon attracted attention from some Irish republicans, with whom she was in touch. This alarmed her closest male relatives. Her brother Richard[1] was a professor of Greek at the University of Cambridge (and later a Conservative MP for the same) and made his unhappiness with the situation known. Tye's husband, Arthur, who initially had been supportive of her HAIA work, was equally concerned. He parted company with the Liberal leader, William Gladstone,[2] on the issue of Irish Home Rule and his own political stance locally was compromised by his wife's public opposition of his view. He began to pressure Tye and in 1884, just two years after she had begun the charity, she stepped back from serious involvement. She still took some local classes, but otherwise withdrew from the cause.

The official reason given for her withdrawal was poor health. Although she was still young, in her late thirties, in the following years she suffered from weight loss, nausea and dizziness. There is no evidence of any physical malady afflicting her, however it may well be that her symptoms were stress-related or perhaps signs of depression and for the rest of her life she remained 'frail'. She was active in the sense of walking and travelling, and she lived to be eighty years old; yet, she was never 'well enough' again to take on responsibilities or duties beyond a limited personal sphere. Whether conscious or unconscious, her reaction to criticism had been absolute and irrevocable. Even after her husband's death, she did not resume the activity that he had not approved in life. She had surrendered her 'purpose' to appease her husband's anxieties, mainly because she loved him so much. Dorothy herself was only three when her mother's public work ceased so she had no direct personal memory of these events. However, the mother she grew up with was the Tye who was thin and delicate and not very well. Emily noted that Tye needed 'constant attention' and Dorothy never knew her mother except in this condition. As we shall see, the retreat to safety behind a call of ill-health would be something that would have similar echoes in Dorothy's life. Tye's setting aside her public cause meant her focus shifted even more onto her children. Later in life, she told her daughter Emily that she had prayed for many, many years that her daughters would all find happiness by having a sense of purpose. Clearly, she did not want them to experience the frustrations of being thwarted that had been her lot and to foster this sense of purpose, Tye knew they needed a broad education.

---

1 Richard Claverhouse Jebb (1841–1905), Professor of Greek, Glasgow University 1873–85, Regius Professor of Greek at the University of Cambridge 1889–1905.
2 William Ewart Gladstone (1809–98), Liberal Prime Minister 1868–74, 1880–85, February–July 1886, 1892–94.

Whilst the two boys went away to school once old enough, the girls were tutored at home. Everyone had to be up and downstairs by 7.30a.m. for family prayers and breakfast. Both took place in the library and lessons began straight afterwards. There was, Emily related, 'no evasion' of the schoolroom routine. In the evening, after dinner and family prayers, all were in bed by 10.00p.m. at the latest. All year round, this scholarly regime was maintained. It started while the girls were young. Dorothy was very keen to keep up with her older siblings and, at aged three, insisted on doing lessons when the five-year old Gamul began them. A week later she was 'learning her ABCD'.[1] There was no shortage of intellectual stimulation and Dorothy's lively mind thrived on it as there were books everywhere, not just in the library. When mixing with other children from the neighbourhood in summer classes, Dorothy came top of her group.[2]

Emily wrote that outside the home the girls were taken to the local Literary Society in Ellesmere, where debates would be attended by solicitors, farmers, the Anglican parson and the congregational minister, along with the stationmaster, clerks, basket-makers, workmen on the rail line, the 'man from the boot shop', and an array of other locals. The subjects on which the discussions were held ranged from state socialism, agriculture and commerce, to the trade in alcohol and Home Rule for Ireland. Emily noted that the 'children kept quiet and listened',[3] yet there was much to stimulate them when thinking about politics. On one occasion, when the family took along their then German governess, the somewhat narrow and self-congratulatory nature of the local society was on show, with one woman delivering, without notes, a 'most fluent & remarkable address on "England's greatness"'. To the enquiry as to the qualities that made British people superior, the witty governess quipped 'conceit'![4] However quiet they were expected to be, this local debating society must have been a window for the Jebb siblings to view the political issues of the day. It was certainly an early stimulus for Dorothy's future interest and pursuit of political causes.

Trips out were not only to intellectual gatherings. Emily related that they all attended dances, once of an age to do so, which lasted until midnight, with quadrilles, lancers, waltzes and polkas sprinkled in with old country dances in which the oldest to the youngest could take part. Dorothy was too serious to find these exciting, but she went along with what was

---

1 Children's letter, 10 May 1884; and children's letter from 'Egland' to 'Um' (Eglantyne to Emily), 18 May 1884, Box 6, 7EJB/B/01/02/01, WL.

2 Eglantyne to Aunt Noney, July 1892, JFA.

3 Emily Ussher (née Jebb), *Notes on our Home and Childhood*, dated 1932, unpublished MS, JFA.

4 Emily to Aunt Noney & Uncle James, 28 February 1896, JFA.

expected. She recalled one occasion with a tone of resigned amusement, 'There was a fancy dress dance at the Chapmans the other day. . . . An ancient dress of some ancestress was rigged up for me & my hair puffed out in a great erection over my head, with the result that even Mrs Tower did not recognize me for some time!'[1]

Back at home, Tye led the girls in drawing and art, and her sister-in-law grounded them in grammar. They had governesses from Europe to teach them other subjects and languages, the most influential being Heddie Kastler from Alsace-Lorraine, with whom Dorothy corresponded for the rest of their lives.[2] Dorothy was less keen on her than Eglantyne was, remembering her as 'the terror of my life', who was 'full of temper and strictness'.[3] The replacement was a German woman, who proved less terrifying, the young Dorothy declaring, 'It is so nice doing lessons with Fraulein, she never gets cross!'[4] The girls' education was not a matter purely of formal lessons, but also a general encouragement to read and write and paint. It was a matter of arousing curiosity about ideas and seeking knowledge. Dorothy would maintain this enthusiasm to the end of her days.

Tye's role was to infuse her daughters with her artistic and intellectual interests and, just as significantly, a religious sensibility. She and her husband were both Anglicans and brought up their children accordingly and Dorothy was confirmed by the Bishop of Lichfield on 26 February 1896 just before her fifteenth birthday, after instruction with the local curate.[5] Religion was not a matter purely of outward conformity to the Jebbs. It was about living out values and having a relationship with God. Daily prayers at the beginning and end of the day were compulsory for all the children and they were brought up to know the Bible. Tye had all the children learn by heart I Corinthians 13, the passage about the nature of love.[6] Arthur's religion remained conventional low-church evangelical, but his wife, whilst adhering to the same path, added a touch of exoticism and for a while, Tye explored the Catholic Apostolic Church. This had begun as an eclectic group in London in the 1830s who combined evangelical fervour

---

1   Dorothy to Richard, 12 January 1898, JFA.
2   Heddie Kastler was a proud Alsatian. She did not approve of the German annexation from France of Alsace-Lorraine (the provinces where she was born) following the 1870 Franco-Prussian War. She spoke both French and German and taught them to her charges. She later went to the USA, but returned to Europe to look after her brothers in the 1930s. She lived in France in her final years. See Heddie to Dorothy, 22 December 1935, BFA.
3   Dorothy to Miss Pullen, 1 April 1935, Box 14, 7EJB/B/C/02, WL.
4   Emily to Aunt Noney and Uncle James, 28 February 1896, JFA.
5   Tye to Aunt Noney, 27 February 1896, JFA.
6   Eglantyne to Aunt Bun, 7 Nov 1925, Box 6, 7EJB/B/01/02/03, WL.

with prophecy – members were led by a set of 'apostles' and some spoke in tongues. By the late nineteenth-century, it had developed an elaborate and rich liturgy and built a grand cathedral in Gordon Square in London.[1] Dorothy remembered her mother taking her to one of the services when she was about ten and she herself heard some of the congregation speak in tongues.[2] Tye certainly became convinced for a while that the advent of the new apostles predicated the 'end of the world', perhaps within her lifetime. Tye joined the CAC in the mid-1890s[3] and, although this attachment did not last long, it illustrates her adventurous nature in exploring religion. She never abandoned the basic tenets or practices of her Anglican faith, but she did explore other avenues of expression. Tye was not a spiritualist, but she became increasingly convinced of her connexion with the 'next world'. Religion for her was not just about right-living, duty or ritual, but about using the imagination to penetrate another realm. All this would influence Dorothy in her spiritual journey as an adult.

For Tye, this religious awakening was another aspect of her determination to educate her daughters to do something useful with their lives and contribute to society. Yet, for all her encouragement and all her love and attention and maternal concern, Tye was nevertheless also somewhat passive, cheering from the side-lines the girls' explorations rather than being at the centre of the action. Her 'delicate' health meant she was more a model for sitting on the sofa dreaming of achievement, reading and thinking about it, rather than an example of vigour and engagement.

For Dorothy and her sisters there was, however, an alternative and perhaps even more influential female role-model. Their father's sister, Louisa, known by them all as Aunt Bun, was the most powerful personality at The Lyth. As already noted, she ran the household for her father and then for her brother and sister-in-law. No one questioned her doing this as she was clearly the best-suited and most adept at fulfilling the role. She was called 'masculine' by her niece Emily; not for Bun the delicacies and sensitivities of the archetypal Victorian woman. She would never be 'dependent' or 'clingy'. In dress, she had no time for frills and bows. Whatever she did, Bun wore the same clothes: a man's linen collar and tie with a long dark jacket.

---

1   It died out during the twentieth century. The last surviving of the 'Apostles' was Francis Valentine Woodhouse (1805–1901) and after his death no further priestly ordinations could take place. It was assumed the 'world was to end' soon and to provide for the continuation of their church was therefore unnecessary. The last priest in the UK died in 1971 and the membership faded away. The Catholic Apostolic Church survived in other parts of Europe as an evangelical church, having shed the rich liturgical inheritance from the Victorian 'Apostles'.

2   Memorandum by Dorothy, dictated 19 May 1962, BFA.

3   Wilson, p. 76.

Louisa Jebb, 'Aunt Bun'

Her only nods to traditional feminine dress were the long dark skirt, instead of trousers, and an occasional brooch. She wore her hair in a shorter style.

Intellectually she was educated and articulate, and was a strong proponent of access to higher education for women, having been one of the pioneers at Newnham College, Cambridge. She played an equal role with Tye in teaching the girls their lessons at home. When the time came, she paid for their tertiary education out of her own income, even when it meant opposing the inclinations of their father who thought that his daughters should stay at home until they married. Bun might have followed an educational career herself had it not been for the draw of country life at The Lyth. Also, her religious and political views were not sympathetic with those of most educational institutions for women. An adherent of the theory of evolution, she was also an agnostic in religion and a radical liberal in politics (although she was far from being a socialist). She was a supporter of female suffrage and had no reason to think of women as in any way a weaker or lesser sex.

She believed strongly in every woman being free to do things for herself and she showed her nieces that a woman did not have to wait for a man to do them for her. She had a workroom in a disused back bedroom at The Lyth and showed the girls how to carve and engrave, how to weave baskets and work in leather or metal. She also taught them domestic skills: when she took them to the family's Welsh home, Tydraw, they went without servants and the children made their own beds, cooked food, cleared the table and washed up for themselves – with the help of the governess and Aunt Bun.[1] According to Emily, Bun taught her nieces how to use boomerangs, kites, popguns, bows and arrows, toboggans, stilts, fishing nets and anything else that caught their eye. She took them on long walks, taught them about nature, how to fish and to ride, and then took them further afield to see castles and Roman ruins. In the family letters that survive from the 1890s, we find Dorothy learning to swim, row and punt aged eleven – indeed she

---

1   Eglantyne to Aunt Noney, [no day] July 1892, JFA.

The Lyth, about 1900

could punt all alone in every direction at this age.[1] She tried skating.[2] She could also ride a tricycle[3] and a horse,[4] and was adventurous in exploring the outside world. Much of this zest came from Bun, who was practical and resourceful and, above all, unafraid. From Bun, Dorothy learned to be intrepid and to take risks, not to believe anything was forbidden her because of her sex and never to fear thinking for herself.

The family were not the only influence on the young Dorothy. There were also her surroundings. The Lyth was a large house with some grand entertaining rooms, set amidst acres of farm land. The original owner of the house, a man called Mathews, had made money in the West Indies and built The Lyth in 1819 in Caribbean style. He had clearly meant the unusual house to impress – the entertaining rooms on the ground floor at least. The morning room was decorated with Dufour[5] wallpaper from Paris, portraying classical scenes, full of young women in floaty costumes and noble Romans in helmets. Eighteenth-century tapestries by John Vanderbank[6] hung in the dining room.[7] He commissioned a lofty cast-

---

1   Eglantyne to Aunt Noney, 12 August 1892, JFA.
2   Eglantyne to Emily, 19 January 1890, WL, Box 6, 7EJB/B/01/02/02.
3   Eglantyne to Aunt Bun, 2 October 1892, JFA.
4   Dorothy to Tye, 19 March 1893, JFA.
5   The French company of Joseph Dufour et Cie was founded in 1797 in Mâcon. They were successful with both panoramic and repeating wallpapers.
6   John Vanderbank (1694–1739).
7   The house was Grade II listed on 27 May 1953: see http://www.britishlistedbuildings.

iron verandah around three sides, and deep windows to the floor in the rooms bordering on the garden. When the Jebbs took over, it is of note that the new owners implemented no grand schemes to re-model the house, or indulge in plush re-decorating in the latest fashion, a sign of both conservatism and a lack of means. Consequently, the house's main ground-floor rooms remain today much as they were when Dorothy was a child.

Yet it was not a luxurious residence. It was cold in winter, with the household all washing in a morning from basins containing ice. Although they 'dressed' for dinner, the evening meals were usually 'meagre' according to Dorothy's older sister Emily. The large tapestried dining-room – which Emily wrote of as 'romantic' – was little used except at Christmas and for significant social gatherings. Most family meals were taken in the smaller library, which was easier to keep warm. So, whilst outwardly comfortably off and a part of the rural land-owning class, the Jebbs only maintained their position by careful use of the funds they had.

The Lyth was an exceptional house not just in its interior appearance, but in its gardens too. The long windows beneath the verandah let in much light to the ground-floor rooms whilst opening out so simply into the garden: one was the continuation of the other. Emily wrote of the trellis 'festooned by clematis and roses'. Japonica, jasmine and magnolia mingled in covering exterior walls. The climax of the colour and glamour of the garden came in June with tree peonies, rhododendrons, azaleas and white broom all combining to create an inspiring display. The whole scene invited Dorothy and her siblings out into the garden, an exciting contrast to the hours with their noses in books. They not only had flowers and leaves to draw, but butterflies and birds. Gamul became fascinated by natural history and Dorothy followed. They spent the late summer of 1892 'continually going about armed with butterfly nets'.[1] They also collected beetles, lichens and mosses.[2] Dorothy grew up half living outside, a passion that never left her, and was always frustrated when she had to stay indoors because of the weather.[3] Many early letters mention her gardening.[4] She fell in love with it and it became a significant means of relaxation for her

---

co.uk/en-260784-the-lyth-ellesmere-rural-shropshire-england accessed 24 January 2014. The house, including the rare French wallpaper, has been lovingly preserved (and restored where required) by succeeding generations of the Jebb family.

1   Eglantyne to Aunt Noney, [no day], September 1892, JFA.
2   Eglantyne to Aunt Noney, 28 January 1893, JFA.
3   For example, Dorothy to Eglantyne, 29 November 1895, JFA. In this letter from her aunt in Hallam, she bemoaned that she had to 'stay indoors & grizzle myself' in a stuffy room' when she wanted to go out to see the hounds. Eventually she was allowed to go out 'with a waterproof & ammoniated quinine'.
4   For example, Dorothy to Aunt Noney, 22 March 1896, JFA: 'We have all been very busy gardening the last week'.

throughout her life. At fourteen, she was knowledgeable about pruning in the kitchen garden, so much so that she taught two of her older siblings the art of currant and gooseberry bushes, before going on to apple and pear trees.[1] She came so to love the outdoors that she revelled in later life in sleeping under the stars whenever the chance came.

Then there were the creatures both wild and domestic that inspired her. She loved to watch birds and took a telescope around with her to see them closer.[2] She became attached to birdsong and wrote of the sensation that came over her when she heard the first thrushes and chaffinches of the year. She called it a 'bit of the glory', 'the dream'. She added, 'But you people who have not got a very particular pal in every sparrow, might not understand that.'[3] It was as if Dorothy, even at this young age, related to nature in a somewhat mystical or spiritual way and that tendency manifested itself in the beliefs she would espouse later in life. The life she observed in nature was a comfort to her: she wrote in 1897 of how whenever she felt lonely and needy, 'there are usually a few trees & sparrows & there are enough' to give her solace.[4] Louisa kept poultry and it was Dorothy who took charge of them when her big sister was away – and she took the duty seriously, reading a book on the subject to ensure she did it properly.[5] She took on feeding two lambs that had lost their mother.[6] In the summer of 1896, aged fifteen, Dorothy also learned how to look after a dog. A friend of the family had bought a puppy and left it temporarily at The Lyth. Dorothy wrote excitedly to an aunt, 'I have just got a new animal, a lovely animal, such as I have always longed for, i.e. a dear, big, ungainly mastiff puppy, who is to be under my care for six weeks.'[7] The dog was named Lion. Within two days of its arrival, Emily wrote that it 'absorbed a great deal' of her youngest sister's 'intellect'.[8] Eglantyne later wrote, 'Outside lessons Dorothy is now rarely to be seen without Lion as an appendage: the dog grows bigger & bigger every day, he is now a huge thing. I don't know whether Dorothy will break her heart when he goes away.'[9] In mid-October, Lion did have to leave, much to Dorothy's sorrow.[10] The episode with the dog was another characteristic example of Dorothy being totally absorbed and committed to the task in hand. With all the animals that she cared for,

1   Dorothy to Aunt Noney, 4 January 1896, JFA.
2   Eglantyne to Aunt Noney, 28 January 1893, JFA.
3   Dorothy to Eglantyne, [no day], February 1897, JFA.
4   Dorothy to Eglantyne, no date but probably 1897, JFA.
5   Eglantyne to Aunt Noney, 11 June 1893, JFA.
6   Dorothy to Aunt Noney, 22 March 1896, JFA.
7   Dorothy to Aunt Noney, 16 August 1896, JFA.
8   Emily to Aunt Noney and Uncle James, 14 August 1896, JFA.
9   Eglantyne to Aunt Noney, 27 September 1896, JFA.
10 Dorothy to Aunt Noney, 18 October 1896, JFA.

she read and learned about the task before her and then expedited it with complete dedication. Even as a teenager, she could not engage in anything half-heartedly, especially when caring for another life.

We can see the stirrings of another of Dorothy's adult interests that began in her childhood. To curiosity aroused from books and from nature was added the awakening that came from travel, something that helped counter any tendency there might have been to rural isolation. The children regularly took trips to Tydraw in Wales, to her Aunt Noney and Uncle James at Hallam, near Marlborough, and also, after 1893, to Aunt Bun's new holiday home, called Rocaburn, near Bridgwater in Somerset. In 1896, when she was fifteen, came Dorothy's first trip to Ireland, accompanied by her oldest sister, Emily. This proved a very exciting experience for the teenager. During the sea crossing, she became enchanted by the captain, who taught her various nautical phrases, introduced her to the machinery and let her see the boat's 'big paddle'. They stayed for an enjoyable week in Dublin, where they saw 'a great deal'[1] and where Dorothy announced very early in the sojourn that 'seeing the world was very nice indeed'. Emily wondered if she would ever be able to get her sister home again![2] They spent some time travelling to friends in other parts of the south of Ireland, before returning home. This trip wetted her appetite for travel and Dorothy would later write in a letter to Eglantyne, 'How I do long to travel; I never read about a place but I am dieing [sic] to go there straight away'.[3]

Dorothy's companions in all these doings were her siblings. To them she was 'Dora', the little sister they protected, petted and entertained. Emily remembered that all six got on well and were not known to have fallen out. There was too much space and too much to explore for them to get in each other's way. Eglantyne was the nearest sister in age to Dorothy, just five years older, and they formed a special bond. Eglantyne took Dorothy and also Gamul (Dorothy's senior by two years) under her wing, inventing stories that she either told or they re-enacted, some of which would go on for weeks, some related in a family magazine they produced: *The Brierland Recorder*. She was their leader, creating,

> wonderful games of soldiers, of kings, robbers, of desert islands & discovery; – the old trees in the garden turned into our 'castles'. Indoor games, too, of endless variety and excitement, notably the charades which were always a feature of our Xmas time. She always inspired and composed these.[4]

1   Dorothy to Aunt Noney, 23 April 1896, JFA.
2   Emily to Aunt Noney & Uncle James, 19 April 1896, JFA.
3   Dorothy to Eglantyne, undated but probably 1897, JFA.
4   Dorothy to Miss Pullen, 1 April 1935, Box 14, 7EJB/B/C/02, WL.

Eglantyne, Gamul & Dorothy with their Aunt Noney, 1889

They were thrilled by their sister's stories. Their habit as they listened of hanging on each of Eglantyne's arms led to a striking image. 'One of father's sporting friends looked back at them in a gig as they drove back from Tydraw. He said they were like a "covey of partridges" as Gamul and Dorothy each clung to one of Eglantyne's arms as she told them one of her yarns'.[1] Dorothy was adept at using her imagination independently too, however, and from a young age copied Eglantyne in inventing narratives. When Dorothy was twelve, Eglantyne wrote: 'The little Towers came over here to tea last Wednesday, & Dorothy amused them by an exciting game of highwaymen, her invention, amongst the bushes on the terrace. Climbing the yews is of course a great attraction, especially in their Sunday dresses.'[2]

In some ways, all her older siblings could be numbered among Dorothy's educators. When Dick was home from school he took her fishing,[3] whilst her sisters were on hand in her youngest days to help her with lessons. Emily helped her particularly with naming plants, German and drawing, and encouraged her with poetry and reading. Louisa (Lill) was more scientific and encouraged her to study nature more systematically. Dorothy joined in with this big sister in studying vegetation under a microscope, and learned as much as she could about the instrument, not just from Lill, but also from a visiting clergyman family friend, for whom the microscope was a serious pastime.[4]

Gamul influenced Dorothy by her following whatever interested him. She began to collect beetles[5] and butterflies and mosses, at first because she

1   Emily Ussher (née Jebb), *Notes on our Home and Childhood,* dated 1932, unpublished MS, JFA.
2   Eglantyne to Aunt Noney, 11 June 1893, JFA.
3   Dorothy to Eglantyne, 6 August [probably 1896], JFA.
4   Dorothy to Eglantyne, 6 August 1896, JFA; Emily to Aunt Noney and Uncle James, 14 August 1896, JFA; Tye to Noney, 16 August 1896; & Louisa to Uncle James, 25 August 1896, JFA.
5   Dorothy to Eglantyne, February 1897, JFA.

was copying his enthusiasms, though later making them her own. Beetles remained a life-long fascination and she was not squeamish about having to search for the special types only found in a decaying animal carcass. Years later she wrote,

> I can remember as a child myself pursuing this search under much larger bodies than that of a hedgehog, when the obstacles of smell etc were really rather formidable. I have often thought since then that those experiences helped me to acquire a certain *scientific* outlook (if that is not too much to claim!) as regards the many things in life before which one's first impulse is to avert one's eyes & to hold one's nose. No, no! let us dig into them & examine them in a detached & observant spirit, searching if there are not by-products of great beauty, like those marvellous beetles, & also many ultimate consequences indispensable to the cycle of glorious life.[1]

Dorothy had learned lessons from Lill's approach and applied them to subjects sparked by Gamul's passion – and the consequence lasted her whole life. So much of her early development then was wrapped up in these relationships with her siblings.

As the years went by in her childhood, these siblings began to leave home and she had to learn to be without their constant presence. Emily studied portraiture in Dresden, Germany; Lill went to Newnham College, Cambridge, to study for an agricultural diploma; Richard, after being away at school, went off to study at the University of Oxford. Eglantyne followed him to the same university in 1894 when Dorothy was thirteen. Gamul went to school at Marlborough where one of the housemasters was his uncle, James Gilmore (husband to his father's sister Emily, or Aunt Noney as she was nicknamed). For Dorothy, this scattering of her siblings was a general withdrawal of companionship for which copious letter-writing could not compensate. A cousin, Kitty Jebb (known as Milly) came to keep her company for a while and share both her lessons and her adventures, but the distancing of the family unit fell hardest on her.

Dorothy's well-being, however, was disturbed by far harder partings than these. First, in December 1894, her father, Arthur, took ill from an infection that turned to pneumonia. He died quickly and unexpectedly aged fifty-five. His youngest child was only thirteen. Many Victorian fathers were distant and quite intimidating to their children, but Arthur had been ever-present, interested in his children and their doings. He read them stories and gave them attention. He was a father who was loved and of whom his children were proud. This was a huge loss to young Dorothy.

1   Dorothy to David, 28 January–4 February 1941, BFA.

Dorothy aged thirteen

Yet more tragedy was to come. At sixteen, her brother Gamul was all set to be a doctor. He was the subject of long debates between his widowed mother and his Aunt Bun as to whether he should read medicine at Oxford or at Cambridge.[1] He was doing outstandingly well at school and was expected to have a brilliant career ahead of him. The teenager, with his dark brown hair and chestnut eyes, was already showing the signs of growing into a handsome and charming man. On 3 March 1896, Dorothy celebrated her fifteenth birthday, writing to her Aunt Noney, 'it is really dreadful to feel so old!'.[2] But a deep maturity would be demanded of her soon after for on the day that Dorothy wrote that letter her mother received word that Gamul had caught a chill at school and it had developed into a serious problem. Tye hurried to her son's bedside

1   Tye to Noney, 27 February 1896, JFA.
2   Dorothy to Aunt Noney, 5 March 1896, JFA.

and summoned a doctor from London. On 10 March she wrote to her other children that although Gamul was in great danger, the situation was not hopeless. She went on,

> I want you all to *rest* in the peace giving assurance that he is in the hands of a Loving Father, and that whether He takes him or leaves him here we may perfectly trust Him to do what is loving & merciful. May God bless you my pets, & make you feel how safe we all are with Him here or elsewhere.[1]

A day later, on 11 March, Gamul died. Tye's approach to her son's death was that it was God's will and whatever sadness and hurt it brought to his family, it was the right thing for Gamul himself – otherwise God would not have let it happen. This must have constrained Dorothy considerably as, if it were God's will, she would have wanted to be 'brave'. As such, her usual routine had to go on and Dorothy continued her lessons the day after Gamul's death. Her mother wrote that she 'has taken the news <u>very</u> bravely and I think she slept a fair amount last night (with me in my room). She is doing her lessons now & at 12 o'clock we are going to put flowers about the rooms for any who may turn up'.[2]

Dick and Lill went with their mother to the funeral at Rhinlas, the little church near the family's Welsh home and where the family burial plot was located – but not Dorothy. Back at home, once more she was referred to as being 'so brave'.[3] The following week, Tye yet again used the same word: 'we must all try to be brave, there is nothing else for it'. Dorothy was being 'very good'.[4] There is no record of tears or anger or lethargy, only a determination and duty to carry on.

All this suggests that Dorothy was controlling the very deep emotions she must have felt about her lost brother. She never forgot Gamul and later in life would say he was one of the inspirations for her work. He had not lived to achieve his 'destiny' – the least his siblings could do was to try to achieve something to compensate for the tragic loss. It was at this time she began to meditate to 'have eyes to see & ears to hear, a heart to understand, & a strength to <u>act</u>'.[5] It was the beginning of her life-long belief that sadness and depression should not be allowed to deflect a person from their chosen

1 Tye to her children, 10 March 1896, JFA.
2 Emily to Aunt Noney and Uncle James, 12 March 1896, JFA.
3 Tye to Noney, 14 March 1896, JFA.
4 Tye to Noney, no date except 'Tuesday afternoon'. It can be presumed from the content that it was written during the week after Gamul's death.
5 Dorothy to David, 10 August 1930, BFA.

path. One must maintain dogged perseverance even when inspiration had fled.[1] This determination seemed to lodge within her during this struggle with grief after Gamul was taken from her.

The death also prompted her to think more about religion. If Christians were not to fear death, then she mused they ought to welcome it – not be sad when it came. Christian doctrine seemed to her to say that death was preferable to the suffering of life and yet people were horrified at death. She mused in a letter written within a year of her brother's death,

> To live seems appalling. To die seems so to some people, but I do not understand that if they are Christians, but then, on the other hand, if one is a proper Christian, to live ought not to be so. A lack of faith seems to be at the bottom of unhappiness, & that makes one still more unhappy to be unhappy, & so on.[2]

These are thoughtful words for a young girl not quite sixteen and they convey the sense of Dorothy's pain and yet also her belief that using her will could conquer it. If she had enough faith, she could overcome unhappiness. Above all she saw her duty as to embrace life. Yet the pain of loss must have still been there buried within her by her fierce will to rise above it. In the short term, her only refuge was to seek comfort in normality and pursue in particular her education. In later years, she would take refuge in concentrated work as an escape from emotional turmoil. Perhaps that habit began when she swallowed the grief at her father's and brother's deaths at such a young age.

Dorothy's education became a preoccupation of her mother's in the autumn of 1896. She had decided that her youngest daughter would benefit from a time away at a school once she turned sixteen. The German governess was to leave by Christmas and then an English one would be employed for a few months with the particular purpose of improving Dorothy's Latin and Greek.[3] Then she could go away to school. Tye decided against Wycombe Abbey School as she thought the town 'slummy' and too near an expanse of water – and she did not take to the head, a Miss Dove.[4] Eventually she decided on Grassendale School at Southbourne near Bournemouth.[5] To prepare Dorothy, a Miss

---

1   Dorothy to David, 18 February 1930, BFA.
2   Dorothy to Eglantyne, February 1897, JFA.
3   Tye to Noney, 1 November 1896, JFA.
4   Tye to Noney, 15 November 1896, JFA.
5   Grassendale School for girls remained open until 1936. Thereafter, the buildings became a Roman Catholic school for boys, first run by the Jesuits (1936–47) and then by the De La Salle brothers. The school amalgamated with others in 1980 and became co-educational. It was still in existence in 2016, the old house that Dorothy would have known being part of its buildings.

Freeman was engaged to live at The Lyth to teach classics and history. [1]
Miss Freeman had taught for three and a half years until she had 'broken
down': she took on this private tutoring role as a way back into working
life. However, life at The Lyth proved too much for her. Emily (Emm),
who was back at home, having created a studio for her painting there,
tried to help. Dorothy wrote of Miss Freeman,

> The fact is that she is such an awful crock that she threatens to
> smash up any day, & has to be taken very great care of! Emmie
> has taken her in hand and rules her entirely, poor Miss F is a little
> rebellious occasionally but has to give in. She does not see the fun
> however of listening to me instead of Emmie in the latter's absence,
> & I have been trying in vain to make her go to bed. Miss F does not
> sleep. . . . Emmie nearly killed her by making her go for long walk
> through deep snow & slush to Hardwick – tried to tire her out so
> she would sleep. [2]

Miss Freeman soon had to go away and supervised Dorothy 'by letter'.
She returned, but then had to leave yet again. The travails of her new
governess were not an obstacle to Dorothy working hard, however. She
read Virgil, Cicero and Caesar in Latin and Xenophon in Greek. Miss
Freeman also gave her a New Testament in Greek and Dorothy worked so
intensely that teacher became alarmed; Dorothy wrote that she 'exhorted
me *not to think* so much, if I went on as I was I w[ou]ld knock myself up
in 3 weeks!!' [3] However, Dorothy was anxious to seize her opportunities for
further education, 'I must work hard & make the most of my opportunities.
I feel it is a frightful responsibility, hence my zeal.' [4] Going away to school
was a new adventure and Dorothy welcomed it, reassuring her brother
Dick that it was her decision not just Tye's, 'I look forward to going, it will
be such a new experience, & girls are such an unknown to me, it will be
amusing to see what they are like! . . . As to knowing my own mind, you
need not be afraid.' [5]

The school at Southbourne gave Dorothy a range of new experiences.
In general, she liked the head, a Miss Tucker, [6] and found her sense of order
satisfactory, 'We are all bits of a very well regulated, well oiled, highly

---

1   Emily to Aunt Noney, 10 November 1896, JFA; Tye to Noney, 15 November
    1896, JFA.
2   Dorothy to Eglantyne, 1 February 1897, JFA.
3   Dorothy to Eglantyne, 1 February 1897, JFA.
4   Dorothy to Eglantyne, [no day] February 1897, JFA.
5   Dorothy to Richard, 16 April 1897, JFA.
6   Dorothy to Richard, 26 September 1897, JFA.

respectable machine; worked by Miss Tucker & Co. She pulls the strings & we dance.'[1] Dorothy felt that this restricted the girls as they were all made docile and obedient, but then the head 'berates them for not having initiative'.[2]

For Dorothy, the freer life she was used to at home at The Lyth meant that the restrictions of school hemmed her in, 'Provision being made for one possible idiot among 40 other reasonable beings, one is tied down to a multitude of aggravating rules, & has scarcely a minute to oneself when one can escape from the gong & breathe freely.'[3] There was church 'at least twice' on Sundays[4] and though she would have preferred the pleasure of reading some Cicero rather than listening to sermons, school authorities would have regarded that as unsuitable for the Sabbath.[5] Instead they felt they made a concession by allowing girls to read story-books on Sundays. Dorothy wrote letters instead.[6]

The other girls were interesting when they were serious, but she found their frivolity and lack of concentration trying, 'That is the best of these girls. Get them serious & they are very nice, – only with many of them to get them so is an unsuperable [sic] difficulty.'[7] She found them to be 'children' and 'narrow minded'.[8] She was even glad when a sore throat for a few days saved her from having to join in some of the entertainments and frivolities.[9] Dorothy's seriousness about life and study, and the fact that she intended to go to university, as well as having an uncle who was a Professor at Cambridge, all coalesced to set her apart somewhat from the majority of the other girls at the school,

> It is somewhat unfortunate having Uncle Dick for an uncle. This, combined with the fact that I am going to college, – for the old-fashioned delusion is a force here that College-girls must be clever out of the common, – made them think I must be very clever at least! So I was put into the top-form, without any questioning as to my amount of knowledge or anything! How long I shall remain there I feel very doubtful, though the standard is very low as it happens.[10]

1   Dorothy to Richard, 12 January 1898, JFA
2   Dorothy to Eglantyne, no date, JFA.
3   Dorothy to Richard, 26 September 1897, JFA.
4   Dorothy to Richard, 26 September 1897, JFA.
5   Dorothy to Eglantyne, no date, JFA.
6   Dorothy to Richard, 26 September 1897, JFA.
7   Dorothy to Richard, 5 December 1897, JFA.
8   Dorothy to Eglantyne, 6 February 1898, Box 7, 7EJB/B/01/02/05, WL.
9   Dorothy to Eglantyne, no date, JFA.
10 Dorothy to Richard, 27 September 1897, JFA.

She was also not used to making friends and socialising so was somewhat awkward in the company of so many other girls, 'I am sure there is a lot to know & that they are very nice & all that, but I never get any further with them, – as to making friends with them I have never known how to set about it.'[1]

She had her first taste of taking examinations in December 1897, and she claimed not to be able to carry the information learned at the beginning of the term through to the end. However, 'if one gives reins to one's imagination the results as a rule seem as satisfactory as facts. In work I find I score best where I can invent.'[2] Dorothy did well academically and clearly her demeanour and maturity compared with some of her classmates commended her to the staff, 'I have been made a "head", – that is to say, am supposed to see that other girls keep rules & so on, – & am consequently in a dilemma, as, seeing I don't approve of the system of rules in the school, ought I to keep them myself, – far less see that others do.'[3]

On reflection, Dorothy did not regret her time at Grassendale School. She wrote to Eglantyne that, 'I am very glad I came here' as she believed the school to be an exceptional one,[4] even if the academic standards were not as high as she would have liked. With the year gone, she returned to The Lyth aged seventeen. There was more travel in her continuing education as she and Eglantyne accompanied their Uncle Heneage[5] to Kissingen, Germany, for two months in the summer of 1900, where he had a chaplaincy. However, more disciplined study beckoned: she had determined to go to Newnham College, Cambridge, to study natural sciences.

---

1   Dorothy to Eglantyne, no date, JBA.
2   Dorothy to Richard, 5 December 1897, JFA.
3   Dorothy to Eglantyne, no date, JFA
4   Dorothy to Eglantyne, no date, JFA.
5   Heneage Horsley Jebb (1850–1913) was a brother of Dorothy's mother and Professor Richard Jebb.

Chapter 2
A soul mate

Eglantyne noted to her mother that Dorothy's 'heart was so set upon going to Newnham'.[1] For a young woman as single-minded as Dorothy that could mean only one thing: dedicated preparation so as to meet the criteria for acceptance. Just a few minutes' walk from Newnham College, in a large Victorian house on the corner of Sidgwick Avenue and Queens' Road, called Springfield, was where Richard Claverhouse Jebb lived. He was the uncle who was a Professor of Classics at the University of Cambridge. It was to his house that Dorothy came with her mother on a long visit so that she could prepare very seriously for her entrance examinations.

'Uncle Dick' was a Greek scholar, eminent and clever, but he did not spend all his time in the library or study. He was an active man, happy to take younger members of the family on cycle rides in the fenland countryside. He liked to dress well and enjoyed company, despite his natural shyness and social reserve. In younger days, he had been prone to drink too much in order to overcome his social awkwardness and consequently fell into debt. However, his life had been changed by a marriage to someone very much his opposite, a vivacious American widow. Born Caroline Reynolds, her father had emigrated before her birth to the United States from England so she had family in Britain. She had been previously married to a soldier who fought in the American Civil War and on his premature death, she had distracted herself from her grief by visiting Europe. She ended her travels with a visit to family who lived in Cambridge. There, her outgoing manner and striking looks meant that the widowed Mrs Slemmer created a stir amongst the reserved British bachelor dons. There was an oft-repeated story that in one house she received three marriage proposals during one evening. When challenged about it, she replied that this was not strictly true – as two of the proposals had been in the garden![2] From amidst many suitors, the glamourous American widow accepted a marriage proposal

1   Eglantyne to Tye, 12 May [1901], Box 10, 7EJB/B/01/03/07, WL.
2   See, for example, Mulley, pp. 72–73.

Dorothy about 1900

from Richard Jebb, after three years of dogged persistence on his part. They married in 1874, when both were in their middle thirties, and Caroline soon put his finances in order, limited his alcohol consumption and organised his social life. Her delight and pride in being married to someone of his academic prowess, and his utter joy at having such an outgoing and dazzling wife, meant their 'marriage of opposites' worked well. Sadly for them both, they had no children of their own and consequently loved to be involved with their nephews and nieces. For Dorothy, her 'Aunt Carrie' was a lively and warm presence, who was happy to introduce the serious young woman to a wider circle. Her Uncle Dick was keen to encourage her further studies, being a supporter of female education and women's suffrage, and he was a supporter of her academic aspirations.[1]

1   This was despite his affiliation to the Conservative Party, which he represented in

From the narrower and more sheltered life of a Shropshire country town and the confines of a Bournemouth school, Dorothy was open to a different world where the power of ideas and arguments would excite her and she would meet a greater variety of both people and views. She was enthusiastic and determined to learn and was supervised one-to-one by an academic tutor, commenting 'I am getting lessons twice a week from a Newnham Don, so I am beginning work in College very early in the day. She is a nice little person.'[1] These pre-Newnham days were not all study, however: Dorothy noted in another letter how her mentor, Miss Sharpley, had taken her to see Jesus College chapel and then on to tea in the combination room at Newnham, where she was surrounded by a 'crowd of dons & Newnham authorities'.[2] It was an opportunity to meet a botanist and a physicist who she expected to be her teachers once she started her course.

All this academic preparation was done in the context of living near family and was a situation that would continue throughout her undergraduate years. For Dorothy's mother, Tye, the prospect of her youngest child, Dorothy, 'leaving the nest' to go to Cambridge had prompted her mother to consider her own living arrangements. Her son, who had inherited The Lyth, had married in 1900 and lived elsewhere when he was not travelling. Emily, the eldest daughter, had married Beverley Ussher[3] in 1898 and was living in London.[4] It would not be long before the other daughters developed lives away from Shropshire. Tye felt it was time to move and so why not Cambridge go to where her beloved brother lived? She asked her children what they thought: most importantly, Eglantyne, who she now insisted should give up teaching (which her daughter did not particularly enjoy) and be her companion. The response was positive.

> Just personally speaking, I should love to live at Cambridge, & that is all I had better say until you hear from Dick & Lill, who have greater stakes in the matter. You *are* a very dear Mother. You know there is no difficulty in creating a happy home, as the one thing necessary is that you should be in it yourself.[5]

---

the House of Commons for some years as a University MP. Many Conservatives were less sympathetic to women's emancipation.

1   Dorothy to Richard, 'Sunday', no date, JFA.
2   Dorothy to Richard, 'Friday', no date, JFA.
3   Beverley Grant Ussher (1867–1956). At one time a professor of philosophy, he was an inspector of schools in 1897–1914.
4   When Beverley retired in 1914, he and his family retired to Cappagh House, Waterford, in Ireland.
5   Eglantyne to Tye, 12 May [1901], Box 10, 7EJB/B/01/03/07, WL.

Richard and Louisa did not raise objections either. The only person discomforted by this proposal was Aunt Bun, but she removed herself from The Lyth to live in a house at nearby Lee, whilst Tye moved her household to Cambridge in the summer of 1901. The Lyth was rented out. The house that Tye took a lease on in Cambridge was called Inchmaholm, situated in Adams Road, off Grange Road, a location then at the outskirts of the city.[1] This was very near Newnham College, as well as her brother's home. This move meant that throughout her undergraduate years Dorothy was able to see and spend time with her mother and sister, Eglantyne, very easily. It facilitated close companionship with Eglantyne, in particular, who remained her best friend as well as sister. She referred to her as 'my beloved own', soon abbreviated to 'Ownie'.

On matriculation in 1901, Dorothy had decided initially to study science, rooted in her love of the natural world. She had written a manual for teachers of botany with Louisa in 1899 called *Observations on plant life*, which was published in 1903. This scientific path was not an end in itself for her, but a foundation course. She noted, 'My plan had been to do a course of Nat[ura]l Science as a preliminary to psychology, ethics etc'[2] as she wanted her study of human behaviour to be rooted in natural science. Study was for Dorothy all about a sense of doing what was right, as she indicated to her brother, 'I shall do science when I go up, but I don't expect to enjoy myself very much there. My reasons for going have got very black & white as I take care to have for everything I do now.'[3]

---

1   Inchmaholm was an eccentric dwelling built a decade before for James Frazer, the scholar who was most renowned for writing *The Golden Bough*. According to Eglantyne, it was 'a charming little magic box of a house, small, neat and compact as a Japanese toy', with a library at its heart. As the lease was due to run out on Inchmaholm in July 1907, Tye had a house built nearby that she called Laharde, where she lived until around 1910, after which she and Eglantyne spent some years travelling. For the building of Laharde, see Tye to Richard, 13 April 1906: 'Not yet signed my agreement for the plot of land – but it's being drawn up – & I think we have pretty well decided about the plan of the house.: and, 29 June 1906: Our agreement with St John's is at last signed under satisfactory conditions, – and now our architect has fallen ill, & is going for a month to Norway. However according to the rate of recent housebuilding there should still be plenty of time before our lease expires (July 1, 07) & the more I think about it the more I believe it is really the best plan. It is quite a common or garden thing among my friends & acquaintances here to do it – three have just finished & two more are hoping to begin. I only hope too many houses won't be built, for then it c[oul]d go down as an investment – however the number of sites round here is limited, and this seems to be considered the most desirable neighbourhood nowadays – being comparatively high – & so very conveniently near the town while there is a belt of country likely to remain such on the other side.' Box 10, 7EJB/B/01/03/07, WL.
2   Dorothy to Eglantyne, 'Sunday', no date, JFA.
3   Dorothy to Richard, 'Sunday', no date, JFA.

Study was not about enjoyment, but a means to achieving something in the world. It was about duty and service, not self-satisfaction. Subject choices had to be justified and relevant to long term goals of public and social service. However, she was impatient for results in her first year (1901–02), and as she later scribbled on top of a letter written to her sister Eglantyne, 'I soon found out my *incapacity* for chemistry & even more so for *physics*, & had to *abandon* them.'[1] Dorothy had the keen observational eye helpful to the scientist, but the theoretical and mathematical side in particular of a science course held little fascination. It was too abstract from the problems of the world and her desire to serve. As such, she was not very happy academically in her first year and, encouraged by her sister, Eglantyne, to whom she confided her misery, Dorothy began to explore a possible change of subject.

Tye's ambition that her daughters should achieve something useful meant that Dorothy had the freedom to consider changing to a field of study that was more relevant to understanding social problems, politics and economics. Yet, whilst Dorothy had inherited from her family a sense of responsibility for the poor, this did not mean she had always been sympathetic to them. At fifteen she complained to her absent sister Eglantyne about the labourers on the land at The Lyth,

> At present I am seeking into the possible motive for us to raise the working classes from their horrid state. – the more I have to do with them the more depressing do I find the condition of their morals: – liars, thieves – indifferent lazy beasts. I w[ou]ld give anything not to have to live surrounded by them. This place wh[ich] I adore is half spoilt by its association with them. . . . I think if I had to look after the men I should be sick every day.[2]

It is plain that at this stage of her life, her attitude was somewhat condescending, calling the men 'lazy' and writing that their presence was 'half-spoiling' the place she loved. She did wish to improve the condition, and especially the education, of those she saw as deprived and consequently lacking in motivation. However, it was a moral cause for her at this age, rectifying a wrong, rather than a personal sympathy. Once at Cambridge, she learned more about legislative proposals for helping the poorer members of society, as distinct from simply charitable actions: ideas such as old

1   Dorothy to Eglantyne, 'Sunday', no date, JFA.
2   Dorothy to Eglantyne, no date but people and matters mentioned in it indicate late in 1896, JFA. She went on to record a conversation with one poor labourer: 'My share – James – bussing good-for-nothing is bad enough. To James gazing over a hedge into space instead of working. "Hard at work James?" "Please Mam – looking for someone to ask the time." "Why do you want to know the time?" "Please Mam I don't know."'

age pensions, land reform, political emancipation and wider educational opportunities. She began to realise that if she were to contribute to society, moral sciences were the area she should study, not the natural sciences with which she was struggling.

Dorothy had already been attending lectures, such as those given by Mary Marshall,[1] the first women lecturer at Cambridge, in relevant subjects like political economy and so asked to swop to moral sciences, which also covered ethics and philosophy. She finally managed to have a conversation with Miss Thena Clough,[2] the college administrator, who then sent her to see Mrs Eleanor Sidgwick,[3] the Principal of Newnham. Dorothy related the interview at some length in a letter to Eglantyne, who was away from Cambridge at the time:

> As regards the training of science she agreed with me that the Polit[ical] Econ[omy] was as valuable as that of chemistry. As regards the subject matter – physics had great bearing on metaphysics – & psychology – but on my enquiry whether physiology w[ou]ld not ultimately explain the psychological processes, she replied than [*sic*] *she* herself had no expectation of it. It was indeed the view of the materialists, it *might* be so, – but she thought not – physiology was indeed interesting in connection with psychology but it was only a minor connection. . . .
>
> Mathematics was more valuable as a preliminary than Nat[ural] Science – not only as a training – but for the mathematical laws themselves who govern the Universe. Of course all subjects contributed interest to moral science, & the Philosopher watched everything & availed himself of all discoveries. But the scientific knowledge he required was always in his reach as he went along – & University courses were not necessary to prevent him falling into scientific errors. Philosophers & Moral Scientists had not usually had scientific training. . . .
>
> Her remarks about Philosophy were interesting: – it was only quite in its beginnings – & she did not seem to think that science w[ou]ld give it the forward step. On the whole therefore she was inclined to think that I w[ou]ld do well to take to M[oral] S[ciences] – unless I gave 1 more year to N[atural]S[ciences] – chiefly physiology. [4]

---

1   Mary Marshall (née Paley) (1850–1944).
2   Blanche Athena Clough (1861–1960), niece of Anne Jemima Clough, the first Principal of Newnham, who took on various administrative roles in the College. She became Principal herself 1920–23.
3   Eleanor Mildred Sidgwick (née Balfour) (1845–1936), Vice-Principal of Newnham College, Cambridge, 1880–1892, Principal 1892–1911. Her husband was Henry Sidgwick (1838–1900), a philosopher and economist.
4   Dorothy to Eglantyne, 'Sunday', no date, JFA.

In the event, the new subjects were embraced and natural sciences left behind. She thanked her sister later in the same letter, 'if it was not for you I sh[ou]ld be still stressing & unhappily. How much you save me from. At all stages I long for your comments: – & all times of depression am buoyed up by the thought of your sympathy.'

In the summer before she began her second year studying her new chosen field, she read more deeply in economics, which suited her. 'This new subject I am starting seems such a familiar beaten track after my sojourn in the strange field of science!'[1] There was also much exploration of politics in her reading, which she linked to her intended concentration on psychology. 'I have been reading up politics fairly . . . & think some more may be managed here. The subject has a great psychological interest – as all subjects connected with human things it is intertwined with psychology. Hence a great hunger seizes me at the outset – a restless longing to compass the whole field!'[2] In her final year, she added more philosophy and ethics to politics and economics, although, as she admitted in one letter, she relied much on what she already knew rather than meticulously studying all the possible authorities and sources, 'I am fearfully busy – having taken at this 11th hour into the subject of Philosophy – & am writing papers on Ethics on the strength of my existing stock of ideas! An audacious method – but I always play for high stakes!'[3]

Dorothy's change of course dovetailed with her extra-curricular interests: one, in particular, was debating. The Political Society at Newnham was the hub of much student life at the College and in a society where women could not even vote let alone stand for parliament, this was a statement of aspiration, as well as a debating club. It was organised like the House of Commons with a government and opposition, Liberal and Conservative taking it in turns for a year at a time to be the 'front bench' and propose bills. The meetings were held weekly during term in the large hall, as they were so popular. Each year there was an election for leader of the two political groups to lead their side through the following year. The Society involved dons, as well as students.

Dorothy's burgeoning political interests made her a leading light of this Society. Known as 'D.F.' by her fellow students – there being too many student women with the name Dorothy for her first name to suffice – she stood for 'Liberal leader' in her second year. According to Mary Agnes Hamilton,[4] who organised the campaign of her opponent, Dorothy was

1   Dorothy to Eglantyne, 22 August 1902, JFA.
2   Dorothy to Eglantyne, 22 August 1902, JFA.
3   Dorothy to Eglantyne, 9 May 1904, Box 7, 7EJB/B/01/02/05, WL.
4   Mary Agnes Hamilton (1884–1966), Labour MP for Blackburn 1929–31.

not a 'co-operator'. She was too dogmatic and full of zeal, unable to see any view other than her own. At the Political Society, Hamilton said Dorothy 'made a fiery maiden speech on the South African question which created a great Impression. To me, it suggested an outlook at once narrow, fanatical and unrealistic: I like D.F. but not as a leader.'[1]

The campaign that followed was 'exciting' with 'endless canvassing, arguing in groups, speeches at the selection meeting'. Dorothy lost and apparently responded poorly to her defeat, thus confirming the distrust of her opponent's supporters. Dorothy stood again in her third year, losing once more, this time to Mary Agnes Hamilton herself, although the victor gave Dorothy a 'Cabinet seat' when she formed her 'government'. She may have lost these student elections, but we see here for the first time her developing the ability to speak in public with fluency and passion, as she had heard others do in Ellesmere. Now, however, the audience – and the opponents – were some of the brightest minds of her generation. No chink in the argument would escape notice. Dorothy, with her sheltered provincial background, must have felt some intimidation and insecurity against such confident women contemporaries. This may have pushed her to speak so strongly and seemingly so uncompromisingly.

It was also, however, a reflection of the way she looked at things, in black and white. There was a moral judgement to be made – something was right or wrong. Once she was convinced of what was 'right' and 'moral', she would not tailor her belief in order to reach consensus with those she felt were supporting a position that for her was 'wrong' or 'immoral'. So, for example, British imperialism was oppressing, in her view, the freedoms of the Boers in South Africa – to her, this was morally wrong and there could be no 'middle ground' or compromise. The Boers were either free or not free – there could not be a halfway position. This mode of thinking would mark her approach for the rest of her life. Every political and economic matter had a right and wrong. The idea of politics as the 'art of the possible', as a pragmatic and earnest search for the 'middle ground', for the practical solution that might hold, was all anathema to her. There was a right and a wrong and right must be advocated and fought for, so that in the end it prevailed. Remember her observation about herself: that she played for 'high stakes'. Her opinions were often intuitive rather than the result of deep and exhaustive research. She did not have the confidence of someone who had mined every bit of information or considered an issue from all sides. Instead she had the dogmatic boldness of the person who is convinced they have right on their side. Dorothy was already showing herself not to be a scholar, but a campaigner. This attitude proved not to

---

1   For this and subsequent references to the elections, see Hamilton, pp. 47–48.

be just a facet of her inexperience or youthful enthusiasm, but an analytical approach that she would carry throughout her life. It did not make her popular or convincing to those with whom she engaged, but it made her confident and fearless as an advocate.

In these undergraduate days, Dorothy was clearly not only a Liberal, but on the anti-imperialist and radical wing of the party. She followed her mother's sympathies and was a supporter of Home Rule for Ireland. She wanted to see social policies such as the introduction of old-age pensions and campaigns to counter poverty and deprivation. She supported women's suffrage and the participation of women in the democratic process at all levels. She also spoke on behalf of the campaign against cruelty to animals, asking her Aunt Bun for old papers she knew she had on the subject.[1]

But Dorothy was not just a talker about social issues and helping the poorer members of society. She was also determined to give of her time to the charitable groups that worked amongst the deprived. One of the ways that women of her class and situation could do this more simply was via the Charity Organisation Society, an umbrella organisation founded in 1869 to coordinate the numerous local charitable bodies and prevent duplication. It also had an agenda to prevent charities being 'hoodwinked' by the unscrupulous and funds being distributed to those it regarded as 'undeserving'. Dorothy's Aunt Carrie gave a great deal of her energies to the work of the Cambridge branch of the COS, and the Sidgwicks and other university members were also supporters. Eglantyne became very involved and developed an interest in sociology, her researches leading to a survey of conditions in Cambridge, which was published. Dorothy as an undergraduate was restricted more to the vacations for her charitable experiences. In 1903 she became the secretary of the Women's University Settlement, its President the following year. This was a project in Southwark which aimed to provide education and training for young women from poor backgrounds. The idea of 'settlements' had taken shape in the 1880s and consisted of property being acquired in inner city locations which became centres for education, as well as social welfare. Many undergraduates, male and female, in Oxford and Cambridge gave time to these centres. Mrs Sidgwick at Newnham College was a great supporter of the settlement movement and the students there became involved from the College's foundation.[2] It was the kind of activity that excited Dorothy.

She was not always happy with the tasks she was given. In the summer of 1903, she found herself being given office work to do and resented this. She wrote to her sister Eglantyne,

---

1   Dorothy to Eglantyne, 9 May 1904, Box 7, 7EJB/B/01/02/05, WL.
2   Beaumont, see especially pp. 41, 59–62, 71–72, 75.

> Yesterday I visited AP's COS office in the City & was appalled at
> his energetic undersecretary, at once handing me a case paper &
> requesting me to write a letter in connection with it. This little
> chore I escaped through lack of time – but she found me another
> in the shape of a Report to draw up wh[ich] is still hanging near
> my bed & alarming me very much! It is appalling the businesslike
> mind one requires for COS work – & mine is just the opposite.[1]

Dorothy wanted to debate and discuss and then act. She felt no aptitude
for the business side of charity and her enthusiasm for involvement in such
projects was diluted as a result. Yet, when asked to give talks these did not at
first go better, confessing to her sister, 'Yesterday was my lecture – no great
success I fear – it was really quite the wrong sort of lecture for a few old
working-women. It is an extraordinary relief to have it over.'[2]

So her zeal for charity work as a concept did not always translate for
her into either success or satisfaction. Nevertheless, she was learning about
her strengths and weaknesses, and how difficult she could find working
with others. Her Cambridge years were therefore not just important for
her intellectual development, but also preparing her for the frustrations of
working in the world of charity and politics. The cosy world of the Jebb
household in Shropshire had been an exciting and challenging one, yet
it was still protected and contained. Now she was seeing a more complex
and dangerous environment for which she would need further skills and
knowledge. Her greatest help in this regard was now at hand, however. For
something even more significant happened for Dorothy whilst at Cambridge,
alongside the activities that formed her politics and social outlook. It was in
these years that she met the person who would be the most influential in her
life: her future husband Charles Roden Buxton.

Their first meeting was at a reading group in the Lake District in August
1902. This had become an annual event some years before and involved
men from Trinity with women from Newnham, an explicit recognition
by the participants of their belief in the equal intellectual contribution of
both sexes. Dorothy's fellow Newnhamite, Victoria Buxton, was one of
the organisers and the usual location was a rented farmhouse on the shores
of Ullswater. The group varied from year to year and Bertrand Russell[3]
joined in one year, Jane Harrison[4] another. Victoria's brother, Charlie
(known publicly by his second name Roden, but called by his family the
more affectionate Charlie), was also a founder of the group and was present

---

1   Dorothy to Eglantyne, July 1903, Box 7, 7EJB/B/01/02/05, WL.
2   Dorothy to Eglantyne, 1 April 1904, Box 7, 7EJB/B/01/02/05, WL.
3   Bertrand Russell (1872–1970), philosopher.
4   Jane Ellen Harrison (1850–1928), classicist and lecturer at Newnham 1898–1922.

Charles Buxton
aged around 30

again in summer 1902. Francis Cornford,[1] a don at Trinity College and
a contemporary of Charlie from his undergraduate years, was one of the
other participants. Thrilled to be invited, having just completed her first
year at university, Dorothy found herself moved by the scenery around
Ullswater, especially the hills, calling it the most enchanting place she had

1   Francis Macdonald Cornford (1874–1943) was a classicist and also became known
    for his poetry. He was a Fellow of Trinity College, Cambridge, from 1899, an assistant
    lecturer from 1902 and two years later became a lecturer. He became Professor
    of Ancient Philosophy in 1931, retiring in 1939. He was a supporter of women
    being awarded degrees (something that did not happen at Cambridge until after his
    death) from his undergraduate days and was throughout his career a mentor to many
    students. He married in 1909, Frances Croft Darwin (1886–1960), a granddaughter
    of Charles Darwin, and like her husband a well-known poet.

ever visited. She loved imitating the hooting of the owls and in an evening it seemed she was conversing with them as they responded to her calls.[1] The intense atmosphere of study and serious conversation also suited her.

> It is an amazing new experience to be on a party like this – but it does not seem strange. We read all the morning. . . . We walk all the afternoon – & in the evening Mr Cornford reads aloud . . . with great appreciation. Altogether it is an ideal kind of life for a time – real work & real play.[2]

It is hard to know how Dorothy and Charlie reacted to each other on this their first encounter, although it does not seem to have been 'love at first sight'. Dorothy was too preoccupied and Charlie too cautious to be likely to be swayed by first appearances. Charlie did write years later that he was slow to 'fall in love'.[3] Nevertheless, they clearly did not find each other's company uncongenial. Charlie was living in London and Dorothy based in Cambridge so their paths would not cross that often, but we can assume they did encounter one another again in the following months.

Charles Roden Buxton was a member of a family that was long distinguished in philanthropy and the espousal of liberal causes, driven by a committed evangelical and Christian faith. His great-grandfather, Thomas Fowell Buxton,[4] had made his fortune in the brewing business and then stood for parliament. As an MP, he followed on from William Wilberforce in being the leader of the anti-slavery campaign. Wilberforce had been the centre of the movement to abolish the slave trade, which was accomplished in 1807. Buxton's task was to lead the fight to abolish the status of slave in the British Empire, the bill going through parliament successfully in 1833, the year that Wilberforce died. Buxton became known as 'The Liberator' and was rewarded by the bestowal of a baronetcy. His grandson, the third baronet, was also called Thomas Fowell Buxton (though using his second name principally), and it was this Sir Fowell who was Charlie's father. He too stood for parliament, but had a lack of personal ambition, so he agreed to stand as a Liberal in seats the party would not usually be expected to win. Only once did he make it to the House of Commons (in 1868), but seemed not to be troubled by his general lack of success. He was a generous supporter of missions and settlements in the East End of London and was a concerned and caring administrator of his estate near London. He served as a County Councillor, chaired the Missions

1   De Bunsen, pp. 29–30.
2   Dorothy to Eglantyne, 22 August 1902, JFA.
3   Charlie, memorandum dated Rome, 31 December 1914, Box 10, 7EJB/B/ 01/03/07-13, WL.
4   See Mottram biography for more information on Sir Thomas.

Lady Victoria & Sir Thomas Buxton

for Seamen and local School Boards, and was a Colonel in a volunteer rifle brigade. At the weekends, he entertained at his country home and regularly these gatherings included African leaders, such as the Katikiro of Buganda[1] and the Alake of Abeokata,[2] who in their flowing robes were exotic visitors to the local people. In 1895, he was appointed Governor of South Australia, where, for the few years he served in the position he was a great success as a consequence of his humility and geniality. Fowell Buxton was known as a nerveless rider of a horse, was rarely ever ill and encouraged all his children to do the 'enterprising thing'.[3] Charlie inherited his father's sense of public duty and a personal lack of fear, in addition to a keen sense of justice and a desire to counter prejudice.

Yet, as his sister Victoria reminisced, none of the ten surviving children of Sir Fowell were 'personally intimate' with their father.[4] Unlike Dorothy's father, Charlie's father was a detached Victorian patriarch, kindly and interested, but not over-involved in the upbringing of his children. The more significant influence on Charlie was his mother. Victoria Noel came from a more aristocratic background than her husband. A daughter of the 1st Earl of Gainsborough, she could trace her ancestry back to medieval and Anglo-Saxon kings of Britain, as well as most of the royal houses of Europe, and through them to Charlemagne himself. For the wealthy baronet of means but inconsequential lineage, Victoria was a socially advantageous match. Yet it seems the marriage was very much one of attraction that led to long-lasting love rather than a mere social arrangement. On their marriage, they moved into Warlies, the house near Waltham Cross that Fowell's father had bought, but then had not lived in as he died relatively young. Fowell moved in with his new bride and had an extensive new gothic-style

1 The Katikiro was the Prime Minister of Buganda (in the south of modern-day Uganda) and was appointed by the Kabaka (or King).
2 The ruler of part of modern south-west Nigeria.
3 De Bunsen, p. 10.
4 De Bunsen, p. 11.

wing built on the back of the eighteenth-century rectangular house with its semi-circular portico at the entrance. The couple soon filled the rooms with a large family. Ten of their thirteen children survived to adulthood and Charlie was the third son and seventh child. They spent part of the year at Warlies, another period at their house in London, and the rest of the year in Cromer, on the Norfolk coast, where Fowell's widowed mother lived until she died in 1911 at the grand age of ninety-seven.

Lady Victoria Buxton began to suffer with a spinal complaint when she was only thirty and, with little medical help available, she became disabled and was in pain for the rest of her life. She had to travel either lying down or kneeling, whilst at home she spent much of her time on a day bed. Yet she never allowed her disability to dampen her spirits. She was interested in everything and everyone and entertained with ease and generosity, known for her laughter and humour. She did not demur at going with her husband to Australia in 1895, where she proved a successful hostess. Unfortunately, her deteriorating health was the main reason the Buxtons returned to Britain in 1897 and then decided not to return Australia, Sir Fowell resigning his office much to the disappointment of the government in Adelaide.

Although unable to do much for her children in practical terms, she took a keen interest in their development. She did not 'baby' her children, ever treating them as more adult than they were – for example, there were few pet names or endearing sentiments. She encouraged them to discuss events and ideas. She taught them to respect different views and not be judgemental. She gave her children much freedom. One daughter noted how her mother did not approve of young women going to the theatre or opera. Yet, having made her views plain, she insisted when they reached the age of eighteen that they could go if they wished, as she wanted them to make up their own minds. She never minded if they were unable to adhere to her views. She insisted they take responsibility for themselves and their decisions, so was content when they did. The only thing she found difficult to tolerate was apathy.[1]

Charlie was a sensitive and thoughtful child, who loved reading and poetry. Yet he was not shy or self-conscious and was a fearless rider of the horse like his father. He was not physically robust. He did play football and cricket at his boarding school with vigour until a doctor insisted his heart was not strong enough. So he concentrated less on sport than intellectual pursuits. He was clever academically and won prizes whilst at Harrow School, where he was also head of his House, before moving on to Trinity College, Cambridge.

---

1   For more detailed information see Russell's book on Lady Victoria, details in the bibliography.

Here he made his mark, taking a first-class degree in Classics in 1897, and being President of the Cambridge Union debating society during his final year. He had hoped for an academic career at first, but his failure to win a Fellowship at Trinity with his essay on the 'Attic style',[1] set him on a different path. He travelled in 1898 – to Australia (where his parents were then living and where he served as an assistant secretary to his father for a few months), to Singapore, the Malay States, Indo-China, Thailand, India, China and Japan. He studied law, but his work was interrupted by a period of ill-health in 1899–1900. He travelled again, including to Texas in the USA, where he worked as a cowboy on a ranch for six months. On his return, he took up the law once more and was eventually called to the Bar in 1902.[2]

It was at this juncture of his life that he met Dorothy at the reading party in the Lake District and it was probably his sister Victoria who invited Dorothy to stay at the Buxton's country house, Warlies, in July 1903. Here, she spent time with Charlie, as well as meeting his brothers – Leland, Harold and Noel. It was an idyllic setting for her with her love of the countryside whilst Charlie provided plenty of lively political discussion.

> It was so nice at Warlies. Summer makes me almost cry with happiness – & the garden there set in a rolling park with luxuriant trees rising out of luxuriant long grass redolent with all enchanting smells, is a place to dream of. It was glowing hot & I spent most of Sunday living on my back in the grass with CB & another agreeable lawyer – who was clever without being alarming so that we c[ou]ld have interesting discussions. I am thankful to people who don't frighten me!
>
> After tea I went for a walk with CB & we continued our standing quarrel on the merits of party Gov[ernmen]t & other political subjects, so you can imagine how I enjoyed myself.
>
> Leland, Harold & Noel were all there & I had interesting conversations[3] with all of them. V[ictoria] . . . was in too great request to have much time for anyone.
>
> It is nice to look back on.[4]

---

1   The Attic style was a type of Greek classical poetry, contrasted with the 'Asiatic style' which was more exuberant.
2   Charlie was admitted to the Inner Temple on 15 November 1898 and called on 23 April 1902. The gap between the dates is partly a reflection of his need to have time away improving his health, including the six months in Texas.
3   This was a type of Greek classical poetry, austere in style in contrast to the Asian style, which was more exuberant.
4   Dorothy to Eglantyne, July 1903, Box 7, 7EJB/B/01/02/05, WL.

Later the same summer, Dorothy visited several counties of Ireland with her mother. From Donegal, she wrote to her sister Eglantyne, 'By great luck too C. Buxton has overlapped us on a visit here, so it has made things extra nice having him to go round with.'[1] This meeting may have been coincidence, but more likely it was Charlie's intention to turn up where she was on vacation in order to gain more of Dorothy's attention. The winter of 1903–04 was when their courtship became serious, as it seems Charlie's feelings about Dorothy grew more intense and more certain.

For Dorothy, the initial attraction of Charlie was his intellectual abilities. She revealed in her letter from Warlies quoted above that she was still lacking in academic confidence and could be frightened by those with powerful arguments. But she was not frightened by Charlie. She also was very taken with his ability to listen to other people. Years later she wrote to her son, David, 'I had always thought that Daddy was the man, who of all others, really listened attentively & respectfully to what I had to say, or indeed to what anybody else had to say.'[2]

In another letter, she remembered that one of her first meetings with Charlie in Cambridge had been at a tea party in Newnham College.

> I was much struck by the fact that he *listened* so well to whatever I had to say (not because I was I – but to everybody). It made me realise that my other men friends – & I had lots – had nothing like the same power of sympathetic attention. The difference lay partly in his sense of *respect* for other people – he made one feel one was really *worth* listening to, & this in itself was very encouraging. Then, secondly, his mind was so *intelligently focussed* on everything one had to say, – the 'attention' was not that of a superficial politeness but genuine & thorough.[3]

Charlie introduced her to people and ideas, broadened her horizons and encouraged her to speak. He wrote ten years later,

> Have I helped her? Yes – why not claim it? She was living in a smaller world when I found her; her intensity of desire and aspiration beating against narrow limits. There was too little choice of direction; she might have chosen a path that would have proved a by-way, and pursued it as if it had been the grand highway of the world. My sweetest thoughts are when I think that it was I who brought her into a wider place and showed her untried paths, and a multitude of new faces – blessing them as well as her.[4]

1   Dorothy to Eglantyne, 23 August [1903], Box 7, 7EJB/B/01/02/05, WL.
2   Dorothy to David, 11 August 1929, BFA.
3   Dorothy to David, 31 October 1930, BFA.
4   Charlie, memorandum dated Rome, 31 December 1914, Box 10, 7EJB/ B/01/

The fact that she could debate with him was significant for her. Although they both were broadly on the radical wing of politics, they had at this juncture differing positions. This was especially so about religion. Dorothy's religious journey will be examined in a later chapter; suffice it to say here that she was at her most atheist in her undergraduate days, whereas Charlie was a committed Evangelical Anglican. In politics he had more faith in the parliamentary political system – indeed he aspired to be an MP like others in his family – whereas Dorothy was distinctly suspicious of the deals and manoeuvring of political parties. This made for stimulating conversation.

She may well have noticed his good looks, but he was not a man who made an effort to be charming to women in a romantic or flirtatious sense. In fact, his reserve could come over as being cool and aloof. Years later, after his death, she confided to her son, 'If Daddy was a young man now I expect the vast majority of girls would think him cold & remote. And yet one knows he was *anything but* that.'[1] His sister, Victoria, told Dorothy around the same time that until she [Dorothy] came along no one had fallen in love with Charlie, to which Dorothy's response was, 'If that is true[,] it is to me an astounding fact!'[2]

Charlie believed friendship came first and then romance might follow. This was certainly how he approached Dorothy. There is no evidence of bouquets of flowers and presents of perfumes, jewellery and trinkets, elaborate dinners or grand gestures. Instead they went to lectures, browsed in libraries and talked about politics over tea. The absence of romantic panache may have been why Charlie was not a favourite of many young women in his circle despite his handsome looks. His more cerebral approach, however, was impressive to Dorothy. She realised that he respected her opinions and was keen for her to have her ambitions. He promised her he would not try to sweep her from her own judgements.[3]

The climax of their courtship came on two successive Saturdays in March 1904: he summed it up ten years into their marriage,

> At times it comes to me with a shock, that I might have missed all this. It was only slowly and with dim eyes that I saw my opportunity. But I did see, surely and clearly at last, the one woman of the world for me, and clung to her and demanded her. Yes, on the bridge over the swirling Thames, and again in the woods of Madingley amid the hyacinthine sea of blue-bells, and once more in the spacious library

---

03/07-13, WL. This quotation is section XVI. Copy also in BA.
1   Dorothy to David, 25 December 1944, BFA
2   Dorothy to David, 18 February 1945, BFA.
3   De Bunsen, p. 42.

with the bright fire and the long low arm-chair, I told her I would have
her for my comrade, mind and spirit, flesh and blood. Words stuck in
my throat, and she thought me cold; she knows I was not, now.[1]

The first Saturday was 19 March 1904 and the meeting took place on
Waterloo Bridge in London. It seems that this was when Charlie declared
his hopes and asked her to marry him. Dorothy was not sure and insisted
on time to consider.[2] One can easily imagine Dorothy's view that she
must make the decision with her head not her heart. It was clear from
what happened subsequently and her reactions to marrying Charlie that
she was very much in love with him. Yet ironically, it would be the very
strength of her feelings that would have made her hold back on saying yes
to his proposal immediately. She had to convince herself intellectually not
emotionally that this was a right thing to do. Would the marriage help her
achieve things for society and fulfil the goals she set herself of being 'useful'
– or was it merely personal satisfaction? If the latter, she would need to say
no in order to keep herself for the higher things she demanded she must
try to achieve. If the former, then she could say yes, as her feelings and her
ambitious aspirations would lead to the same conclusion.

Dorothy did decide that week that the marriage could be part of the
larger scheme of things and so the following Saturday (26 March), when
they met in the Backs and walked to Madingley near Cambridge, she put
Charlie out of his misery and said a definite yes.[3] By his own admission,
words stuck in his throat: he found it hard to express the depth of his
love for her. But this may have helped his cause as Dorothy would have
judged an ardent and silver-tongued wooer as too swayed by overpowering
yet shallow emotions. Charlie's more reticent approach suggested a more
reasoned decision that would have ultimately appealed to her.

Charlie loved literature and wrote poetry so these events resulted in a
piece of verse, which he entitled: In the Backs at Cambridge, 1904, the
last two lines of which were: 'And here one came, in her brown woodland

---

1   Charlie, memorandum dated Rome, 31 December 1914, Box 10, 7EJB/
    B/01/03/07-13, WL. This quotation is section XIII. Copy also in BFA.
2   Charlie to Dorothy, 20 March 1918, BFA: he referred in this letter to the Waterloo
    Bridge meeting as being 'painful'.
3   Charlie to Dorothy, 18 March 1912, BFA. 'I wonder if you have remembered that
    tomorrow is the day for ever to be known in connexion with Waterloo Bridge,
    1904? A great day, but not the best, because spoilt by uncertainty in some strange
    way. The *best* was March 26, the following Saturday when we met in the backs at
    Cambridge, and walked out along the Madingley Road, and said and did glorious
    things in the wood by the side of it. Eight years since then, and ever better and
    better years.'

dress, And opened the wide gates of blessedness.'[1] If this was Charlie's view, what of Dorothy's? Her letters show her swept away by her feelings for 'her boy'. A week after she said 'yes' she wrote to Eglantyne, saying how Charlie understood the importance the sisters had for each other and how he wanted to meet Eglantyne. To her delight, Charlie took a great interest in her friends too and what she was doing. She wrote to her sister,

> I do so wish I was with you, my beloved, that you might read all my letters & know how glorious my boy is, & that I might tell you how different everything looks & how changed the world is altogether.
>
> I find new heights & depths in him on closer acquaintance – he must have a great power of sympathy for he seems so quick to see into one's heart & mind, & to lay hold of what is important & dear to me. . . .
>
> We write to each other every day – but he is so busy that the correspondence becomes a matter of my yarning & his responding – so that he really knows far more about me, my history & ideas than I know about his. Quite the reverse of the usual state of things I am sure! But we will get level in time. . . .
>
> He has such a big heart: – I have seldom known anyone so gentle, only my Ownie I think. How impossible it is to tell you 1/100 part on paper. . . . The chief joy of my circ[umstance]s is, I think, to have found someone whom it is easy to love so completely. For he does seem to me [to be] so extraordinarily good. I only guessed at it before.[2]

Within a few weeks, finishing off her studies[3] seemed utterly trivial now she had a vision of life with Charlie before her. 'Oh this stagnant experience! Newnham now is a very different place. I walk through it like a ghost – I see & hear things all the same as of old – but *feel* nothing! I only *feel* – when

1   The full text of the poem is: 'Here a boy's heart, by sickly dreams oppressed, / Turned, once for all, from Fancy's childish quest. / Here in his brain, long fallow, dull, and chilled, / Thoughts' drawing world – life's new ideal – thrilled. / And here one came, in her brown woodland dress, / And opened the wide gates of blessedness.' He later elucidated this poem by identifying 'Fancy's childish quest' as a woman called Betty on whom he had had a crush for some time in the mid-1890s. The second two lines refer to the intellectual awakening that came from his time studying at Cambridge. Then the fulfilment of his life came with meeting Dorothy.

2   Dorothy to Eglantyne, 3 April 1904, Box 7, 7EJB/B/01/02/05, WL.

3   It should be noted that women could not take degrees at the University of Cambridge until 1948, even if they had passed the final Tripos examinations. Consequently, some women students in earlier years completed their course of study, but did not trouble to take the examinations at the end. Dorothy was one of them and so did not have examinations to sit in May/June 1904.

of old I c[ou]ld only *see* – the vanity of things that troubled me.'[1] Charlie's weekly visits from London were the centre of her world and all thought of study was abandoned once he arrived. 'My boy comes here every Sat[urday] afternoon at 2.30. From that hour till Monday Morning I do no stroke of work – a most unprecedented state of things. We walk & talk – & don't get tired of either strange to say!'[2]

The families approved of the match. Dorothy's Uncle Dick and Aunt Carrie were full of congratulations. Tye and Eglantyne were away and not back in Cambridge until the end of April, so she had to be told by letter. Aunt Bun received a personal visit from Dorothy early in April at Lee in Shropshire. Charlie's sister, Victoria, and her fiancé[3] were equally welcoming of the match. His brother Noel kissed Dorothy's hand and made her feel immediately part of the Buxton family. Charlie's parents, however, proved a more complex challenge for Dorothy when she went to meet them at their London residence in Princes Gate, especially his father who was hampered by deafness.

> The only trying thing so far was a visit to Princes Gate on Tuesday. I met Charlie first & we had lunch at a restaurant together – & afterwards went to the Macedonian Conference together – where various people (–including Mrs Burkitt!) eyed us somewhat curiously! We had to come out together in the middle to go to Prince[']s Gate – there I had a long interview with Lady Victoria who did not alarm me at all – The alarming person is old Sir F[owell], whom I can't make hear – & who hates people who can't make him hear – in the first place, of course, I had not anything I wanted to make him hear![4]

Most significant for Dorothy was her sister Eglantyne's approval. She had this most warmly and Eglantyne saw Charlie as the perfect match for her sister. Eighteen months into the marriage, Eglantyne wrote, 'You & Charlie are the only people whom I have ever been able to think of as *one* in my prayers.'[5]

The engagement brought approval not only from close family. Jane Harrison wrote to Charlie's sister, Victoria – Jane thought Victoria's own recent engagement would be a wrench for her brother as they were close and hence the use of the word desertion in the quotation below.

---

1   Dorothy to Eglantyne, 26 April 1904, Box 7, 7EJB/B/01/02/05, WL.

2   Dorothy to Eglantyne, 9 May 1904, Box 7, 7EJB/B/01/02/05, WL.

3   Victoria was engaged to Lothar de Bunsen, a widower with a son. He was fifteen years older than her. Some in the family had been concerned about this, but Dorothy's doubts about Lothar were swept away by the warmth of his reaction to her own engagement.

4   Dorothy to Eglantyne, 1 April 1904, Box 7, 7EJB/B/01/02/05, WL.

5   Eglantyne to Dorothy, 21 December [1905], Box 7, 7EJB/B/01/02/05, WL.

If it were anyone but Dorothy Jebb, I should say Charlie was marrying in despair at your desertion, but those two were made for each other – it is a dream marriage – I quite understand that to you no girl is good enough, but on my side I have always been a good deal laughed at for having a sort of 'culte' for Dorothy, – the extraordinary purity of her face has always moved me strangely, and I have sometimes felt that marriage would be desecration, she is so original, – but with this marriage I am content. I have often planned it in my mind, but I always thought it was so eternally fit that it would never be.[1]

And what of sexual attraction? According to one of Dorothy's contemporaries, Newnham students were generally ignorant about sex at that time and it meant the subject was never discussed even in intimate conversations between close friends.[2] Sex outside marriage was taboo and sex inside marriage was not something to be spoken about. Years later, Dorothy wrote of sexual feelings,

I remembered that my mother had told me that no 'good' *woman* ever felt this physical desire at all; it was only prostitutes – or the like – who acquired it! With *men* on the other hand it was natural & inevitable. My mother probably reflected in this a very general outlook of her age – at least among the 'refined' bourgeoisie. I cannot subscribe to it. [3]

Dorothy's love of nature and her scientific education meant she was fully aware of the 'facts of life' and did not agree with her mother's outlook. Sex was a part of life. Nevertheless, aware of convention, she hid any inclination to include sexual desire in her motivation for wanting to be married. This meant Dorothy's fellow undergraduates approved of the match too as they saw it as 'one of mutual dedication to high ideals and good works as we could understand and talk about; there was no uncomfortable evidence of physical passion'! But on ideals, Mary Agnes Hamilton recalled how Dorothy seem to skirt around the different positions on religion she and Charlie held, worrying instead that they disagreed about Old Age Pensions, Charlie being for a non-contributory scheme and Dorothy for a contributory one.[4]

Finding a date for the wedding took a while, especially with the competing advice and requests coming from family members.

---

1   Jane Harrison to Victoria Buxton, [undated] 1904, Box 10, 7EJB/B/01/03/07.
2   Hamilton, p. 45.
3   Dorothy to David, 25 December 1944, BFA.
4   Hamilton, p. 45.

We are still quite indefinite about plans – no decision can be made till we see how we get on next term with our respective work – how possible it is to resist distraction. I sincerely hope we *shall* find it possible – it is unsatisfactory to feel one is at the mercy of any circumstance. At present friends & relatives are heaping upon me their contradictory advice – which amuses me very much & puzzles me not a little. For I have had no opportunity yet of escaping into a sufficiently solitary place to think things out for myself.[1]

Eventually, 11 August 1904 at 2p.m. was set for the marriage at St Giles' Church in Cambridge. Neither Aunt Bun nor Dorothy's eldest sister Emily, were able to come, but Eglantyne was the bridesmaid. The two sisters and their mother had the usual flurry over fittings for 'the dresses'.[2] It was quite a traditional wedding, but not elaborate. Dorothy wore 'a simple gown of white satin with a Brussels lace veil', her bouquet being of white flowers. Her older brother, Richard Jebb, 'gave her away', whilst Noel Buxton served as his brother's best man, and Dorothy's Uncle Heneage took the wedding service, assisted by Charlie's cousin, Conrad Noel.[3] The reception was at the University Arms Hotel.

The bride 'went away' in brown Tussore silk,[4] smocked and embroidered in brown and gold, with a brown picture hat. They went to Ireland for the first part of their honeymoon and then on to Monte Fiano in Italy. Unusually, we have Dorothy's own account, in a letter written many years after to their son, of what happened when they were journeying to Ireland.

[We] were *immensely lucky* in finding each other; & our impersonal interests – & the underlying attitude which made them possible – bound us mightily together. But I can well imagine that with a more 'modern' mode of outlook I might have cooled off rather rapidly. I remember rather vividly how, after our wedding, we set off to Ireland for our honeymoon, & he explained to me, as night approached, that he thought we better not have any intercourse until we were both in a state of greater physical fitness, i.e. that this part of our life together should be subordinated to the interest of

1   Dorothy to Eglantyne, 1 April 1904, Box 7, 7EJB/B/01/02/05, WL.

2   Dorothy to Eglantyne, 20 July [1904], Box 7, 7EJB/B/01/02/05, WL.

3   Conrad le Despenser Roden Noel (1869–1942), Vicar of Thaxted 1910–42, well-known for his left-wing views so nicknamed the 'Red Vicar'. He founded the Catholic Crusade, a pressure group combining Anglo-Catholic religion with strong socialist politics. He was Charlie's first cousin, son of his mother's brother the poet Roden Berkeley Wroithesley Noel (1834–1894).

4   Tussore silk is a type of Indian silk woven from the cocoons of wild silk worms feeding on mountain shrubs. It is naturally brownish in colour and light in weight. It is a traditional wedding fabric.

the possible *child*. . . . This appealed to my *reason*. At the same time I felt some disappointment that Reason should play so decisive a part on this occasion! And along with this I felt shocked with myself that my sexual instincts should play so strong a part as to *cause me* to be disappointed! I felt I must be rather a low-down creature compared to him.[1]

It is very easy for the twenty-first century Western mind to be bewildered by Charlie's attitude. Indeed, some might even use this as evidence of his not having felt much sexual passion or even that he was really homosexual. However, this is to misunderstand the contemporary attitude to sex. Charlie was brought up with the very same approach that Dorothy had been and so to him sex was something men 'imposed' upon women as the woman may well not enjoy it. So for Charlie, if he loved Dorothy as much as he did, sparing her the 'ordeal' of sex on their wedding night was an act of loving consideration. Clearly, in time this misunderstanding was overcome and they came to have a mutually fulfilling intimate relationship. Yet, here was a glimpse of the ignorance and caution about sex that even educated Victorians and Edwardians suffered through the prevailing attitudes of the time.

Dorothy and Charlie's marriage proved the rock on which both could build their lives and their public work. From the beginning of their life together they were determined that how they lived should reflect their personal views and political stance. It meant that however traditional their wedding had been, they took some less conventional choices on the return from their honeymoon.

---

1   Dorothy to David, 25 December 1944, BFA.

Chapter 3
Married life and politics

The society that Dorothy and Charlie wished to serve was one deeply divided by class. Movement between classes was possible, but limited owing to the significance of the family into which a person was born and the consequent access to certain types of education. Those in the lower ranks of this stratified social structure struggled to survive, not just those living in abject poverty, but also the artisan working-class. They had jobs, but wages were low, resulting in those at the top of society being able to live in comfort, even extravagance, without large expenditure. The servant class had to work long hours, living in their place of employment in small rooms and with few facilities or days off. Even those with considerate employers felt constrained not to ask for better conditions in case they forfeited their job, which might result in being forced to take work with a far harsher employer. The long hours and routine made it hard to escape their position through training or education, as there was little time or opportunity. Between the leisured and working classes, the middle class tried to copy the fashions and fads of the upper classes, yet lived in fear of falling into poverty and sliding into the lower classes. So they espoused thrift and economy in a determined effort to prevent such a fall. Their fear often led to overt deference for those above them in the social hierarchy and a nervous contempt for those below. Class was reflected in how someone spoke, how they dressed, where they lived. Small indications of social status were magnified to an importance that they did not warrant. It was a system that bred insecurity, which in turn led to snobbery.

Charlie's private income, derived from shares in the family brewery, would provide the Buxtons with a comfortable life-style. However, both Dorothy and Charlie believed that the social structure was unfair and wished to change it instead of perpetuating it by living as their own class would expect them to do. They desired a more equitable distribution of wealth so that all could enjoy a decent standard of living. For Charlie the way to fight for change in society's economic structures was through being elected to parliament and influencing government policy. Ironically to do this, he could not surrender his income because, as MPs were not then paid a salary, a parliamentary seat required a private income or a wealthy benefactor.[1] Otherwise such a career was impossible. So giving away their wealth was not an option. Nevertheless, they were both convinced they should live in a more modest way. Retaining control of their income did not mean the newly-married couple had to live opulently; they could choose simplicity.[2]

So what could Dorothy and Charlie do at the outset of their marriage to demonstrate this? One of the most significant gestures was where they chose to live, as the type of dwelling you lived in and its location was significant in indicating where you stood in the social hierarchy. Some people would pay dearly in rent in order to live in a house that was outwardly decorative, even if this meant a very simple life inside. London streets had filled with rows of bay-windowed terrace houses,[3] with elaborate corbels and plasterwork on the outside. Yet, inside only the entrance hall and front reception room would be full of detail, the rest of the house where the family lived might well be quite bare and unadorned. It was common knowledge that such houses were not full of moneyed people. Some joked that such streets were 'bread and butter lane', as the residents had no funds left for food because their social pretensions meant they spent their income on rent.

It was not necessarily a rebellion against their class for Charlie and Dorothy to live in a terraced house as such. A terraced house would be considered acceptable if: the house was substantial in size and served by

---

1   Charlie was on record as supporting salaries for MPs, for example, see CRB1, p. 72, Salaries for MPs were introduced in 1911.

2   Charlie's views were articulated in a speech to the Church Congress at Weymouth on October 1905, a speech entitled 'Increase of Luxury and its Effects'. He defined luxury as a 'superfluity' of furniture and furnishings, carriages and horses, gardens and the tyranny of ever-changing 'fashionable' clothes, the maintenance of all of which entailed an 'enormous increase' in the number of domestic servants. It was 'a social injury' and was indulgence 'at the expense of the poor' in his view. It also produced, he believed, a difference in social habits as well as education that kept society class-ridden and divided. Accumulating 'treasures on earth' prevented the finding of the 'lost sources of spiritual strength'. CC1905, pp. 80–84.

3   Charlie's friend and fellow Liberal politician Charles Masterman described it as, 'miles and miles of little red houses in little silent streets, in number defying imagination. Each boasts its pleasant drawing-room, its bow window, its little front garden, its high-sounding title – "Acacia Villa," or "Camperdown Lodge" – attesting unconquered human aspiration.' Masterman, p. 70. This book, based on previously-published articles in *The Nation*, was popular on publication and ran to three editions in its first year.

staff; located in a desirable and even fashionable area; regarded as a *pied à terre* in the city, with more time being spent at another home in the country. Charlie's parents' London residence in a grand terrace in Princes Gate met these criteria. So did 14 Grosvenor Crescent where Charlie had been born in 1875.

The place that Dorothy and Charlie chose to live however did not. It was a terraced house south of the River Thames in London, in Kennington Terrace.[1] The location was convenient for parliament, should Charlie be elected, and also near a college where Charlie had taken up some teaching, but it was not a fashionable area. Nevertheless, suggestions that Charlie and Dorothy moved into a 'working-class district' are misleading;[2] 7 Kennington Terrace was not in a street housing poor people. Indeed, in 1902 Charles Booth in his survey of wealth and poverty in London classed Kennington Terrace as well-to-do.[3] This did not mean people of similar background to Charlie and Dorothy, but did include those who had made money through business. Their neighbours fell into several categories: those with their own businesses, those in professions and the retired.[4] Most of the householders had live-in servants. So whilst the accepted social snobbery of the time would have made this unsuitable as an area for those with inherited wealth like the Buxtons, it was certainly not working-class. The house itself looked out on Kennington Park, so had a pleasant outlook and was not in a crowded street. It was true that it was adjacent to a more mixed area, where residents were, for example, clerks, leather workers and cooks. The Buxtons' new home was therefore near a district where most inhabitants had to budget carefully from limited resources; and it was this standard of living that the

1 This is no longer standing. The terrace of houses overlooked Kennington Park and in the 1920s was acquired to provide an extension to the park area. The local Liberal MP from 1916 to 1924, J.D. Gilbert, was chair of the extension committee and he himself resided at No 25. Over the years the tenants vacated the houses; once all the dwellings were empty, the whole terrace was demolished. The new extension to the park was opened in 1931 (see for example *The Times*, 31 July 1931, p.10), first being used as the site for a swimming pool and later for tennis courts.

2 For example: De Bunsen, p. 43; Mahood, p. 156; Mulley, p. 90.

3 Booth – see main map.

4 The 1901 census listed the householder at No 7 as a printer, but he was an employer with a business in Fleet, Street not an employee. Other employers with their own businesses and professionals in the street included a leather trim manufacturer, a coach ironmonger, a builder, a tailor, a professor of music and a sanitary engineer. The retired included a former gas engineer, a manager, an elderly spinster with a private income and a widow living on her own means. All had at least one live-in servant, usually a cook. At No 1 was a man who worked as a fruit salesman and clerk, but he and his wife appeared to pay the rent by taking lodgers and not having any servants – they are the exception, however, in the terrace as a whole.

Dorothy as a young married woman

newly-married couple initially aspired to share. They intended to shed the daily comforts that their backgrounds had made familiar: plush furnishings, a large wardrobe of clothes, personal carriages and taxis for transport and, above all, household staff. The other income they had could then be spent for charitable and political purposes.

For Charlie this need for simplicity stemmed from his religious convictions, which in turn formed his political stance of championing the working classes. Dorothy agreed with his politics and came to understand the significance of his religious motivations. She now felt able to share the latter and attended a daily early morning service with him at the church[1] near their new home.

In a fit of naïve idealism, Dorothy decided to cover the domestic work herself, so as to forego the need for servants – something she had rarely experienced in her life previously. Her intentions were announced to her sister some months before her wedding whilst still studying for her degree. '[I] shall start learning cooking if possible the moment term is over.'[2] Despite her good intentions, illustrated in her attending the School of Domestic Economy in Buckingham Palace Road, this hope never came to fruition. Dorothy proved to have no aptitude for the kitchen and she soon gave in to the need for someone else to make the meals. She could not after all dispense with the need for servants and would never be able to do so. Others in time joined the cook. This was why Charlie's sister noted they led a 'simplified' life in Kennington Terrace not a 'simple' one![3]

---

1   It may be assumed this was St Mark's, Kennington, the Vicar of which was John Darlington (1868–1947). He was an intellectual man with a DD degree and remained the incumbent of the parish for fifty years: 1897–1947. His wife Lilian (1870–1961) was a daughter of Frederick William Farrar (1831–1903), a well-known Dean of Canterbury Cathedral.
2   Dorothy to Eglantyne, 9 May 1904, Box 7, 7EJB/B/01/02/05, WL.
3   De Bunsen, p. 44.

In any case, Dorothy could not combine her political and social work with the full-time role of running a household. What time she had for household duties tended to see her gravitate towards the garden, where she relaxed by digging and planting and indulging her love of the natural world. Once they had the garden in order, they even slept there in a wooden shelter in summer rather than inside in a bedroom. 'They have been sleeping (not for economy but pleasure!) in a revolving shelter in their back garden & find themselves benefitted thereby.'[1]

Dorothy saw her early married life as a continuation of much of what she had been doing before with respect to social work. In May 1904, she wrote, 'I purpose some COS [Charity Organisation Society] work in the autumn. . . . '[2] Francis Cornford put her in touch with one of his mother's old friends, so as to give her an introduction to the poorer London neighbourhood north of the Thames as well as to give more information about Kennington.

> I went to see a wise & good friend of mine who lives on twelve shillings a week in Stepney & gives her life to making friends with & helping on the people there. Her name is Miss Elliott. She lives at 20 Rectory Square, Stepney. She has known me all my life & was a devoted friend of my mother's. I made so bold as to say that I thought you would like to know her. She can tell you a great deal about South London life & I am sure you must like her.[3]

Such an introduction was a way of Dorothy finding out more about social conditions so she could, when opportunities arose, fulfil the joint aspiration to speak out for the poorer sections of society. The fact-finding was not only local. In August 1905, she and Charlie joined a group going to Denmark to look at approaches there to education and employment. Dorothy's sister, Louisa (Lill), who was also in the party, concentrated on agriculture in which she was evolving into an expert. She was initially hosted by the aristocratic Baroness Rosenkranz at her palatial home.[4]

---

1   Tye to Richard, 1 June 1906, Box 10, 7EJB/B/01/03/10, WL.

2   Dorothy to Eglantyne, 9 May 1904, Box 7, 7EJB/B/01/02/05, WL.

3   Francis Cornford to Dorothy, 8 October 1904, Box 10, 7EJB/B/01/03/07-13, WL.

4   Dorothy to Eglantyne, 13 August 1905, Box 6, 7EJB/B/01/02/01, WL. 'Here we are in a huge 16th century castle, surrounded by . . . [a] duck-frequented moat; I sit in a tapestried room, on the age worn leather of an ancient carved oak chair – & spread my elbows & scatter my papers over the great expanse of a massive oak writing table. . . . It is an enchanting house to stay in, palatial, full of winding ways, vast corridors & spacious old world rooms with medieval looking furniture & nothing small or finnikin.'

In time, they moved on to Copenhagen for lectures, a tour of a button factory, a school and a labour bureau and then saw something of less privileged people.

> The proprietor & his wife of one of the leading People's High School put 9 of us up for a night in the High School the other day – & fed & lectured & explained things to us in thorough manner for 24 hours, introducing us at the same time to the inside of Danish life in a strata of society less aristocratic than that of the Rosenkranzs. It was Sunday & we dined at a long table in the student dining room with the hosts & guests at one end – the servants at the other end – & the children at another. . . . The lady of the house wore a regular peasant's dress in the time of the Saxons – & seemed equally at home in the capacity of Hausfrau or of reader in Danish literature to the students of the High School (she illustrated her husband's lectures). C & I are much inflamed by the High School spirit – & the bold abandonment of examinations, paperwork, & the exacting academic standard. We have devoted ourselves principally to educational matters & to Poor Law. Lill went off with a separate agricultural party on Sunday to visit an agricultural authority. . . .
>
> The labour bureau *appears* to be a striking success. 24000 persons have been found employment through it in the last year. . . . We are really not working at things very hard – & very often only *me* of us attending the lectures etc. & hands on information to the other – according to our cooperative principles! I am enjoying it all very much.[1]

Other travel was more for pleasure. In May 1905, Dorothy went on a five-week tour in Spain with a cousin. She saw Granada, Tangiers, Gibraltar and Madrid among other places. She was taken not only by the scenery, but also by the paintings of Velazquez.[2] With Eglantyne, Dorothy planned trips to Somerset and France.[3] Later in the year, Dorothy and Charlie followed up the trip to Denmark with time in Northumberland visiting friends and

---

1   Dorothy to Eglantyne, undated but soon after 13 August 1905, Box 6 7EJB/
    B/01/02/01, WL.
2   Dorothy to Eglantyne, 11 May & 15 May 1905, Box 7, 7EJB/B/01/02/05, WL.
    On Velazquez: 'no pictures that overwhelm me with their force and truth as these
    do'. On the trip in general: 'This time in Spain (& in Africa!) has been a great
    education, new worlds have been opened up – vast & captivating beyond my
    hopes.'
3   Dorothy to Eglantyne, 25 December [1904], Box 7, 7EJB/B/01/02/05, WL

then in early September a reading group in the Lake District and then walking in Scotland.[1] Most of this travel was done cheaply as both of them were happy to stay in third-class hotels and they went about without elegant clothes. Indeed, on their walks, they could often look quite shabby and be thought by onlookers to be people of straightened circumstances. This was another example of the Buxtons wishing to cast off the expectations of their class background.

These trips were times of escape from the more pressured life that evolved for Dorothy, as she was helping Charlie with his work in both education and politics. By the time of his marriage, Charlie had found being a barrister emotionally draining and the concentrated work proved physically too strenuous, as his health was not robust. He therefore soon gave up taking cases and looked for other avenues in which to serve. The first was in education. In January 1905, he accepted the position of Principal of Morley College[2] in the Waterloo area of London, where he had been giving lectures on English Literature and had been appointed to its executive Council. He had also been active in its Political Debating Society.

The College had been founded in the 1880s to help improve the educational opportunities for the poor in the area. Coupled with concerts and musical evenings, penny lectures by scientists were organised from 1882, given in the dressing and rehearsal rooms of the Royal Victoria Hall (the 'Old Vic'). The Old Vic had had a reputation as a bawdy and raunchy theatre, but with this endeavour its owners attempted to promote education alongside any entertainment. In 1889, the programme was incorporated into a college structure, with an endowment given by Samuel Morley MP,[3] and it later found its own premises. The College was unusual in that the first two principals were women and the College was run almost entirely by women, although some of the trustees were men. One of the founders and the second principal was Caroline Martineau.[4] When she

---

1   Dorothy to Eglantyne, undated but soon after 13 August 1905, Box 6, 7EJB/B/01/02/01, WL.

2   De Bunsen, p. 34, gave the year 1902 as the time Charlie took up this appointment. This date has then been used subsequently by a host of other writers and editors when referring to Charlie's life, including the online *Oxford Dictionary of National Biography*. Indeed, 1902 was used in a *curriculum vita*, compiled by a member of the family, which is in the BFA. However, this is not the correct date. See the *MCM*, Vol XIV, No 4 (January 1905), p. 49, and also the history of Morley College – Richards, p. 148 and elsewhere – both of which unequivocally record that the date was early 1905.

3   Samuel Morley (1809–86), Liberal MP for Nottingham (1865–68) & Bristol (1868–85).

4   Caroline Martineau (1843–1902), Principal 1891–1902, died 21 February 1902.

died in 1902, the trustees found it impossible to find a suitable female successor, the main problem being that it was an unremunerated position. The administration of the College was expedited by the capable Vice-Principal, Mary Sheepshanks, but she could not afford to work without a salary and so was not able to step up to the top position. The difficulty was therefore finding someone with a private income who also had the interest and qualifications to lead the College. After nearly three years of vacancy, the trustees decided to offer the post to Charlie and break with the feminine tradition.

The choice was a tribute to Charlie's record as a believer in education for all, men and women on an equal basis, and access for the working classes. He lived locally too and would not require a salary. The historian of Morley College noted that Charlie was 'young, active, good-looking, deeply religious and idealistic, talented, likeable and leisured'.[1] Dorothy was appointed to the College's Council[2] and would take a full part with him in engaging with the students socially and in encouraging their commitment to study. Some of this was for more superficial duties: Charlie attended the College Flower Show;[3] the Swimming Club social;[4] welcomed new students at a tea;[5] chaired debates at the Debating Society and used his contacts to invite speakers.[6] Dorothy contributed to debates;[7] presented prizes for sporting achievements;[8] and was a general support to her husband. Their innovation, however, was the 'At Homes', social events they hosted about once a month in College rooms. Dorothy's mother noted in May 1906 in a letter how extensive this was. 'They have invited in the course of the winter & spring 700 people from Morley College to their hospitable board – of course all have not come.'[9] But many did and the events were much enjoyed. As an example, one on 19 January 1907 was described as 'a quite brilliant affair' and included music as entertainment. On this particular occasion, Charlie even persuaded his father to be present and meet the students.[10] For all the success of these College activities, Dorothy did not find them easy. 'Other evenings we attended Morley College for Committees, Debates or

---

1   Richards, p. 148.
2   She resigned from the Council in 1906 when she gave birth to her first child.
3   *MCM*, Vol XVI, No 1 (October 1906), p. 5. Charlie confessed to having learned that day for the first time the difference between a buttonhole and a spray.
4   *MCM*, Vol XVI, No 2 (November 1906), p. 47.
5   *MCM*, Vol XVI, No 4 (January 1907), p. 58.
6   *MCM*, Vol XVI, No 6 (March 1907), p. 88; Vol XVI, No 8 (May 1907), p. 114.
7   *MCM*, Vol XVI, No 6 (March 1907), p. 91; Vol XVI, No 8 (May 1907), p. 114.
8   *MCM*, Vol XIV, No 5 (February 1905), p. 63.
9   Tye to Richard, 4 May 1906, Box 10, 7EJB/B/01/03/10.
10 *MCM*, Vol XVI, No 5 (February 1907), pp. 73–74.

"Socials", or we entertained the students in "at homes" from 8-10, & these functions were a great strain to me.'[1] This was mainly because they were in addition to political activities that Dorothy understandably regarded as more significant. Indeed, the couple's political aspirations were creating increasing pressure on their time and energies.

Dorothy had become involved in Liberal politics and the women's wing of the party. She had spoken at Liberal women's meetings and in July 1904, a month before her marriage, went to speak in Oswestry in her native Shropshire in support of the Liberal candidate in a by-election there. This was Dorothy's first speech during an election campaign and was favourably reported in the local press. It was given in the market place in Ellesmere, her family's home town, which was part of the constituency. She spoke in support of free trade, espoused by the Liberal candidate, a topic made pertinent because of the Conservative candidate's advocacy of protectionist tariffs on imports. Dorothy's argument was that free trade supported jobs and employment and she backed her case with examples of how Germany had damaged its shipping industry through imposing import taxes.[2] The by-election took place at a time when the Conservative government of Prime Minister Arthur Balfour[3] was unpopular and the Liberal candidate won by 385 votes. It was the first time the Liberal party had been the victor in this particular seat and Dorothy must have been thrilled to have participated in the triumph.[4]

Her next campaign was on behalf of Charlie's older brother, Noel. He had stood unsuccessfully in the 1900 General Election, but in June 1905 had the chance to stand in a by-election at Whitby in Yorkshire. With the government still unpopular, he had a chance of winning despite this being natural Conservative territory politically. Dorothy clearly loved campaigning and was not at all intimidated by her being a 'lady speaker', which was a novelty at the time. Her account illustrated the excitement of it all:

> Up to the last *2 days* I really rather enjoyed the time; the country is so exquisite & the people so charming – & I do so love whizzing in a motor car; – & then all accounts augured well of our success. The last 2 days however the strain & tension became more acute & the last morning was agonising when I sat through the counting of the votes in the same room with Noel & the rival candidate & friends!

1   Dorothy's memorandum on her pregnancy with Eglantyne, BFA.
2   *Oswestry Advertiser* & *Montgomeryshire Mercury*, 16 July, 1904.
3   Arthur Balfour (1848–1930), Prime Minister 1902–05, Conservative MP for Hertford 1874–85, for Manchester East 1885–1906; for City of London 1906–22.
4   The Conservatives recaptured the constituency at the next General Election in 1906 with a majority of 503.

I made 15 speeches in the course of the week varying from 10–35 minutes in length! The last day I made 4 & you sh[ou]ld have seen the last meeting. Driving home after 10pm I & some others passed through a village which had just endured a long open air meeting & nearly everyone had dispersed homewards. A handful of people remained in the road & on seeing *my* arrival (!!) one of them rushed off full split to try & call back the audience to hear me speak! In about 5–10 minutes dozens of people came *running* up the road as fast as they could & collected enthusiastically round the carriage. It is seldom one has such a glorious sight as one[']s audience *running* to hear one[']s words & at that time of night! The fact was, a lady speaker was very much of a novelty to them & they were all excited the last night before the poll. I spoke for about 15 min.; & left them singing Lib[eral] songs in a great state of enthusiasm.

If one is not too anxious an election is really great fun. The common cause puts one straightway on the most friendly footing with politicians flocking in from all parts to help in the work, & with all the local Liberals too. We all act under the orders of the local subagent & are sent off in all directions every evening to collect again towards midnight & compose notes over all the exciting news of the day[']s work.[1]

Noel Buxton proved the victor[2] and following this, it was time to work towards Charlie's election to the House of Commons so he could join his brother. Charlie had been adopted as the Liberal candidate for East Hertfordshire with considerable enthusiasm. The local constituency party members had given Dorothy and Charlie a large portrait of the former radical Liberal MP John Bright,[3] as a wedding present and as a sign of their esteem. Although women did not have the vote, their influence on the decisions of their husbands was acknowledged by the involvement of many women in election campaigns. It was also important to show women's considerable interest in politics as part of the pressure to grant them the vote. Especially in influencing women in the constituency, Dorothy recognised that she would be needed there, most crucially once a general election was called. So the nursing of the constituency began as soon as they were married and intensified in late 1905 as the Conservative

1   Dorothy to Eglantyne, 5 June 1905, Box 7, 7EJB/B/01/02/05, WL.
2   1905 June, by-election Whitby (electorate: 10,857) 79.7% turnout: Noel E. Buxton (Liberal) 4,547 (52.6%); William G. Beckett (Conservative) 4,102 (47.4%); Liberal majority 445 (5.2%).
3   John Bright (1811–89), parliamentary orator and MP for: Durham 1843–47; Manchester 1847–57; Birmingham 1858–89.

government resigned and the new minority Liberal government under Sir
Henry Campbell Bannerman[1] immediately called an election for January
1906. Dorothy wrote about this period:

> The autumn of 1905 found me deeply engrossed in our usual round
> of work. Our order of life up to this time was a fairly strenuous
> one: Church before 8 o'clock breakfast; afterwards housekeeping &
> discussion of plans etc till 9.30; then letter writing & preparation
> of speeches; & other head work of various kinds. At this time I
> was studying the history of England during the 19th century. The
> evening[']s business often meant a political meeting in East Herts
> & the imminence of the General Election gave them at this time,
> special interest & importance. It was an arduous business, leaving
> home to catch a train between 6 & 7 [p.m.], sometimes having high
> tea before, or else sandwiches in the train, or tea in a pub or the
> house of a supporter just before the Meeting: the meeting itself an
> affair of 3 h[ou]rs winding up with a short speech from me; then
> home by a 10.30 train, & bed after midnight. Other evenings we
> attended Morley College for Committees, Debates or 'Socials', or we
> entertained the students in 'at homes' from 8–10, & these functions
> were a great strain to me. One evening in the week we tried to
> keep for a dinner party either here or elsewhere & weekends we
> frequently spent in the country, staying with friends or relations. An
> evening at home by ourselves was the rarest thing, often many weeks
> elapsed between such treats. By the end of November [1905] this
> manner of life was becoming very laborious to me, & the strain of it
> culminated in a long promised political tour in the Whitby division
> (N[oel] E B[uxton]'s at that time). 5 Meetings with speeches often
> an hour[']s duration were crowded into 2 days & 3 nights, a labour
> to which I felt quite unequal beforehand & my anxiety was doubled
> by my doubts as to the justifiability of incurring such a strain; . . .
> Then the same question, – as to the desirability of working – arose
> with far greater seriousness in connexion with the Gen[eral] Election
> which was to take place in January. I knew that my presence & work
> in E[ast] Herts during the Election could not but increase CRB's
> chances, & conceivably might make the difference between defeat
> & victory, between failure & success in the object to which we had
> given so much time & hard labour.[2]

---

1   Henry Campbell-Bannerman (1836–1908), Prime Minster 1905–08, Liberal MP
    for Stirling Boroughs 1868–1908.
2   Dorothy, memorandum January 1907, BFA. This is one of the opening paragraphs.

Nationally, the 1906 General Election proved a landslide for the Liberal Party, who formed a government with a huge majority, but it was not a happy one for the Buxton brothers. Noel lost his Whitby seat to the Conservatives whilst Charlie failed to take East Hertfordshire by the slim majority of just eighty votes.[1] It was a blow, although East Herts had never been a Liberal seat – indeed the party had not even put up a candidate to oppose the Conservatives in the previous two general elections. The 1906 election was the nearest the Liberals ever came to capturing the constituency so Charlie had no reason to feel a failure. But to both him and his wife, it was deeply disappointing: success had been so close, but had eluded them. Eglantyne tried to comfort Dorothy, saying principles are what matters. One stood for ideals – whether successful or not in a worldly sense – and it was these that counted. She saw this as part of the sacrifice her sister and brother-in-law were making with their lives and that disappointment and suffering was an inevitable part of the political fray. 'Charlie's mission, as everyone knows, is to advance God's kingdom on earth: to hasten the day of juster social relations, greater equality of opportunity, a wider diffusion of happiness & well[-]being. I shed no tears – this time – over his not getting into Parliament.'[2] Dorothy wrote an open letter to the Liberal women in the constituency, commending their work and urging them not to be discouraged. Part of her own disappointment – and indeed guilt – was that she had been unable to participate in the campaign. 'It will be a lasting regret to me that I was prevented from standing by you to share in all your feelings in the time of trial and disappointment.'[3]

The reason for her absence was simply that towards the end of 1905 she had discovered that she was pregnant. When she found out, it left her in emotional turmoil as she knew she was 'letting others down'.

> Great therefore was my agony of mind when informed by Dr McAlister of Cambridge, that, for the child's sake, my absence from the Election was imperative. . . . Accordingly, from the middle of December onwards my whole manner of life was changed, & mapped out for the one supreme end – the benefit of my Child to be. On the 18th [December], I attended my last meeting in E[ast] H[erts]; a meeting to instruct & encourage the women as to the part they were to play in the Election. I could not but feel very sad & downcast. The crowning moments of what had been so long a

---

1   1906 January, general election East Herts (electorate 11,124) 86.7% turnout: Abel H. Smith (Conservative Unionist), 4,836 (50.4%); C. Roden Buxton (Liberal), 4,756 (49.6%); Conservative Unionist majority of 80 (0.8%).
2   Eglantyne to Dorothy, Box 7, 7EJB/B/01/02/05, WL.
3   Open letter from Dorothy to E. Herts Liberal Ladies, 9 February 1906, BFA.

struggle were now so near, – the long-awaited – much thought of – dreamt of battle must take place, the momentous issue must be decided – without my being able to lift a finger in the cause I had so fervently at heart. At the close of the Meeting the horrid truth leaked out that I was not to take part in the Contest. The women were dumbfoundered [*sic*] & aghast at this news, & in the midst of this bewilderment I hastily made my escape, – never – so far as I yet know – to attend another Meeting in E. Herts.[1]

She and Charlie then went on a week's break to Rottingdean on the south coast for some sea air and relaxation before spending Christmas at Warlies, after which Charlie started his election campaign without his wife. Despite the disappointment of the timing, having a child was something both she and Charlie longed for. 'She has longed, equally with me, to have children of our own, hers and mine, mine and hers.'[2]

In January 1907, Dorothy wrote a memorandum chronicling her pregnancy so that her child would have a record of it all. She related how she had decided to go and stay somewhere remote where she could be cut off and insulated from all the emotions of Charlie's campaign. This way she felt she could stay calm and this would benefit her unborn child. Otherwise she would have been hopelessly agitated.

> Though disappointed, more than words can express, in the matter of the Election – still I felt something of the thrill of being launched on another & a new enterprise – mysterious, great, & not to be foreseen in all its fateful consequences. . . .
>
> I knew that for my child's sake, peace of mind was essential to me, & joy & happiness the thing to seek. There appeared to me only one possible way of attaining it & that was to cut myself off completely from the world, from all news of CRB's campaign or anything political whatsoever, I was in too incendiary a condition to allow any spark to come near me; I must therefore *bury myself.* To this end I sought out a lonely Inn, the Snake Inn, in the Peak district, 7 miles from Glossop on the one side, & 10 miles from the nearest town on the other, a place so inaccessible that letters were only delivered 3 times in the week. It was a beautiful & desolate country, the Inn overlooking the lower slopes of the peak & surrounded on all sides by heather clad hills; fold beyond fold.

---

1   Dorothy, memorandum January 1907, BFA. Subsequent quotations in this section are from this same document.

2   Charlie, memorandum dated Rome, 31 December 1914, Box 10, 7EJB/B/01/03/07-13, WL. This quotation is from section XII. Copy also in BFA.

The rush of the stream in the winding valley below the Inn, & the crow of the grouse, were constantly in one[']s ears, wild sounds, soothing as the voices of home, to the ear of a Londoner.

With Charlie so preoccupied, her natural companion was the sister to whom she was closest, Eglantyne, and it was she who came to spend the three weeks with Dorothy, with short walks, reading and discussion to keep them occupied. Despite the self-imposed banishment from the news, eventually her sister collected the telegram that contained the news of Charlie's result to take back to Dorothy.

> I cannot dwell upon the hours of trial that preceded the arrival of the fatal telegram – nor on those that followed. E[glantyne] brought it to me in our bedroom in the late afternoon at one of the hours when I used to stay daily to pray for CRB. 'It is time to be brave' she said, her own face quite pale, & sitting together on the bed we opened the telegram. The fatal words & the sensation they gave me live all too vividly in the memory: 'Smith wins, majority 80'. Somehow I had numbed myself against the news.

She was full of angry frustration and worried about whether she could have made any difference had she been there.

> All the influence of mere wealth, – with its appeal to the snobbery of one class, & the sense of dependence of another, had been used against us, & used without scruple; – & had prevailed. From the first moment of course the thought had come to me 'had I been there, might it not have turned the scale?' Many people, as I afterwards learned, thought it might have, – but it was a vain speculation – fruitful only of unprofitable torment. Under the circumstances I could never for an instant regret the course I had chosen.

Charlie joined Dorothy for ten days of holiday and his 'cheerfulness & patience never failed', although the night of his arrival they had to cope with the news of Noel's defeat.[1]

> In the midst of the almost universal & almost unparalleled Liberal triumph consequent in the Election, the few failures seemed to stand out as all the more sad & disappointing, & among those few exceptions it seemed hard that *both* the politician members of our family should be numbered. The year came in with bright hopes

---

1   1906 January, general election Whitby (electorate 11,263) 84.2% turnout: William G. Beckett (Conservative) 4,780 (50.4%); Noel E. Buxton (Liberal) 4,709 (49.6%); Conservative majority 71 (0.8%).

for the Liberal party & for the country to whose service so many were genuinely devoted, not least among such, NCB & CRB, but for them the door was shut & the career which seemed to them – above all others – to offer the greatest opportunities for effectual service, was closed.

In February they were back in London taking up their usual routine, albeit with the absence of the to-ing and fro-ing to Hertfordshire. In April, Dorothy spent time at Barmouth on a holiday with her Aunt Bun.[1] However, as the time for the birth approached, Dorothy began to spend more time relaxing – in fact, it was remarkable how the usually somewhat fretfully busy Dorothy became so calm and unhurried. She spent some time at Warlies enjoying the countryside, but mostly she revelled in her own garden in London. She as good as lived in that garden, sleeping there in a shelter, made possible because it was an exceptionally hot summer.

> It was a new & delicious experience to breathe the night air, pure and fragrant then almost as the air of the country; to wake up in the morning to look out onto daffodils & tulips shining like stars out of the growing grass, & to hear the thrushes singing in the trees close to us. In the day time I would take my books & papers out to the shelter, & go to sleep on the bed there after lunch. Sometimes I would spend hours sitting there simply to contemplate the flowers, & how I revelled in the luxury of leisure for such a purpose! As the summer grew daily more rich & beautiful I devoted myself more & more to sheer enjoyment of it.

However, she found Kennington stressful nevertheless. She became intolerant of the people who came round, the servants who lived alongside her, as she felt they were not people who shared her outlook. Dorothy's upbringing had made her like space around her with few demands from other people bearing down.

> I was moreover only *partially* successful in my endeavour to preserve a tranquil & harmonious state of mind. There remained in my life certain sources of worry & disquietude which up to that time I had entirely failed to eliminate. To be obliged to share one[']s house & home[,] one[']s *very life* (outwardly), & to live on quasi-familiar terms with persons whose ideas & ideals are necessarily widely disparate from one[']s own, persons with whom I found it impossible to be really in sympathy, who do not understand me

---

1   Tye to Richard, 13 April 1906, 20 April 1906 and 28 April 1906, Box 10, 7EJB/B/01/03/10, WL.

& whom I do not understand & for whom notwithstanding all this I am in a position of the most serious responsibility, this is a deplorable state of things, & I doubt whether I can even get completely hardened to it. At the time of which I write it worried me to an extent which even then I fully recognized as morbid. The thought of it constantly overshadowed me & I never completely escaped from its malign influence till I had put many geographical miles between myself and Kennington!

Another worry was a crisis in the Buxton family brewery business, which (temporarily) threatened their income, as Dorothy's mother wrote,

We had Charlie & Dorothy to lunch with us on Saturday, both looking very well, and cheerful, despite the unlooked for Brewery crisis, which deprives them of the greater part of their income. It was well they chose to live in a way which enables them to go on as they are, notwithstanding! Unless things look up, however, Parliament & holiday travels are no longer feasible. Charlie will doubtless I hope be able to get remunerative work & I hope find a career worthy of his abilities.[1]

However, the financial threat proved temporary. Instead, Dorothy received the comfort of her mother, Tye, arriving to stay in early July 1906. Tye proved able to shield Dorothy from some of the intrusions. A midwife was also employed, a Mrs Paddie, who Dorothy described as the 'most wonderful & loveable of women'. On 4 August 1906, Dorothy gave birth to a daughter, who was named Eglantyne, after both Dorothy's mother and her own beloved sister. According to Tye, Dorothy was given chloroform on and off to help her with the pain of giving birth during the last hours of labour. Charlie, she noted, was 'immensely pleased' the child was a girl.[2] Dorothy's prior conviction was that it would be a boy.[3] In September, Dorothy went off to a farmhouse at Byfleet, Surrey, with a nurse for the baby, in order to have a complete rest.[4]

Long afternoons in the garden with lunch provided by a cook, a paid nurse, chloroform, a long holiday afterwards – these were important for Dorothy as she awaited and then gave birth to her first child, but they were not supports available to most women. However, the fact that she had availed herself of them showed that, for all her longings, Dorothy could

1   Tye to Richard, 6 June 1906, Box 10, 7EJB/B/01/03/10, WL.
2   Tye to Richard, 7 August 1906, Box 10, 7EJB/B/01/03/10, WL.
3   Dorothy's memorandum on her pregnancy with Eglantyne, BFA.: 'I was all along convinced that the child would be a son!'
4   Tye to Richard, 13 September 1906, Box 10, 7EJB/B/01/03/10, WL.

Dorothy and her daughter, Eglantyne

not yet live as working-class women would of necessity have had to do. She could give up the luxuries of her class background (fashionable clothes, exotic food, convenient transport), but not as yet the comforting supports.

Charlie joined her initially at Byfleet before going walking in northern England with one of his brothers in October. He also attended the Church Congress in Barrow in Furness, where he made a speech arguing for Christian convictions to result in political and social action.[1] The defeat at East Hertfordshire had not dampened his parliamentary ambitions, but made them even more insistent. The search was on for another seat to contest. The Liberal Party officials guided him towards the constituency

1   CC1906, pp. 247–250.

of Mid-Devon also known as Ashburton. This had returned a Liberal MP since 1885, even in years when the party lost power at the national level, and this despite a strong Conservative Party locally. In the January 1906 election, H. T. Eve[1] had retained the seat with a majority of 1,289. Eve was very popular locally, as he was involved in farming in the constituency as well as being a lawyer, and so had garnered support amongst agricultural workers. However, in late 1907 he was appointed a judge in the chancery division of the High Court of Justice and had to resign as an MP. Hence there was a by-election called for January 1908. The Liberal Party felt that Charlie would be a suitable candidate. Despite his radical views, he was moderate in his approach, ever seeking to persuade people to his opinions rather than denouncing those with whom he disagreed. He was of a well-known family and was the kind of Liberal candidate acceptable to the more traditional electorate of an essentially country seat. He was adopted as their candidate by the local Liberal association with some enthusiasm.

However, Charlie did not necessarily start out as a strong favourite. He was 'parachuted' in from outside the constituency whereas the Conservative candidate, Captain Ernest Morrison-Bell,[2] was well-known locally, as a resident of Chudleigh. Indeed he had fought the 1906 General Election and polled well even though losing. He had used the two years since to cultivate the electors by, according to *The Times* correspondent, 'talking to them at public meetings and by fireside chats and wayside amenities'. Charlie on the other hand had no such ties and was an 'unknown' candidate, although in campaigning he would prove to be a 'well-equipped antagonist'.[3]

Although the writ for the election was not issued until the first week of January 1908, Charlie was already active, addressing meetings after Christmas in December 1907. The Women's Political and Social Union, campaigning for votes for women, announced they would canvas against Charlie, because the Liberal government had not passed a bill for women's suffrage, as the Prime Minister, Herbert Asquith[4] did not support such a move.[5] Charlie was in favour of votes for women, as was Dorothy, but in the context of all adults, male or female of any class, being enfranchised – that is, universal adult suffrage. For them it was not a gender issue, but one of political rights for the working classes, of whom women made up fifty per cent. Some suffragettes, however, were fighting for women's votes

1   Harry Trelawny Eve (1856–1940), Liberal MP for Ashburton 1904–07.
2   Ernest Fitzroy Morrison-Bell (1870–1960).
3   *The Times*, 14 January 1908.
4   Herbert Henry Asquith (1852–1926), Prime Minister 1908–16, Liberal MP for East Fife 1886–1918, for Paisley 1920–24.
5   *The Times*, 1 January 1908.

on the same terms as men, even if that meant continuing the restrictions that excluded for example live-in household servants. So the Buxtons did not join the WPSU, but instead in 1909 supported a new group called the People's Suffrage Federation, which represented the universal position.[1]

Another problem for Charlie was that the Socialist and Independent Labour organisers, whilst having no candidate of their own, advised their members to abstain rather than vote Liberal.[2] The newspaper reporters detected a swing amongst some electors in favour of Tariff Reform and import controls against Charlie's staunch Free Trade position. These factors and trends all made for a prediction that conditions were favourable to the Conservative candidate and that 'he ought to be able to reduce the Liberal majority towards vanishing point'.[3] In the event, he did so and won the by-election by 559 votes.[4] Charlie was gracious in defeat, but there was uproar from both sets of supporters, who were overjoyed and furious respectively at the unexpected result.[5] Fights broke out and Mrs Pankhurst[6] (the suffragette leader) was knocked down and injured her ankle whilst being pelted with mud. With a certain defiant air, Charlie pledged himself to fight the seat at the next general election.[7]

This loss for Charlie was far more devastating than that of East Hertfordshire. At the latter, he had been contesting a safe Conservative seat and nearly won. Here he had been defending a traditionally Liberal constituency and had lost. Dorothy accompanied Charlie to meetings during the latter part of the campaign. Local press reports record her being present, sometimes receiving a bouquet, but she spoke only occasionally and then just 'a few words'. There is one report of her addressing Liberal women supporters in Dawlish.[8] However, her presence was appreciated: local Liberals thanked her for whatever she did do by giving her a carriage clock.[9] At the result, she

1 Clarke, pp. 138–139.
2 *The Times,* 14 January 1908.
3 *The Times,* 17 January 1908.
4 1908 January, by-election Ashburton (electorate 10,976) 89.5% turnout: Captain Ernest F. Morrison-Bell (Conservative Unionist) 5,191 (52.8%); C. Roden Buxton (Liberal) 4,632 (47.2%); Conservative Unionist majority of 559 (5.6%).
5 The by-election was illustrated by a page of drawings entitled 'The Turbulent Mid-Devon Election: The Polling Day', in *The Illustrated London News* 25 January 1908.
6 Emmeline Pankhurst (1858–1928), founder of the Women's Political and Social Union 1903.
7 *The Times,* 20 January 1908.
8 *The Western Times,* 10 January 1908.
9 The inscription on the clock (still in the family's possession) reads: 'Presented by the Kingsteignton Women's Liberal Association to Mrs C. R. Buxton in appreciation of her efforts during the mid-Devon by-election January 1908.'

Dorothy & Charlie in their 'Devon' period

must have felt deflated and miserable. As we noted in her undergraduate days, she did not take defeat well. It was now clear Charlie would have to 'nurse' the constituency so as to have a chance of winning at the next general election and that meant moving to live in Devon. Dorothy would also have to be a full partner in the political work ahead and she determined to throw herself into this, even though it would involve activities that might not be congenial, such as large social gatherings.

On 21 March 1908, the couple moved to a house called Braeside in Bovey Tracey, and were met by a cheering crowd of supporters at the train station when they first arrived.[1] As well as a round of political meetings, Charlie accommodated the expectations of his potential electors: he grew a dashing moustache favoured by gentlemen in the Edwardian period, kept a groom and horse, hunted, went to the cricket matches and joined the Devon Yeomanry, which involved camps and military exercises on Dartmoor. Most of this he much enjoyed.[2] Dorothy for her part made speeches and chaired meetings for the Women's Liberal Association, attended teas and bazaars, even laid the foundation stone of a new Wesleyan chapel in Newton Abbot in 1909. She donned smart clothes and the enormous hats then fashionable and played the 'county lady'. It was a style that she had thought she would never have to espouse, so most of this she loathed. The couple had kept the Kennington house for when they were in London – and indeed if Charlie did get elected he would need a base there for when parliament was sitting. However, Dorothy was resident mainly in Devon, where her consolations were the countryside and its natural beauty, as their house was near to the edge of Dartmoor. For the rest, she made sacrifices for her husband and for the causes in which they both believed.

The year 1909 was a turbulent one in British politics as the Chancellor of the Exchequer, David Lloyd George,[3] presented his 'People's Budget', including (amongst other measures) the introduction of old age pensions and an increase of taxes on the wealthy. The Liberal-dominated House of Commons passed this radical budget, but it was much opposed by the Conservatives, who still had a majority in the House of Lords. The rejection of the budget by the Lords meant a general election was called for January 1910. As in 1906, Dorothy found herself unable to help with Charlie's campaign in person, as she was heavily pregnant with her second child and stayed in London. She did write circulars that were used in the constituency.[4] In the event, all the hard work and numerous sacrifices finally proved worthwhile as Charlie was returned, beating his previous conqueror Morrison-Bell by 247 votes.[5] At last, he was a Member of Parliament.

---

1   *Western Daily Press*, 23 March 1908.
2   De Bunsen, p. 51.
3   David Lloyd George (1863–1945), Prime Minister 1916–22.
4   Charlie to Dorothy, 9 January 1910, BFA.
5   1910 January, general election Ashburton (electorate 11,976) 92.6% turnout; C. Roden Buxton (Liberal) 5,668 (51.1%); Captain Ernest F. Morrison-Bell (Conservative Unionist) 5,421 (48.9%); Liberal majority 247 (2.2%).

I didn't want you to be here for the contest – but oh I do wish you could have been here for the victory! The wild enthusiasm tonight – & above all at Newton, & at the final reception here at Bovey – would have done your heart good. It is not *mere* fanaticism. All the little crushed people everywhere have felt a sudden exaltation – they are the masters here – *their* work has got their champion in![1]

Charlie wrote to his mother of how after the poll result, he had,

a sort of triumphal progress round the division, including torchlight processions at Newton and here. The final welcome here from my 'fellow townsmen' was most moving, ending up with my being *carried* into my house shoulder high![2]

For Dorothy, there was elation at her husband's success. However, she remained for the time being in London as she expected to give birth early in March. On the evening of 24 February, Dorothy entertained friends at Kennington Terrace until 10p.m., but then in the early hours of the next day, the baby decided to arrive a couple of weeks earlier than expected. Charlie chased all round London in a taxi cab picking up the doctor and the nurses and at 4a.m., after a very short labour, Dorothy gave birth to a boy. This time she did not need chloroform. They toyed with calling him 'Devon' to celebrate Charlie's constituency, but then settled on David – for both the Psalms and David Lloyd George according to Dorothy, symbolising religion and politics.[3]

By this time, the Buxtons had a cook and several maids in attendance at Kennington Terrace plus a German nanny, Frieda Bour, who looked after little Eglantyne as well as the new baby. But Dorothy found having staff around still irritating, 'within 4 hours of baby's arrival I had to be interviewing the servants & hear the agitated housemaids suggesting I should immediately see about getting in a different cook!'[4]

---

1   Charlie to Dorothy, 26 January 1910, BFA.
2   Charlie to his mother, 29 January 1910, BFA.
3   Dorothy to Victoria, March 1910, BFA; Charlie to Victoria, 2 March 1910, BFA.
4   Dorothy to Victoria, March 1910, BFA. The difficulties with servants were a constant complaint of the middle classes among whom Dorothy had chosen to live. Masterman noted this in describing the women of suburbia, 'The women, with their single domestic servants, now so difficult to get, and so exacting when found' and later, 'His wife is harassed by the indifference or insolence of the domestic servant.' The suburban man, 'refuses to mourn over the sufferings of the factory girl when he is offering a desirable position as general "help" and can find no applicant'. Masterman, pp. 70, 71 and 73. Dorothy's exasperation was shared by many others.

Life was also complicated by Charlie's health which, on occasion, began to be of concern. His eyes began to weaken and trouble him.[1] It was clear that he had to be careful not to take on too much, so he shed some of his pre-election responsibilities. He resigned as Principal of Morley College.[2] In April 1910, Dorothy encouraged him to take a complete break in Switzerland – she stayed behind with the children. It seemed to do him good as he reassured his wife.

> Doing nothing is one of the most difficult arts; but I think I have been very successful at it! I have idled away all the time I could – read nothing, hardly, & written nothing. I look on this holiday as a precaution rather than a necessity. It is very jolly so long as one can feel that one's past exertions entitle one to an easy time. I should not like it for very long, tho' I am enjoying myself hugely. [3]

Politics was exciting and time-consuming in 1910, with the final passage of the controversial budget, the government considering resignation in April over House of Lords reform, the death of King Edward VII in May, and then the need for a second General Election in December 1910 as the government sought an electoral mandate for curbing the veto of the House of Lords. Charlie, as one of the radical wing of Liberal MPs, supported the proposed changes with conviction, whilst learning how the House of Commons worked. His brother Noel was also there as he had been returned at the January General Election for North Norfolk.[4] Dorothy helped Charlie and his colleagues by doing research and helping to write speeches – and her husband valued this greatly. 'Every time I see the swarm of *wives* on the Terrace [of the House of Commons], I think with more & more pride of *my* wife, who is *cooperating* in the work!'[5]

The second 1910 election was the first of Charlie's campaigns in which Dorothy was directly and continuously involved throughout. As Charlie travelled about the constituency, Dorothy acted as his secretary, opening his letters and forwarding relevant papers to help him for different meetings.[6] He wanted her also to make speeches and be a visible presence, and he gently urged her not to fuss over details, but instead spread an optimistic 'bonhomie'.

---

1   Charlie's eyesight remained troublesome. See for example Charlie to Dorothy, 25 April 1913, BFA, in which he wrote of consulting yet another oculist and trying new spectacles, after having to have letters read to him as his sight was so poor.
2   *MCM,* Vol XIX, No 7 (April 1910), p. 101.
3   Charlie to Dorothy, 11 April 1910, BFA.
4   1910 January, general election North Norfolk (electorate 11,169) 87.7% turnout: Noel E. Buxton (Liberal) 5,189 (53%); H. Douglas King (Conservative) 4,604 (47%); Liberal majority 585 (6%).
5   Charlie to Dorothy, 14 June 1910, BFA.
6   Charlie to Dorothy, 1 November 1910, BFA.

Everyone is in excellent spirits about the election: it is most fortunate that I have just completed a tour of the division – & exceptionally lucky that you should have arranged your meetings just now! Nobody has got such a helper as I have, to hold the fort. We are in for a historic contest, & it *is* jolly to think of you being in the field this time! We shall have grand fun.

But all this makes it trebly important that you should take it easy. Remember, the time has now come when *educational* work ceases altogether, & agitation begins. So that it is not a time for preparing material for speeches with elaborate care. The absolutely vital thing now is to move about among our friends with an encouraging air – *feeling* happy & vigorous & making *them* feel so. It matters less than ever what the details of our speeches are, or how often we repeat ourselves. Let us have a thoroughly enjoyable time.[1]

Dorothy could not do anything by halves and her intensity was unavoidable – she either did nothing or else everything. She threw herself into the task. Yet her anxiety that Charlie should be re-elected meant this campaign could not be 'fun'. So much of her own sense of fulfilment was at stake unlike those early campaigns of 1904–05 in which she had spoken. Sadly for them both, the efforts of December 1910 brought disappointment. In round three of Buxton versus Morrison-Bell in Mid-Devon, the Conservative won by 354 votes.[2] It was a terrible blow. In their political aspirations, Dorothy and Charlie felt they were back to 'square one'.

What became clear in the aftermath was that Dorothy was ready to move on from Devon: Charlie would not fight there again. He could shave off his moustache and she could return to simpler clothes. They did not leave immediately as Charlie had a foreign affairs trip abroad in January and then Dorothy went to help look after her Aunt Bun in Shropshire, who had a bout of ill-health. Finally, however, in June 1911, the house at Bovey Tracey was vacated and Dorothy had no qualms about relinquishing the 'county lady' role. Charlie, staying at Warlies afflicted with a strained hand and arm, acknowledged Dorothy's relief as she packed up their house at Bovey Tracey for the last time.

I am thinking very much of you, dearest one, in these last few days at Bovey, & wondering if you feel any sadness at the departure. Beyond the breaking of the bond with numerous loyal friends,

1   Charlie to Dorothy, 18 November 1910, BFA.
2   1910 December, general election Ashburton (electorate 11,976) 90.2% turnout: Captain Ernest F. Morrison-Bell (Conservative Unionist) 5,579 (51.6%); C. Roden Buxton (Liberal) 5,225 (48.4%); Conservative Unionist majority 354 (3.2%).

I don't think you do – very much. And the rush of preparations probably prevents you from thinking even of that. . . .

My simple creed at present is 'look to the future'. We are very young, and certainly have a part to play which will be altogether apart from Devon & our Devon friends. About that there can be no doubt whatever. It may be a big part: it may be a small one.[1]

In the next months, Charlie immediately began looking for another constituency to contest. The Government Whips said they wanted him back in the House of Commons as soon as possible.[2] When Sir Charles Dilke[3] died suddenly in February 1911, Dorothy warned him off Dilke's Forest of Dean constituency as it was another 'county' seat – although it had a strong mining community amongst the electorate.[4] She felt he should look for an urban seat which would better suit their situation and inclinations. He took an interest in West Ham North, where the Liberal MP, his friend Charles Masterman,[5] was unseated owing to illegal election expenses,[6] but Charlie was not chosen to fight the by-election. He was also in the mix of possible candidates for North-West Norfolk but, in the end, was not chosen.[7] He was not out of touch with the House of Commons though, as his brother Noel was still there (he had retained his Norfolk seat in the December 1910 election),[8] as were other close colleagues. As Charlie had been active in looking for ways to address the problems of agricultural workers, who suffered poverty

1   Charlie to Dorothy, 17 June 1911, BFA.
2   Charlie to Dorothy, no date but early 1911, BFA. At Prime Minister Asquith's one evening, he was told by one of the Whips: 'I'm not going to leave you out for long!'
3   Sir Charles Wentworth Dilke, 2nd Baronet, (1843–1911), Liberal MP for Chelsea 1868–86 and for the Forest of Dean 1892–1911.
4   Charlie to Dorothy, 27 January 1911 and undated (but end of January/early February 1911), BFA. The by-election on 24 February was contested by Henry Webb for the Liberals who held the seat with an increased majority of 3,068 over the Conservatives. Charles Dilke's majorities in the 1910 elections had been 2,862 and 2,724 respectively.
5   Charles Frederick Gurney Masterman (1873–1927), Liberal MP for West Ham North 1906–11, for Bethnal Green South West 1911–1914 and for Manchester Rusholme 1923–24.
6   Masterman had been re-elected to West Ham North for the Liberals at the December 1910 election. However, a petition to unseat him on grounds of illegal expenses and declare the election void was filed. It proved successful and in the by-election on 8 July 1911 Baron Maurice de Forest increased the Liberal majority from 897 to 1,031. (Baron de Forest was a hereditary Baron of the Austrian Empire and authorised to use his title in Great Britain.) Masterman was returned for Bethnal Green SW at another by-election in July 1911.
7   The Times, 24 April 1912.
8   1910 December, general election North Norfolk (electorate 11,169): Noel E. Buxton (Liberal) 5,187; H. Douglas King (Conservative) 4,491; Liberal majority 696.

Dorothy elegantly attired in August 1912 for the Golden wedding celebrations of her parents-in-law

as much as the urban working-class, David Lloyd George asked him to be the secretary of the Land Enquiry Committee in 1912. Charlie threw his energies into this with enthusiasm, quickly becoming an expert on the various types of tenancy agreements. This work kept him very much in the stream of parliamentary life and in his office in Westminster. The Committee's report came out in two volumes, published in October 1913 and April 1914.

Dorothy pushed herself to remain involved in politics. In mid-1911, she attended the annual Women's Conference of the Liberal Federation, held at the Manchester Reform Club. Despite her experience of speaking, going back nearly ten years, she was clearly still diffident, as Charlie extolled her to enjoy herself and make friends. He also suggested she stop worrying about her speech and not to spend her time refining details. He offered to send her notes on land reform issues to be of service. 'Don't sit po[u]ring over leaflets all your spare time. *Have complete confidence in yourself.* You *cannot* make a bad speech if you try. You are quite certain to impress people, (so don't worry about it) even if you do no more preparation. Feel that you are a swell. (You *are*). *Expect* people to bow down before you – don't grovel to *them.*'[1]

Dorothy did not seem convinced: she had yet to feel completely comfortable in the world of a political party. She wanted to be free to express her own ideas and concerns instead of upholding the 'party line' in order to maintain party unity. Such a discipline was too restrictive for her passionate spirit. As it was, she was more comfortable with writing. Two pamphlets from her pen were published by the Women's Liberal Federation in their Crusade Leaflets series: in January 1912 on 'Peace and War' and April 1912 on Irish Home Rule. In the former she noted the financial cost of war, as well as the human one – she added that it would take Britain a generation to recover even if victory were achieved. She argued for a policy of friendship towards Germany and its aspirations.

1   Charlie to Dorothy, 5 May 1911, BFA.

We must let by-gones be by-gones, and encourage our Government to give Germany practical proof that an honourable friendship with her, as with all other nations, is what we want. We must recognise that she has a perfect right to build a large navy to protect her growing trade. We must not deny her the opportunities for growth, which in her place, we should desire ourselves. There is plenty of room in the world for both Peoples.

On Ireland, she argued that self-rule elsewhere had led to 'prosperity and loyalty (even in the newly-conquered Boer countries) and to the peaceable settlement of religious differences'. Ulster Protestants could not be allowed to dictate to everyone else in Ireland. Remembering the rowdy behaviour of election crowds in Devon, she noted that Winston Churchill[1] had been shouted down in Belfast and denied free speech, so that the political leaders in Ulster, 'have shown that they share the political methods of the rowdy youths who sometimes obstruct village Election Meetings in the less enlightened parts of England'.

In many respects, whether speaking or writing, Dorothy still worked in her husband's shadow, in his field of activity, and could not find her own sphere of influence. She wanted to speak on land reform at the Women's Conference, for example, because that was the area of expertise Charlie was working on. So, it was still Charlie's parliamentary aspirations and his political agendas that shaped Dorothy's own.

In 1912 Charlie finally found another constituency and was adopted as the prospective parliamentary candidate for Hackney Central, then a Liberal seat where the incumbent was to step down at the next general election. As a consequence, the couple began to consider the location of their home and whether a move north of the river in London might be appropriate. Both of them were aware of the Garden City movement, advocated by Ebenezer Howard[2] in his 1898 book *To-morrow: A Peaceful Path to Real Reform* (re-published in 1902 under the more familiar title: *Garden Cities of Tomorrow*). He argued for urban landscapes to be less crowded and brutal. He advocated each dwelling having its own garden and there being plenty of space in housing developments with wide streets and verges. In short, he wanted city dwellers to have the benefits of the countryside – and this meant all city-dwellers, including the poor.

This was an idea that was almost tailor-made for Dorothy – combining the improvement of working-class conditions with an advocacy of gardens and the significance of the natural world for human well-being. Charlie

---

1   Winston Spencer Churchill (1874–1965), Prime Minister 1940–45, 1951–54; at this time he was a Liberal and serving in cabinet as First Lord of the Admiralty. In the 1920s he joined the Conservative Party.

2   Ebenezer Howard (1850–1928).

had led a party of Morley College students to see the first town developed on Howard's lines – Letchworth Garden City – in 1907.[1] Around that time the social reformer Henrietta Barnett[2] founded a similar project in Hampstead, north London, arranging for 243 acres of land to be bought from Eton College. It took some years before progress could be made as a bill had to go through parliament to allow the planners to ignore local by-laws and create a lower housing density than was usual. The idea was to mix the social classes in a variety of housing and this objective fulfilled many of the Buxtons' aspirations: they determined to purchase a house there. Dorothy was particular that it should be a house which had the largest back garden available and Erskine Hill, one of the new streets, had houses that fitted her brief. The house they took was Number 6, part of a substantial terrace, with a garden twice as long as the next along the row, and which also backed onto one of the two woods in the development. Erskine Hill led off from the Central Square, where the famous architect Edwin Lutyens[3] designed two magnificent churches – one Anglican and one Free Church. On the revised plans of 1912,[4] their house was laid out on three floors with two reception rooms, four bedrooms on the first floor and a large attic at the top, divided into two rooms, thus giving substantial accommodation. Dorothy and Charlie however kept the house frugal by not having such items as stair carpet, whilst Charlie would always walk the considerable distance to Golders Green Tube station and rarely take a cab. They anticipated that working-class people would live as neighbours in some of the less costly housing being built nearby. The house took some time to be completed and the move did not take place until the end of 1914.[5]

Ironically, this experiment in mixing classes and housing in a countrified setting was not sustainable in the long term. After the First World War with building materials scarce and a changed social outlook, the developers had little choice but to concentrate on housing for the wealthy if they were to make the project economically viable. As a result, Hampstead Garden

---

1   *MCM,* Vol XVI No 10 (July 1907), p. 146.
2   Henrietta Octavia Weston Barnett (1851–1936), social reformer, educationalist, co-founder of Toynbee Hall in 1884.
3   Edwin Landseer Lutyens (1869–1944), architect, renowned for designing country houses, government buildings in New Delhi and The Cenotaph in Whitehall.
4   See ACC/3816/P/01/191, ACC/3816/P/01/194, ACC/3816/01/06/357, ACC/3816/01/06/359, LMA.
5   The Buxton household left Kennington Terrace in September 1914 and lived temporarily in rented accommodation in Willifield Way, Golders Green, until 6 Erskine Hill was available at Christmas 1914. Tye's journal of the early weeks of the First World War, BFA.

Suburb developed into one of the most expensive parts of London, a desired residential area for many well-off people. However, it is important to remember that when Charlie and Dorothy decided to move there, it was with a very different social vision in mind.

6 Erskine Hill became Dorothy's retreat from all that made her despair in the world outside. The large garden especially provided this sense of a haven amidst the pressures of work. As the years went by, she found solace in the attic, which the couple made into their studies and work room, and from here the various projects that consumed her in the next decades took shape and their progress was directed. In this way, the house in Erskine Hill became her home, as 7 Kennington Terrace had not been, and it also allowed her an office, at last a work space of her own. Charlie had such an amenity in Westminster: she now had her own where they lived.

The back of 6 Erskine Hill in 1915, the windows all open illustrating Dorothy's love of fresh air

In the first decade of the Buxtons' marriage, the other important component of Dorothy's life was travel. Walking and climbing, dressed in simple clothes, she could cease being the politician's wife and feel freer from social restrictions. Some of the most adventurous trips were taken with Lawrence and Barbara Hammond,[1] who like the Buxtons were committed Liberals. Lawrence and Charlie had known each other before Charlie's marriage. From 1899, Lawrence was the editor of *The Speaker*, a Liberal publication which took an anti-Boer War position. After seven years, he handed the editorship on and then he worked briefly as assistant editor on *The Daily News*, but this still gave him little opportunity for the research and study he longed to do. Taking a civil service job in 1907,[2] as Secretary to the Civil Service Commission, allowed him time

---

1 John Lawrence LeBreton Hammond (1872–1949) and Lucy Barbara Hammond (née Bradby) (1873–1961). They married in 1901.

2 Charlie's letter of congratulation to Lawrence Hammond, dated 16 September

for historical work and he and his wife Barbara researched and wrote a series of influential books on the social and economic history of the labourer.[1] Charlie and Lawrence were both on the editorial committee that produced a series of essays in *The Speaker* in 1904 entitled *Towards a Social Policy*, reproduced in book form a year later.[2] Barbara and Dorothy got to know each other during the same period and the two couples remained good friends for about ten years.[3] The Hammonds' diaries show regular dinners and lunches and weekend walks.[4] They had two long trips on the continent together. One of which in 1909, leaving on 6 April, returning to London on 5 May, was spent in the region between Milan and Florence. The other from 9 September to 9 October 1911 was to the Italian and French Alps. Decades later, after the husbands had both died, Barbara wrote to Dorothy:

> some of the happiest days of our lives were spent with you & Charlie. Someone was talking lately about Aosta & Courmayeur & it brought back most vividly that exciting day when from Pre' S' Didier we went over the Little S' Bernard's Pass, in spite of warnings ab[ou]t the coming snow. The snow came on & you & Charlie came behind & saw a Pole cat or marten & we went ahead & got up to my neck in the snow just outside the hospice. What fun it all was.[5]

At the time, Dorothy wrote of the glorious views of the 'panorama of jagged mountain tops'. Mostly walking, but sometimes taking a tram when the heat was very powerful, they climbed up to nearly 7,000 feet and Dorothy as ever revelled in nature, '17 miles downhill seemed a mere nothing after the previous days of uphill & I never enjoyed a walk more, for I found *gentians* for the first time in my life.'

1907, can be found at MS Hammond 16, 76, HP.

1   *The Village Labourer* (1911), *The Town Labourer,* (1917), *The Skilled Labourer* (1919).

2   Weaver, p. 79.

3   The friendship was disrupted by the First World War, which took the couples in different directions. The Hammonds were convinced that Britain had to enter the war after the invasion of Belgium, the Buxtons were not. But also it seems Barbara (who was unable to have children of her own) found the Buxton children tiring. For example, 'somehow I don't feel up to David & Eglantyne so I am glad the distance prohibits'. (Barbara Hammond to Lawrence Hammond, 2 October 1913, MS Hammond 4, 178, HP.) 'I've got a snorting dripping cold tonight. . . . It derives from David Buxton's germs seizing on a lowered state.' (Barbara Hammond to Lawrence Hammond, 27 October 1915, MS Hammond 4, 178, HP). After 1915, the couples appear to have had less chance to see each other, although they were still in touch by letter and occasional social visits.

4   MS Hammond 37, 49, HP.

5   Barbara Hammond to Dorothy, 9 August 1949, BFA.

When not walking, the couples read aloud from Thackeray and Scott novels, whilst Dorothy for the first time tried embroidery – on dresses for her children. She seemed content to have time away from little Eglantyne (now five) and David (just twenty months), but did not forget them. 'I get excellent accounts of the children & feel free to enjoy myself to the utmost – so am having a really first rate holiday.'[1]

It was a healthy lifestyle for them even though hard work. They carried what they needed in knapsacks and washed clothes in streams like the local women.

> The peasant women seem to spend a large part of their time at this occupation & I did not feel my experience of the country was complete till I had seen what it felt like! It is I must say however a very back-breaking occupation!
>
> We have been having a splendid time.
>
> The Hammonds say that C[harlie] & I eat like 'boa constrictors' & 'what digestions those Buxtons have got'! C[harlie] often eats 4 eggs at a sitting when we are having our midday meal near a mountain top. He looks a lovely ruddy colour and so I believe I do too.[2]

They met up with Dorothy's mother and sister Eglantyne at Lake Como for two nights before returning home.

These were happy interludes amidst their busy lives and were necessary for Dorothy to escape from her tendency to overwork and worry. In some ways these trips proved the most carefree days of her adult life and as Barbara, quoted above, commented years later, the happiest. In the summer of 1914, Dorothy and Charlie had been married for ten years. They had two children and a new home and they enjoyed their travels and friends. They worked together towards their ambitions, had experienced successes and failures in the joint endeavours, centred on supporting the governing Liberal Party. It seemed that their aspirations would continue along the same path for many years to come.

Then the world changed. On 28 June 1914, the heir to the Habsburg throne of Austria-Hungary was assassinated on a visit to Sarajevo by a Serbian nationalist. Just over a month later, the intricate web of diplomatic alliances in Europe, stoked by fears of other governments' secret intentions, drew all the major nations into the First World War. As for most of her generation, this war would change Dorothy's life forever and it would redefine her politics, her religious views and her work. Through this world catastrophe, she was to find her own voice and sphere of influence, parallel yet distinct from Charlie's.

---

1   Dorothy to Aunt Bun, 17 [September 1911], Box 6, 7EJB/B/01/02/03, WL.
2   Dorothy to Aunt Bun, 1 October [1911], Box 6, 7EJB/B/01/02/03, WL.

Chapter 4
Experiencing the struggle

The outbreak of the First World War in early August 1914 was a profound shock to most British people. Indeed, that summer all the preparations for conflict, both military and political, had concerned Ireland. The Irish Home Rule Bill had been passed in 1912, but its implementation was delayed for two years by the House of Lords. The delay could not be further extended and the creation of a 'home rule' parliament in Dublin was expected to provoke armed rebellion from Protestants in Ulster who had been establishing volunteer fighting units and holding drills in Belfast in acts of threatening defiance.[1] In Dublin and the south of Ireland, Irish nationalist militias were arming themselves too and civil war loomed. On Sunday, 26 July 1914, a jeering crowd baited a group of British soldiers in Dublin who had seized a cache of arms belonging to Irish nationalists. The soldiers fired at the unarmed crowd and three people were killed and thirty-two injured.[2] This was the immediate emergency for most British citizens, not Austria's conflict with Serbia, and an outbreak of war in continental Europe had been far from people's minds. A European war erupted with great speed in the dying days of July. When the Germans attacked France via an invasion of neutral Belgium, the British government believed they had to protect Belgium and therefore declared war on 4 August. Many people accepted this decision as morally justified. Among those who did not were some MPs of the governing Liberal Party.

A significant element of the Liberal Party had always opposed involvement in any war. They were vociferous in opposition to the war in South Africa at the turn of the century and thereafter were wary of British foreign policy being wedded to imperialism and the use of force rather than diplomacy to

---

1   For an illustration of the then preoccupation of the popular press with Ireland, see for example: Angell, p. 179. The outbreak of war caused the implementation of Home Rule for Ireland to be suspended.

2   Marlor, p. 4.

secure its ends. They also believed that negotiation with Germany before the events of 1914 would have been more constructive than engaging in an arms race. They saw the strengthening of British ties with both France and Russia in the same period as a threat to Germany, which increased the likelihood of war instead of keeping a 'balance of power' to prevent it. The secrecy with which much diplomacy was practised was also seen by this group as equally destabilising to peace in Europe and the European colonies worldwide. They were suspicious of what military agreements had been made without recourse to parliamentary approval by the long-serving Foreign Secretary, Edward Grey.[1] As early as November 1911, a group of around seventy-five Liberal MPs had formed the 'Foreign Affairs Group', which was critical of their government's conduct of foreign policy and pressed for changes. It was unsuccessful in its aims, but was an indication of the anxiety amongst the more radical section of the Liberal party. One of the MPs who formed this group was Noel Buxton and he was its first chairman.[2]

Undoubtedly Charlie would have joined his brother had he still been an MP. Outside parliament he supported causes for peace and was a contributor to the journal *War and Peace*, launched in 1913.[3] He participated in efforts to oppose the naval rivalry with Germany and the build-up of armaments. He was involved with lobbying for Britain to keep out of any European conflict and joined a group called the British Neutrality Committee. In the days before war broke out Charlie was vociferous and unequivocal in the position he took, a stance fully supported by Dorothy. A letter to *The Manchester Guardian* was published and he wrote,

> Now is the time for every Liberal to declare that he protests against the idea of this country being drawn into war in order to support Russia and France against Austria and Germany. . . . [we should not] give an opportunity to those who believe in the false and dangerous superstition of the 'balance of power'.
>
> It is a Tory doctrine, but Liberals have been rushed into a Tory policy before now. Let us emphatically declare that we are under no obligation to support one European group against another.[4]

---

1 Edward Grey (1862–1933), Foreign Secretary 1905–16, Liberal MP for Berwick-upon-Tweed 1885–1916, Viscount 1916.
2 Arthur Ponsonby succeeded as the chairman in 1913 and was in that position on the outbreak of war. However, the committee's activities had diminished and when Ponsonby called a meeting of the group on 29 July, only 11 MPs turned up. Marlor, p. 42. On 30 July, with matters becoming more critical, there were 25. Marlor, p. 55.
3 Angell, p. 169.
4 *The Manchester Guardian,* 1 August 1914.

When war did break out, the Neutrality Committee dissolved itself because they felt that if an early opportunity occurred to pursue peace, any conciliation movement would be best run by a new group rather than those who had opposed entry into the war.

The new group was named the Union of Democratic Control.[1] Its founders included two liberal MPs: Charles Trevelyan,[2] who was one of those who resigned from the government as a consequence of the declaration of war, and Arthur Ponsonby,[3] who had refused government office precisely because he wished to speak out on foreign affairs. Ramsey Macdonald,[4] the chairman of the Labour parliamentary group, resigned his position when his fellow Labour MPs decided to vote for war credits and he too joined the fledgling UDC. The other leading founders were E.D. Morel,[5] a prospective Liberal parliamentary candidate, who became the UDC's secretary and organising force, and Norman Angell,[6] who was less involved in party politics, but was the most well-known of pre-1914 peace campaigners. The group published their aims as: parliamentary control over foreign policy; negotiations after the war to promote understanding between governments; peace terms that did not humiliate the defeated or re-arrange frontiers so as to leave cause for further wars. By June 1915, the UDC had 107 affiliated organisations supporting it, with a membership of 300,000, and by the end of the war this had increased to 300 and 650,000 respectively.

Charlie and Dorothy were both horrified that Britain had declared war instead of seeking to mediate. Therefore, it was unsurprising that Charlie was an early recruit to the UDC. He served on the UDC executive committee for much of the war and he was one of the most generous financial donors to the cause.[7] Charlie was a moderating influence, as

1   For a detailed history of the UDC, see: Swartz; Harris.
2   Charles Philips Trevelyan (1870–1958), Liberal MP for Elland 1899–1915 and then as an Independent 1915–18, Labour MP for Newcastle Central 1922–31.
3   Arthur Augustus William Harry Ponsonby (1871–1946), Liberal MP for Stirling Boroughs 1908–18, then Labour MP for Sheffield Brightside 1922–30, when he was given a peerage and transferred to the House of Lords. Ponsonby remembered how he and Charlie sat on a bench in St James' Park in 1914 wondering how they could bring a stop to the war, Jones, p. 229.
4   James Ramsey Macdonald (1866–1937), Labour MP for Leicester 1906–18, for Aberavon 1922–29, for Seaham 1929–35, for Combined Scottish universities 1936–37. Prime Minister January–November 1924 and 1929–35.
5   Edmund Dene Morel (né Georges Eduard Pierre Achille Morel de Ville) (1873–1924), Labour MP for Dundee 1922–24.
6   Norman Angell (1874–1967), author of the influential *The Great Illusion*, which argued that war was irrational and would be economically disadvantageous to both the victors and those defeated.
7   Swartz, p. 55 and note 35.

ever, on the UDC's policies as he believed denunciations and aggressive condemnations achieved little. He believed in negotiations even with a pro-war government, just as he did with the country's enemies.

Dorothy and Charlie may have been horrified, but they were not surprised by the outbreak of conflict. This was partly because the Balkans, where the initial conflict occurred that ignited the First World War, had long been of keen interest to Charlie and his brother Noel. As far back as the 1870s, the Buxton family had supported the small mainly Christian nationalities in the Balkans, an area mainly ruled by the Turks as part of the Ottoman Empire. Charlie's father had deplored the government's policy under the Conservative Prime Minster, Benjamin Disraeli[1], which had seen Russia as more of a threat than Turkey. He believed that the Ottoman Empire was the perpetrator of much injustice and maladministration amongst the Balkan peoples, with a 'divide and rule' policy that set the nationalities one against another. Gladstone's famous campaign in favour of the Bulgarians in 1878 had resonated with Sir Fowell Buxton: and his sons had been brought up to share his position. The way to counter the Russian threat to the eastern Mediterranean (and the 'route to India' so precious to the British) was to have the Balkan nations rule themselves as free peoples, not to prop up the despotism of Turkish rule there. Charlie in his politics consequently espoused the cause of small nations.

Noel first visited the Balkans in 1899 and was especially moved by the plight of the Macedonians. When they rose in rebellion against the Turks in 1903, he and his brother were among a group that formed the Balkan Committee to lobby the British government to support the Macedonians. In 1904, Noel Buxton visited Macedonia again, part of the time with his sister, Victoria,[2] and the cruelty they witnessed in terms of burned homes and wounded villagers, mourning others who had been killed by the Turkish authorities, led them to set up the Macedonian Relief Committee.[3] Charlie's first trip to the region came in 1906–07 with his brother and Charles Masterman, after which they reported both the progress and setbacks in the region.[4] He went again in 1908, to Constantinople following the 'Young Turk Revolution', a political development which in its early days promised a reform of the Ottoman administration. He published articles on his return in *The Economist* and other journals, regretting that the British

1   Benjamin Disraeli, 1st Earl of Beaconsfield (1804–1881), Prime Minister Feb–Dec 1868, 1874–80.
2   Victoria would later travel in Turkey and published a book called *The Soul of the Turk*.
3   For this and subsequent points, see more in Anderson, especially 32–41, and De Bunsen, especially pp. 54–55.
4   See for example, *The Times*, 29 November 1907.

government did not see the need to encourage the new developments in Turkey. In January 1911, he and Noel returned to Constantinople to see for themselves if the new Turkish government was reforming or relapsing to its old ways. After the Balkan wars of independence broke out in 1912–13, Dorothy's sister Eglantyne travelled to Macedonia in 1913 to help with the Macedonian Relief Committee's work.[1] All these first-hand accounts from the region meant that Charlie and Dorothy were well-informed of the political dangers there long before the events of summer 1914 enfolded.

Dorothy with her children & Frau Schoene, Crowborough, summer 1914

That summer had promised much, being one of glorious warm and sunny weather. Dorothy's mother, Tye had had a house built in the Sussex countryside near Crowborough, and called it aptly Forest Edge as the accompanying land bordered a wood.[2] She had arrived to take up residence in June 1914[3] and Dorothy arrived with her children on 28 July 1914 for a few days, intending to travel to Germany with Charlie for a holiday at Wiesbaden on Saturday 1 August. When Russia declared war on Germany however, Charlie sent a telegram to his family saying the proposed trip must be abandoned. He came to Crowborough and he and Dorothy worked into the night writing letters and peace leaflets.

---

1   Mahood, pp. 148–149.
2   Tye's brother, Professor Richard Jebb, had died in 1905 and his American wife had returned to the USA. With Dorothy now married and living elsewhere, Tye had fewer contacts in Cambridge – so the place became less interesting for her and she desired to move. She let her Cambridge house whilst she went travelling on the continent on and off in the years 1910–14. She then sold it, and had this house built at Crowborough, a five-bedroom detached property with large grounds.
3   For this and other detail for this section, see Tye's journal for the first weeks of the First World War, BFA.

Charlie had returned to London the day before Britain declared war, whilst Dorothy had remained at Forest Edge. Dorothy sent him a telegram and Charlie responded that he found it difficult to write straight away because of 'the horror of the hour'. He noted that they could not know how much work they would be called to undertake or even what kind.[1] During the following weeks, Charlie's only solace amidst all the anxiety was when he was able to visit Forest Edge, spend time with his family and help implement the planned garden at Tye's new house. He later recalled,

> That month in England, [after] the outbreak of war. . . . was a nightmare. . . . Crowborough was the only bright spot, and I shall never forget the relief of returning there time after time, the walks across the common to Forest Edge, the digging in the garden, and the many mechanical and other works performed with E[glantyne] and D[avid] in the attic and the wood. But London and the county generally were almost unbearable – no clearly marked task for me (the tasks I was presumably most fitted for being needed in the future rather than in the present) and meantime the tide of hatred rising daily, truth & honesty at a discount everywhere, even one's own friends losing all sense of evidence, and generally, the crumbling away of civilisation.[2]

Both Dorothy and Charlie were dismayed by the upsurge of jingoistic enthusiasm for the war, with crowds cheering in the streets of London, and the popular press indulging in innuendo, rumour and downright untruths in whipping up support for the conflict. The hatred expressed for the German people rather than the policy of their government was, for the Buxtons, an appalling descent into crude racialism, exemplified by the homes and businesses of Germans and those whose names merely sounded Germanic being daubed with slogans and threatened. Dorothy in particular was distressed by the internment of German nationals who were living in Britain. She saw this as unfair as none of these people had committed a hostile or criminal act. They were being imprisoned purely because of their nationality. She offered her services via a scheme run by the Society of Friends (Quakers) that organised the sending of handicraft work to German civilian internees. Already having a German nanny resident in her household,[3] Dorothy offered

---

1   Charlie to Dorothy, 5 August 1914, BFA.
2   Charlie to Dorothy, 30 October 1914, BFA.
3   This was a Frau Schoene, who was Swiss-German and married to a German. Dorothy met up with her again in 1934 and commented that she was 'quite unchanged' after nineteen years and that she had kept a lock of David's 'bright yellow hair' that he had when he was very young! Dorothy to David, 5 June 1934, BFA.

7 Kennington Terrace as a place to be used for other 'internal refugees', and she moved out with her children to rented accommodation at 28 Willifield Way, not far from her new but as yet unfinished house in Erskine Hill.[1] The offer of the house in Kennington Terrace as a hostel was gratefully accepted and soon the house was full of German women stranded in London who had lost their employment. One of the German guests was given the task of 'managing' the house. Some of the guests stayed a short time, others for longer, but all were there at the Buxtons' expense, although they had to do their own housework.[2] For this use of her home, she courted criticism from some quarters, but she would not surrender to what she saw as distorted prejudice whipped up by irresponsible and dangerous newspaper reports. The Buxtons also shared their new house at 6 Erskine Hill with refugees, especially as they were away regularly, and they sometimes stayed elsewhere themselves to accommodate these guests. They had to book in to their own home on occasions to ensure there was a bed available, as people came and went.[3] Such refugees became fewer as the war progressed.

The main political concern in the war's first weeks for anyone with anti-war views was how to stop the fighting and such an endeavour had different strands as the agendas in the war were many and complex. In the first months of the war, the Ottoman Empire was not a combatant, but had strong ties with Germany and was antagonistic towards Russia. It seemed only a matter of time before it joined the Central Powers (Germany and Austria-Hungary) in order to help defeat Tsarist Russia. In the event, Turkey did join the war at the end of October 1914. The Balkan Committee in London feared that when Turkey joined the conflict, it would draw in Rumania, Bulgaria and possibly other countries. It also believed that creative diplomacy might be able to prevent this escalation. Someone needed to visit the Bulgarian and Rumanian governments in particular to persuade them to stay neutral or even to join the Triple Entente (Britain, France and Russia) and if so on what terms. Noel Buxton persuaded Winston Churchill (First Lord of the

---

1   Tye's journal of the first weeks of the First World War, BFA. Tye found that the local territorials set up camp near her new home in Sussex and the sound of marching soldiers became familiar by both day and night. On 5 September 1914, 'Two officers called to ask if I should be "incommoded" by their occupying the adjoining field, & to enquire if I meant to occupy the house through the winter.' She decided to let the house to the army and rented a small house at 66 Willifield Way, near Dorothy, for the next winter. She moved back to Forest Edge in May 1915 when the army had completed its local training and no longer needed the house.

2   Testimonials about this were published in the German press, translations of which are in BFA.

3   For example, Charlie to Dorothy, August 1916, BFA: in which he asked her to arrange for the family to stay at 6 Erskine Hill when he returned with the children from a sojourn in Yorkshire with his sister Victoria and her family.

Admiralty) and David Lloyd George (Chancellor of the Exchequer) that such an initiative had value and that he could lead it, given his great knowledge of, and many contacts in, the region. These two ministers supported him, but Edward Grey (the Foreign Secretary) was doubtful and therefore insisted any 'mission' to Rumania and Bulgaria would not be official. From the beginning Noel wanted Charlie to accompany him and indeed Charlie was present at Noel's initial meeting with Lloyd George.

Eventually permission was given for a non-official visit[1] and the two brothers set out on 1 September. The beginning of the journey was tumultuous as they had to pass through Paris at a time when the German army was advancing swiftly towards it.[2] However, they reached the capital of Bulgaria, Sofia, by 11 September.[3] Dorothy could not have been happy about her husband leaving the country at such a time, but initially at least she appeared to be supportive, as Charlie wrote, 'You *were* splendid from beginning to end, above all in seeing my point of view about coming here – no easy matter at the time.'[4] However, seeing Charlie's point of view was different from agreeing with it. Throughout Charlie's months in the Balkans, his letters all contained a certain tone of self-justification as if he knew he had repeatedly to ensure Dorothy understood his reasons for travelling. After noting the effusive reception Noel received in places along the Struma valley that they visited, he continued,

> I hesitate to stay, because I feel I might be doing more work at home (as well as longing to be with you) but on the other hand it seems that things might arise in which we might make a difference, & if so it would be a great mistake to have left. You may be quite sure that N[oel] does make a difference, difficult as it is at a distance to realise it.[5]

News soon leaked of the brothers' trip and the Greek press publicised it, speculating that the reason behind it was to promise territory to Bulgaria if they supported the Triple Entente and that this territory would be at the expense of Greece and Serbia. The Foreign Office issued a public denial at the end of September, insisting that the visit by the Buxtons was a 'private' one and that there was no foundation in the rumours about offering Bulgaria territory.[6]

1   For more on the political manoeuvres among ministers on the issues, see Fry, pp. 280–286. The government did provide the brothers with berths on a warship when they needed to cross the Adriatic Sea, so there was tacit support for the mission. Tye's journal of the first weeks of the First World War, BFA.
2   Anderson, p. 64.
3   Charlie to Dorothy, 11 September 1914, BFA.
4   Charlie to Dorothy, 30 October 1914, BFA.
5   Charlie to Dorothy, 29 September 1914, BFA.
6   *The Times*, 29 September 1914.

Charlie was anxious that Dorothy represent him and his views if questions were asked back in London in his prospective constituency or else in wider society. He was particularly concerned about the Foreign Secretary's reaction.

> The main point about anything that's said on the subject in England is that we are not on an official mission, but that we are endeavouring to use our influence in the Balkans, where we know great numbers of people & have studied the situation, in such a way as to help England's cause. From the constituency point of view it would be useful to use the words 'at Grey's request', but this you cannot do, as it might lead to Grey or our ministers here trying to repudiate us or refuse to help us, – & we need their cooperation.[1]

A few days later, he acknowledged a postcard from his wife and praised her 'sound & permanently valuable works', adding, 'Mine is of a less tangible kind – still it is also of value.'[2]

Charlie's first letters home were very guarded because of the Bulgarian censors. Some were even written in French. He restricted himself to describing trips the brothers had made and sights they saw. However, early in October, he took advantage of a 'diplomatic bag' to write a more frank letter to Dorothy, which outlined the reasons for the trip from the brothers' perspective.

> Our object is to secure Bulgaria's friendly neutrality towards the Entente, so as to liberate Roumania to fight against Austria for Transylvania (peopled by Roumanians) and to free Servia from the fear of Bulgarian attack in the rear – also to get Bulgaria to resist Turkey by force of arms if Turkey attacks the entente. The question is what terms Bulgaria will accept for this. She ought to get back Macedonia from Servia, & Dubrutscka from Roumania, if these other powers are aggrandised. It would be possible to get the whole Balkan question settled on a basis of nationality; as well as assisting our cause, if only our government would play the proper cards. Things are so uncertain that we feel we ought to stay on until the situation is clearer. We can make some real use of (a) N[oel]'s influence, which is considerable, (b) by the power which non-diplomats have of getting into touch with unofficial circles, & of bringing people together in one way and another. It is all vague,

---

1   Charlie to Dorothy, 5 October 1914, BFA.
2   Charlie to Dorothy, 1 October 1914, BFA.

but there is some reality at the bottom of it, & we still think we *may* effect something of more importance than anything we could now do at home. The difficulties however are very great.[1]

Politically, Bulgaria's government was complex. Its monarch, Ferdinand I,[2] had been born in Vienna into a branch of the Saxe-Coburg family, and was distantly related not only to Kaiser Wilhelm II of Germany, but also to Prince Albert, the consort of Britain's Queen Victoria. He was also related to the Belgian Royal family amongst others. Ferdinand had been made Prince of Bulgaria as far back as 1886, when he was in his mid-twenties, and eventually declared himself king or tsar in 1908. Charlie assumed that the king and his government were pro-Austrian.[3] Yet, the government had a slim majority in the Bulgarian Parliament thanks only to the support of Turkish deputies and, as such, keeping Bulgaria neutral promised to be a difficult task. The English ambassador (or 'minister') was very pro-Serb, which did little to help the brothers' cause, as the Serbs and Austrians were already in conflict with one another; it was their antipathy that precipitated the European war. However, as King Ferdinand was a mercurial character and not guided by fixed loyalties, he and his government were open to persuasion, depending on what territory they might gain from supporting a specific side. Charlie saw progress being made and was eager to note this to his wife:

> We think we have already accomplished something of bringing the English minister up to the point of suggesting to Grey a policy more or less in line with what we think right. He would not have done without our being here. Also our coming gave rise to an outburst of pro-English feeling in the press, etc., which has had some effect in counteracting the pro-Austrian tendencies of the Government.[4]

The brothers decided to leave Sofia as some of the Bulgarian newspapers were becoming more negative than at the start of their stay. They went on to Rumania, which was also not politically straight forward. King Carol I[5] was in his seventies and had ruled Rumania since 1869, although constitutionally his powers were limited. He was born Prince Karl of Hohenzollern-Sigmaringen, so of German descent and a cousin of Kaiser Wilhelm; he made no attempt to hide his pro-German feelings.

---

1   Charlie to Dorothy, 5 October 1914, BFA.
2   Ferdinand I (1861–1948), Prince of Bulgaria 1887–1908, Tsar (King) of Bulgaria 1908–1918.
3   Charlie to Dorothy, 5 October 1914, BFA.
4   Charlie to Dorothy, 5 October 1914, BFA.
5   Carol I (1839–1914), Prince of Rumania 1869–81, King of Rumania 1881–1914.

However, the Rumanian people tended to be more pro-French – indeed Bucharest externally 'aped Paris' in Charlie's view. This was partly because the Rumanian regime was not democratic and the 'west' was associated with freedoms they did not enjoy.[1] The rebellion by many peasants in 1907 had been suppressed with some ruthlessness. In August 1914, the Rumanian government had opted for neutrality against the wishes of the king.

In the second week of October, Noel and Charlie went on a trip to Sinaia, near the border with Hungary,[2] where the king and queen had built their summer home, Peleş Castle. Here in the afternoon of 9 October 1914, Noel and Charlie had tea with the royal couple and were served caviar sandwiches.[3] They were especially captivated by the charm of Queen Elizabeth.[4] It was a memorable meeting and the brothers felt they had established a rapport with the elderly couple.[5] To their surprise, the very next day they heard the tolling of bells and discovered the news that the king had died during the night. The heir to the throne, Carol's nephew Ferdinand,[6] was married to a granddaughter of Queen Victoria.[7] Consequently, the new king was believed to be more open to British influence and the German press insinuated that the Buxton brothers had poisoned the old king!

King Carol's funeral was held five days later on 15 October in Bucharest. The brothers travelled to the capital and that morning they were getting into an open car outside their hotel, when a man three feet away fired a gun and shot six bullets. Their host, a son of a former Prime Minister, suffered only a hole through his hat, but both Buxton brothers were hit. The chauffeur knocked the would-be assassin to the ground so that he could be arrested. The gunman was a Turkish radical, who accused the Buxtons of stirring up enmity towards his country.

1   Charlie to Dorothy, 5 October 1914, BFA.
2   Charlie to Dorothy, 7 October 1914, BFA.
3   Noel later drew a sketch from memory of Charlie speaking to the King and Queen whilst being served the sandwiches, which is in BFA.
4   Queen Elizabeth of Rumania (1843–1916), born Pauline Elisabeth Ottilie Luise zu Wied, married Ferdinand 1869. Their only child, Princess Maria, died in childhood. They were estranged for many years during their marriage, but in old age became companions again. She wrote with facility in German, Romanian, French and English and, under the pseudonym 'Carmen Sylva', she published poems, plays, novels, short stories and other writings.
5   Anderson, p. 66.
6   Ferdinand I (1865–1927), King of Rumania 1914–27.
7   This was Marie (1875–1938), daughter of Victoria's second son, Alfred, Duke of Edinburgh. She became Queen Marie on her husband's accession.

Noel took a bullet in the jaw, but was not seriously injured.[1] Charlie, however, took a bullet that entered in the front of his torso and came out the other side, grazing one of his lungs during his passage. The brothers were hastily carried back into the hotel. Noel thought at first that Charlie was dying. There was pandemonium in the hotel room, culminating in the gunman, guarded by soldiers with fixed bayonets, being brought handcuffed before the brothers so that they could identify him as the man who shot them.[2] Eventually, the Buxtons were taken to St Elizabeth Hospital where Charlie's condition gradually improved with the help of the skilled nurses. He claimed to have little pain, just 'raging indigestion' and fatigue, and having to lie still on his back made sleeping difficult.[3]

The incident made the British papers the day after the shooting,[4] and this is how Dorothy learned of the event; further information came via the Foreign Office and telegrams, and eventually some letters also came through.[5] Her anxiety can hardly have been relieved by Noel's initial jocular communication, typical of the then fashionable male dismissal of any hardship. 'You will have had wires – private & in the press – & I now send newspapers to give the story. It was a marvel that this man shot so badly, but as we *did* escape we are delighted with it all politically & personally! Nothing could have been better arranged. It was exciting! Do write & tell us what you think & hear about it.'[6]

What Dorothy wanted was her husband home. She wrote to him on 19 October – and his reply suggests it was a strong letter:

> How I have read & re-read your beloved letter of Oct[ober] 19. It was indeed a joy. How well I realise (indeed I did already, but the letter renewed the impression) of all you felt about the attack – deeply and strongly, & reaching out to me – Trotz der Ferne [despite the distance] – with powerful & timely aid – and yet without the enfeebling fear & anxiety to which so many are slaves. It is not necessary for you & me to use many words on this subject.

1   He hid the scar that it left by growing a beard, which he sported for the rest of his life.
2   Anderson, pp. 66–67. De Bunsen, p. 66. The gunman's name was Hassan Tahsin Receb (born Osman Nevres) (1888–1919).
3   Charlie to Dorothy, 19 October 1914, BFA.
4   See for example *The Times*, 16 October 1914.
5   Tye's journal of the first weeks of the First World War, BFA. 'Days of anxiety followed – some of the papers seeming to suggest a danger of "complications" arising from the wounds. Two of Charlie's friends offered to go out to him – but it was felt this would be useless. The post was very slow & delivery of letters doubtful – News came chiefly through the Foreign Office or in letters send [*sic*] along in the govt. dispatches.'
6   Noel to Dorothy, 17 October 1914, BFA.
7   Noel to Dorothy, 17 October 1914, BFA.

Rest satisfied that all is going very well. We will return the first
moment our work allows. All sorts of precautions are taken for our
safety, but personally I believe the occurrence was an isolated &
unique thing, the sort of thing which doesn't recur.[1]

However, the brothers felt that their work was not complete – indeed the
attempted assassination had enhanced their credibility with the Bulgarians.
Once Charlie was well enough, the two returned to Sofia to a rapturous
welcome. The city even named a street after them – still so named to this
day.[2] Dorothy wrote again and must have put further pressure on him to
come home quickly. Although the letter has not survived, she must have
been insistent given Charlie's reply.

Your second beloved letter has arrived. They *are* bliss! Also your
telegram. What you say is very important for I know you would
not have wired unless you had formed a well[-]considered opinion
based on all the facts. I simply *long* to come home but there are
very strong reasons which detain us a little longer. These you
would appreciate if you knew them. It is difficult to balance all
the considerations, but I have made up my mind without much
hesitation, for the present. . . .

These late events have made me think more of you than ever. I
have thought much about your thoughts & feelings at the time of
the outrage, & I think I understand them all.

Did she hint to him that he was not thinking of her feelings? Certainly,
he went on to acknowledge that he had not always done so:

Also my mind has travelled back very much to the past. I have
especially thought – I don't know exactly why at the particular
juncture – of my own grievous want of sympathy at certain grave &
critical times in the past, especially E[glantyne]'s & D[avid]'s births
& their *operations*. I hope it was more a want of outward sympathy
than inward: but outward sympathy is just as important in its way.
Calmness can be carried too far. I carried it much too far. I should
not do so again: I feel that I was wanting in real appreciation of what
you went through, & I blame myself much for it. Better things shall
be done in the future, tho[ugh] we must grieve over the past.[3]

---

1   Charlie to Dorothy, 9 November 1914, BFA.
2   The whole area around Buxton Brothers Boulevard is now referred to as the district
    of 'Buxton'. The road in south-west Sofia is notable for still being paved with setts
    rather than being surfaced with tarmac.
3   Charlie to Dorothy, 20 November 1914, BFA.

He wrote again justifying why he was not coming home before Christmas.

> The reasons for our still staying on is that things have reached a
> very important stage here, & probably in the next few days Bulgaria
> will make the most important decision of all. When that occurs,
> we think from the position we have got here, we shall be able to
> exercise some influence, & we are confirmed in this by the opinion
> of others. We feel that this is really a case where duty outweighs all
> inclinations – & they are very strong – on the other side. We might
> be leaving our work just before putting the finishing touch to it –
> a finishing touch which *we* could put & also could not. – I don't
> forget your opinion about my being needed at home. I know it's
> carefully formed, & that *I* cannot judge the matter. On the other
> hand it is only I who can judge the matter here. So I must make
> the best choice I can.[1]

Charlie & Noel on the way home after the escape from assassination

In the event, Noel and Charlie's Balkan expedition did not achieve all for
which they had hoped. Grey would not follow their advice in announcing
an overall Balkan policy, but preferred to keep options open for individual
negotiations, something the Buxton brothers opposed as it was likely to
lead to competition between the small nation states, all to the detriment of
the Triple Entente. Eventually, Bulgaria would declare war on the side of
the Germans, Austrians and Turks in October 1915, whilst the Rumanians
joined the war in 1916 on the side of the Russians, British and French. Yet,
this could not have been certain at the time so the Buxton brothers were
convinced that their efforts had been worth the hardship.

1   Charlie to Dorothy, 24 November 1914, BFA.

Before they left the region they had another encounter with their would-be assassin. They visited him in prison. He turned out to be in his mid-twenties, an attractive and educated young man who had read philosophy at the Sorbonne in Paris. He insisted to Noel and Charlie that he was a Turkish patriot who wished to punish those whom he felt were enemies to his country. He claimed his reason for shooting at the brothers was because they were 'responsible' by their political work for shedding Turkish blood. He acted alone and tried to encourage his contemporaries by an act of bravado. His failure to kill the brothers he put down to bad cartridges rather than his poor aim.[1] Noel placed a revolver on the table and invited the young Hassan to aim again! The gun was unloaded, but the Turk declined Noel's offer.[2] For the Buxtons, this was proof that talking to people made violence less likely.

The brothers arrived back in Britain in January 1915 after visits to Rome and Paris. Dorothy met Charlie at Victoria Station and then he visited his mother-in-law that evening, showing off 'the two holes neatly darned by his nurses, where the bullet had gone in on[e] side of his body & come out at the other'.[3] Whilst staying in Rome, Charlie wrote an appreciation of his wife. The separation and the brush with death had certainly made him reflect on his marriage and its importance. He wrote that the absence from Dorothy had made him see her more clearly.

> I am glad that I have been separated from her through four months of travel and active work. I have been able to see her life as a whole. I have escaped from the tyranny of the moment. It seems possible now to say what I have desired to say – but could not say, because I could not detach myself sufficiently from little things. I have desired to say what I knew and what I felt about this woman, one of the chosen spirits of the world, with whom my life has been linked by a strange and happy chance. I am the only man who can tell the truth about her. If I do not tell it, it will lie buried, with all the other good things that have perished for want of words.

He went on to extol her spiritual strength, her lack of fear, her love of nature and then her advocacy for those fallen into misfortune and need.

> Yet she does not live in the spiritual world as a spirit, in the nature world as a bird. These worlds do not make the world of men and women an unsubstantial thing to her; she is in it and of it. She

---

1   Anderson, pp. 68–69.
2   NRB4, p. 128.
3   Tye's journal of the first weeks of the First World War, BFA.

shares the weaknesses of the world; she yields to fatigue, and irony, and anger. She sees in our world, too, her true sphere of action. She is the friend of the unbefriended, meeting them on the ground of their own needs, spending herself without stint to help and strengthen them. She would mould this world of ours if she could, nay, break it and recast it. She has equipped herself for it. She has made her brain a keen sword, and kept it sharp. She is a fighter in our human battle-ground, clear in the choice of ends, relentless in the pursuit, not sparing the men and women who wince at the defiance of custom, or the exposure of their own cherished opinions. A champion of God, smiting without hesitation, without fear, without even sober self-retreating.[1]

It was this championing of the underdog and the neglected that would rise to the fore in Dorothy's life. The events of the opening months of the First World War had had a profound effect on Dorothy. She had had to cope without Charlie's presence for four and half months and with him being too far away to consult. She had had to take responsibility and decisions for their children, home and finances, including organising the move to their new house – and even more significantly, she had not been involved with his work. She had had emotionally to face the real possibility of losing him and being a widow. When Charlie returned, their personal relationship remained strong, if not stronger because of what they had been through. However, significantly, these months were crucial to breaking the pattern of Dorothy acting primarily his helpmate and her work being principally an extension or support of his. Things would now develop differently. She had no part to play in the Balkan negotiations and she did not take a significant role in his political work for the rest of the war years. He edited and published books about his Balkan experiences and the political situation,[2] but Dorothy had little involvement with them. Charlie was not a pacifist,[3] but he made speeches advocating a negotiated peace, during

---

1   Charlie, memorandum dated Rome, 31 December 1914, Box 10, 7EJB/B/01/03/07-13, WL. These quotations are from sections I and VIII. Copy also in BFA.

2   With Noel, he wrote CRB4; books he edited include: CRB3 – Charlie's own essay in this is called 'Nationality'; CRB2.

3   He did not believe he should fight in the First World War, but realised his health would mean he would never be accepted in any case if he volunteered. Later he was 'called up' when conscription was introduced and consulted his doctor again: 'He says the notice "calling me up" has been issued in the ordinary way to every one of military age, & without reference to, or knowledge of, my medical examination & its result. So that when I go up I confront them with a *fait accompli* in the shape of my classification card showing that I am passed only for "sedentary duties." He says that they will then say they don't want me. I hope he is right. He strongly urged me

which he was sometimes shouted down and vilified.[1] Dorothy supported his stance, but did not join him as a speaker on the platform. He was involved in by-elections all over the country in the later stages of the war,[2] campaigning for candidates who were in favour of a negotiated peace, yet Dorothy was not at his side.

Instead, Dorothy had found something she regarded as her own mission, stemming from her work with German internees, which absorbed most of her energies. She reached the conclusion that the only way to counter the appalling jingoism of the press and public discourse was to illustrate how those on the other side of the conflict felt. She wanted to show that the citizens of the Central Powers were also human beings, who suffered from anxiety and distress and bereavement – that they, too, were being swept away by the fear incited by their own governments and press. She also wanted to reveal that there were those amongst the enemy who also saw the possibilities of a negotiated peace – that they, too, longed for the conflict to cease and were willing to participate in dialogue. For this, Dorothy's remedy was to reveal what was being written in foreign newspapers. She had a strong knowledge of German and French and translated articles, but recruited others to help with additional languages, one of the first recruits being Mosa Anderson,[3] who had studied Russian in Paris. Mosa moved into the Buxton household and practically became a member of the family. She has been referred to as Charlie's 'secretary', but this was in the sense of a personal assistant, with others employed to come in during the day to do any typing.[4] Although distributing the translations to a large audience would initially be difficult, Dorothy could easily do so within her own circle of friends and acquaintances and, from there, onto others with influence in government or the media or academic.

---

not to appeal to a tribunal for exemption. I had come to this conclusion myself, on reviewing all the pros & cons.' Charlie to Dorothy, 24 June 1916, BFA.

1   See for example *The Times* 11 January 1916 and 18 January 1916.

2   Including Rossendale (Lancashire), Stockton and Aberdeen in the early months of 1917 and Keighley in April 1918, details of which are in letters Charlie wrote to Dorothy, BFA.

3   Mosa Isabelle Anderson (1891–1978). Mosa remained an important help and friend to the couple throughout their lives and was buried in the same cemetery as Charlie and Dorothy at Peaslake in Sussex. She wrote the biography of Noel Buxton.

4   'And by degrees she was taken over by my father as his assistant (though described as his 'secretary' she was much more than that; also *less*, as she could hardly type). One way and another she was practically adopted by my parents & usually lived in the house as a member of the family. She was also strongly influenced by them and I believe they so scorned the advances towards her of some young man that she gave up all thoughts of matrimony for good.' David Buxton, autobiographical notes, BFA.

She had two problems in trying to fulfil this idea. First, she had to obtain the newspapers printed on the Continent. The government had granted itself draconian powers of censorship and control of propaganda at the outbreak of war – it seemed hardly likely it would allow her to translate and distribute words from the enemy camp. According to Charlie's brother Harold Buxton, Charlie used his influence with David Lloyd George in particular, so that the Board of Trade issued a licence to import continental newspapers, which were obtained through neutral Scandinavia.[1] Even though some in the government would have been wary of granting such a freedom, in many ways Dorothy and her team would do something which otherwise civil servants would have to do. The resulting consequence of this information being more widespread was not sufficiently dangerous enough to bar the activity. To ensure that this balance of interests was not tipped against her, Dorothy ensured that none of her translations were of articles to do with military matters. She concentrated on social conditions and political issues. Throughout the rest of the war, the government did not intervene to stop Dorothy continuing this work.

Dorothy's second problem was how best to distribute what she had produced. At first, she brought the material out as leaflets.[2] Then she decided to approach Charles Kay Ogden,[3] the editor of a weekly publication called *The Cambridge Magazine*. Ogden was a talented classicist and linguist, best remembered today for his campaign for basic English, the idea that the English language could be cut down to an essential vocabulary so that it could be used as the international medium for communication. He was something of an outsider and a little eccentric, but he was respected for his wide learning and interests. He had started *The Cambridge Magazine* when he was still a student in Cambridge as a general weekly for the arts and literary pieces as well as politics, attracting contributions from literary giants such as George Bernard Shaw, Thomas Hardy and John Masefield. On the outbreak of war, Ogden pursued a more political line, principally commenting on the war and the international situation. His impaired health meant he was unable to fight himself, but in any case he was sympathetic to the pacifist position and wanted to oppose the jingoistic tone of the daily newspapers. Dorothy's material fitted his purposes well and he offered space in every issue for her 'Notes from the Foreign Press' (later renamed 'Foreign

1   Wilson, p. 170, note 4.
2   Mosa Anderson wrote a memorandum about the history of the Notes in *The Cambridge Magazine*, copy in BFA. Also, there is extant a copy of the circular letter Dorothy sent out with the early leaflets. Dated 12 August 1915, it requested that recipients keep the Notes confidential and did not make the issuing of the circular publicly known 'as this might give rise to misrepresentation'. However, they could make use of the information the Notes contained.
3   Charles Kay Ogden (1889–1957), read Classics at Magdalene College, Cambridge, Editor of *The Cambridge Magazine* 1912–22.

Opinion: a weekly survey of the foreign press'), beginning with the issue for 28 October 1915. It was more than a mere column for it came to fill between one third and more than half of each issue during the university terms. In the vacation time, it occupied almost the whole issue. Circulation of the magazine rose to an estimated 20,000 copies per week.[1] The cover cost of a mere one penny made it cheap relative to other journals.

Coverage included articles from neutral countries such as the Netherlands, Sweden and Switzerland plus Britain's allies France and Italy, not just the German and Austrian enemy countries.[2] In time, when translators became available, items from Russia, Hungary, Poland and the Balkan states were included. Views on war aims in different countries were an important topic covered, as was the presence of pacifist views even in countries like Germany where there was no provision for conscientious objection.[3]

As weeks turned into months and then years, the scale of the translation operation grew and Dorothy had a team of volunteers covering a range of languages. One of her team from early 1917 was her sister Eglantyne, who came to help after recovering from a thyroid operation and she lived with Dorothy and her family. Their mother, Tye, sold her car to provide money for hiring an additional typist.[4] The large attic at the Erskine Hill house became a place of continuous activity to which all other calls were subordinate, something which had a large impact on Dorothy's children as we shall consider in a later chapter. Mid-week was always the heaviest time as copy had to reach *The Cambridge Magazine* for Friday as the publication came out on a Saturday. Dorothy would work with few breaks and then when the latest issue was done, she might recuperate with a day in bed.[5] Charlie helped her with some issues when he wished to collect items on particular subjects of significance to him[6] and when she needed to go away.[7] This was an interesting reversal of roles from their pre-war work. He now helped her.

'Notes from the Foreign Press' annoyed some people, but was much praised by others, including General Smuts from South Africa.[8] Many

1   Florence, p. 58.
2   A list of publications covered can be found in Florence, pp. 59–60.
3   See Florence, pp. 61–66; also Hammond, pp. 50–51.
4   Eglantyne to Tye, 'Wednesday', no date but from 1917–18, Box 12, 7EJB/ B/01/03/22, WL.
5   'Mind you have your <u>day</u> in bed tomorrow, dearest.' Charlie to Dorothy, 29 January 1917, BFA.
6   Charlie to Dorothy, 16 April 1918, BFA.
7   'I can undertake complete responsibility for the *C[ambridge]M[agazine]* for the weekend Sept 14–16. And if necessary, 21–23.' Charlie to Dorothy, 27 August 1918, BFA.
8   'By the way, Smuts told me he has read the *C[ambridge] M[agazine]* throughout the war, & in E. Africa it went regularly round his staff too! He was enthusiastic about

Cover from an edition of Foreign Opinion

eminent people were known to read the Notes.[1] In advertisements for the magazine in *The Times*, a dozen or so quotes from MPs are used in commendation without names being identified.[2] Thomas Hardy, the novelist, allowed his words to be used with his name, saying he read the Notes every week as they 'enable one to see England bare and unadorned – her chances in the struggle freed from distortion by the glamour of patriotism'. George Bernard Shaw and Sir Arthur Quiller-Couch are others who supplied similar named commendations.[3] What became clear was that *The Cambridge Magazine* became essential reading for anyone serious about understanding the war and wanting to be fully informed. This included journalists and editors of British newspapers, local as well as national. The editor of the North Eastern Daily Gazette at Middlesbrough noted to Charlie: 'Thank your wife for the C[ambridge] M[agazine]. I set it down as one of the things that *must* be read.'[4] A non-conformist divine preached a whole sermon at Brighton about the magazine.[5] Workers at a by-election, supporting a 'peace' candidate, 'vociferously applauded' when Dorothy's name was mentioned.[6]

you, and said "She must be a *great* woman!'" Charlie to Dorothy, 15 May 1917, BFA.

1   Wilson, pp. 170–171; Mulley, pp. 220–221.

2   *The Times*, 17 October 1916 and 20 October 1916. In a duplicated list of early subscribers to be found in BFA, the following MPs are named: Hastings Lees-Smith (Liberal for Northampton); Richard Denman (Liberal for Carlisle); John Dillon (Irish Parliamentary Party for East Mayo); Noel Buxton (Liberal for North Norfolk); Willoughby Dickinson (Liberal for St Pancras North); Joseph King (Liberal for North Somerset); Sir Alfred Mond (Liberal for Swansea); Arthur Ponsonby (Liberal for Stirling Boroughs); Aneurin Williams (Liberal for North-West Durham); Philip Snowden (Labour for Blackburn); Charles Trevelyan (Liberal then Independent for Elland); Sir Ernest Lamb (Liberal for Rochester) and Sir Henry Fitzherbert Wright (Conservative for Leominster).

3   *The Times*, 1 November 1916.

4   Charlie to Dorothy, 4 March 1917, BFA. In Stockton, a Sunderland friend said to Charlie that he could not help reading every page of *The Cambridge Magazine*; 'One sees how your work tells.' Charlie to Dorothy, 10 March 1917, BFA.

5   Charlie to Dorothy, 16 April 1918, BFA.

6   Charlie to Dorothy, 22 April 1918, BFA.

It was used more particularly by those wishing to advocate for a negotiated peace, as its contents revealed that there were those on the opposing side who might respond positively. For this, both the magazine and Dorothy's section were castigated for being pacifist. One group to make such an accusation was the 'Fight for Right' organisation which wished to 'refuse any temptation, however insidious, to conclude a premature peace'.[1] Britain was 'right' and therefore needed to fight to a successful finish whatever the sacrifices. The leaders were Sir Francis Younghusband[2] and Sir Frederick Pollock,[3] but others who spoke at its meetings included the Bishop of Winchester[4] and the Chief Rabbi.[5] Such 'pro-war' and 'patriotic' groups deplored in particular *The Cambridge Magazine* because to them it appeared to be formally connected to the University of Cambridge (which it was not) and therefore was attributed a false official status.[6] Such concerns led to a question being asked in the House of Commons in November 1917.[7] Others supported *The Cambridge Magazine* because of freedom of the press even if they were not in agreement with its content.[8]

Dorothy's work had significance for both sides of the argument as it provided unbiassed and direct evidence of the views and events

1   See for example *The Observer* 5 March 1916.
2   Francis Edward Younghusband (1863–1942), British army officer best known for his 1904 expedition to Tibet. He was also President of the Royal Geographical Society 1919–22 and was a founder in 1936 of the World Congress of Faiths.
3   Frederick Pollock (1845–1937), Professor of Jurisprudence at Oxford 1883–1903, and a prolific editor and writer on legal matters.
4   Edward Stuart Talbot (1844–1934), Bishop of Rochester 1895–1905, of Southwark 1905–11, of Winchester 1911–23.
5   Joseph Herman Hertz (1872–1946), Chief Rabbi 1913–46.
6   Dorothy and Ogden refuted the claims of Sir Frederick Pollock to Charlie's satisfaction: 'Yours & Og[den]'s return blow at that snuffly old Pollock is simply crushing! I never thought you'd do so well.' Charlie to Dorothy, 26 March 1917, BFA. Pollock had been a lead signature in a letter to *The Morning Post*, dated 23 February 1917, published under the heading 'Insidious pacifist propaganda'. The letter complained that the Notes were 'remarkably free from any exhilarating belief in the victory of the Allied arms or predominating righteousness of their cause'.
7   This was from John Butcher (1853–1935), MP for York 1892–1906, 1910–23. He objected to the government paying for adverts for war loans in *The Cambridge Magazine* as he judged the publication a 'vehicle for pacifist propaganda of a kind repugnant to the great majority of members of Cambridge University and of the people of this country'. The reply was that the advertisements had been stopped as soon as the contents of the magazine had been made known to the National War Savings Committee. *The Times,* 13 November 1917.
8   For example, the letter published in *The Manchester Guardian*, 24 March 1917, signed by many literary figures including Thomas Hardy, Rebecca West, Arnold Bennett and Jerome K. Jerome.

in the enemy countries. However, whilst informing many people and countering popular prejudices, it did not succeed in changing many hearts and minds. The bitterness that many people felt having had relatives killed in the conflict, and the experience of their lives being irrevocably changed, meant they could not abide the thought of not eventually emerging as 'victors'. Peace was longed for, yet not at the price of making their loved ones' ultimate sacrifices appear to be in vain. Germany and its allies had to be crushed and 'made to pay'. For Dorothy and Charlie this was a short-sighted view. It was understandable in emotional terms, but not when viewed from a more neutral political stance, when long-term consequences were considered. As they judged, the pursuit of 'Victory at all costs' by the coalition government would only lead to humiliation and enmity that would far outlast any potential outcome and lay the foundations of another conflict. Charlie wrote prophetically in late 1914 that whilst he believed a victory for the Triple Entente would be the best outcome of the war, nevertheless, 'I have many misgivings about an Entente victory – e.g. the excessive crushing of Germany, leading to another Armageddon, and the excessive strengthening of Russia, leading to more powerful tyranny than before.'[1]

The war brought other significant changes too for the Buxtons beyond their work. Charlie's father died in October 1915 and his mother in August 1916. They had been a fixture in Charlie's life, interested yet not interfering, in all his and his family's doings. Their last great celebration had been their Golden Wedding in 1912,[2] marked with a family gathering at Warlies, in the photograph of which occasion the elderly couple are surrounded by their descendants, including Dorothy, Charlie and their children.[3] The family house was little used after the outbreak of war and the Buxton parents died when living at Cromer. Charlie took time to visit his mother in her last months and to participate in a rota of relatives to keep her company. When she died, Charlie took it in his stride, grateful that she had survived so long:

> No, there is no tragedy about all this: it is natural, beautiful, and there is nothing in it that one could wish otherwise. The tragedy which arouses fierce indigestion & pain is the tragedy of the young, slain in the flower of youth through the folly & vileness of men. But here, all was peace and satisfaction.

1   Charlie, memorandum sent to Dorothy, written 30 October 1914, with revisions (including this quotation) added 26 January 1915, BFA.
2   *The Times*, 5 August 1912.
3   10 children and 28 grandchildren.

What one feels is the strange break in the family life. Mother *was* the family home – in the local sense, that the real feeling of home was wherever she happened to be for the moment: & also in the spiritual sense, that one thought of her and felt her as the true centre of the life of the family. In this second sense, she still continues to be what she was for us. But in the other, the local, sense, all is changed – and that's the element of sadness in it all. That is what makes her death a sort of milestone in one's life. Most people pass this milestone much earlier than we have done. Ours has been an exceptionally fortunate family life in that respect.

For Charlie, the death of Sir Fowell and Lady Buxton may have symbolised the end of the family's old pattern of living, a pattern that was being destroyed by the First World War. The country house life-style in which Charlie had been brought up and the trappings of privilege that went with it had been laid aside by him and his wife, but with these deaths they could be abandoned forever. There was no going back to the old life, but there would be now no echo of it either. Warlies ceased to be the 'family seat'. Charlie's elder brother, Victor,[1] who inherited the baronetcy, decided not to move there during the war and died in an accident soon after it ended. His young heir in turn took the decision to sell it and for many decades afterwards it served as a Dr Barnardo's Home for orphaned and abandoned children.[2]

Other mainstays of the Buxtons' world also 'died'. Charlie and Dorothy could no longer feel comfortable in the Church of England, however nominal their membership had become. They had long been unhappy about the closeness of the Church of England's leadership to the Conservative Party. Then during the First World War, they felt the bishops had colluded too cosily with the government's decision for war and its resolution to continue it. In London, the bishop, Arthur Winnington Ingram, held recruiting drives for the armed forces on the steps of St Paul's Cathedral and too readily appeared to associate with the jingoistic language that the Buxtons deplored. Archbishop Cosmo Gordon Lang of York also supported the campaign for recruiting soldiers in 1914–15. Nevertheless, in one public speech, he expressed reservations about a vulgar lampoon of the German Emperor. Yet he soon allowed himself to be rebuffed as his passing and mild criticism of anti-German sentiment created a furious reaction in the press and he was vilified. The incident dogged him for the rest of the war

---

1   Sir (Thomas Fowell) Victor Buxton (1865–1919).
2   It was converted into offices in more recent years, but the outside of the house and its grounds have been preserved.

and he thereafter remained silent on the subject.[1] This kind of reaction was not the morally courageous witness against shallow nationalism for which they had hoped from the representatives of the Church. With the Church of England leadership so compromised in their eyes, the Buxtons had inevitably felt distance from their Anglican roots.

Dorothy's religious views were evolving, as we shall examine in a later chapter, and she was not sure how she would describe her position, so she found it simple enough to stop going to church. But for Charlie, who remained a mainstream Christian in his beliefs, the issue of religious allegiance weighed heavily: he needed to be part of a community of Christians. The obvious home was the Society of Friends, the Quakers, even though there were aspects of the Society he found difficult.[2] He had attended their services on occasions even before the First World War[3] as he was attracted by their anti-war position and he had Quaker ancestry. He was also drawn to the lack of ritual and 'constant words', as he had become uncomfortable with finding in church 'something always going on'. He had come to find even architecture, music and liturgy spiritually distracting.[4] Both Buxtons knew the Friends from their social work too. When war broke out, the stance of the Quakers in opposing it became even more significant. In addition, there was a Friends' meeting house in Central Square, round the corner from 6 Erskine Hill. Early in 1918, the Buxtons took the step to take up Quaker membership. Eglantyne wrote to Tye,

> You'll be interested to hear that Charlie & Dorothy are now Quakers! Dorothy had not felt at all sure whether they would take her, considering her higher thought views, but the lady who was sent to talk with her had them herself!! A man & a woman came together as a sort of deputation . . . Charlie & Dorothy began by explaining that they didn't agree with *each other* at all, but their interviewers correctly replied that there wasn't any necessity for that.
>
> I am very happy about it all. I feel that Charlie & Dorothy have been so very warmly welcomed by people who already had a great respect for them, & who were sincerely glad to form this link with them, that their association with the Quakers has at once brought them a great deal of happiness. The Quakers, I suppose, had long realised that Charlie, if not Dorothy too, agreed with them a good deal, just as Charlie & Dorothy knew that the Quakers thought

---

1   Lockhart, pp. 248–251.
2   De Bunsen, pp. 97–98.
3   Dorothy to Tye, 11 March [1918], Box 10, 7EJB/B/01/03/10, WL.
4   De Bunsen, p. 96.

much as they did. But the avowal of sympathy seems to have led to the discovery on both sides, that the unity went far deeper than they had supposed – & this was, of course, a very inspiring discovery.[1]

Political party allegiances had changed even earlier in the war. When Charlie attempted to address a series of public meetings in London in the early months of 1916 to advocate for a negotiated peace, the unpopularity he courted alarmed the members of the Hackney Liberal Association. Fearing Charlie was making himself unelectable, they de-selected him and he was no longer their candidate for any future election.[2] Lawrence Hammond sent him letter of commiseration when the news eventually reached him; Charlie's reaction showed a certain resignation, 'it was very good of you to sympathise about Hackney. The whole thing seems very trivial when compared with the vast issues at stake. The future is so uncertain that it is not worth calculating upon it.'[3]

Charlie and Dorothy were not as disappointed as they might have been had this move made even a year earlier. By 1916, they perceived the Liberal Party as being too pro-war.[4] Prior to 1914, their own radical wing of the party had been represented at the highest level of government by David Lloyd George, but his commitment since then to winning the war outright instead of trying to negotiate a peace had disappointed them. Lloyd George's bellicose attitude would propel him into the position of Prime Minister by the end of the year, replacing Asquith. In December 1916, he rejected a possible offer to negotiate from the Central Powers and an invitation to discuss peace terms by President Woodrow Wilson of the USA (whose country was still at that time neutral).[5] This approach deeply depressed Charlie and Dorothy.[6] The change of leadership also marked a deep split

---

1   Eglantyne to Tye, 7 February [no year given but 1918], BFA. I am grateful to Ben Buxton for confirming that Charlie and Dorothy's reception was recorded in the *Westminster & Longford Monthly* meeting minutes for 1918.

2   *The Times*, 18 February 1916.

3   Charlie to Lawrence Hammond, 28 April 1916, MS Hammond 8, HP.

4   For example, when Trinity College, Cambridge, blocked the Union of Democratic Control meeting in which Charlie was to talk about the Balkans in November 1915, the Liberal Club in Cambridge also cancelled a replacement booking for the meeting. Charlie was in no doubt of his unpopularity in the Liberal Party in general, not just Hackney. (With a huge audience, the meeting was eventually held in the Guildhall.), Florence, p. 36.

5   In his memoirs published in 1930, Edward Grey (Foreign Secretary in 1916) admitted that in hindsight this may have been a lost opportunity. However, he doubted Germany would have agreed the terms so the British rejection was irrelevant. He believed speculation about a possible ceasefire in 1916 was a case of 'building castles in the air; and if the future is too clouded for this, we build them in the past'. Grey, pp. 131–132.

6   Charlie to Dorothy, 21 December 1916, BFA. Lloyd George, now Prime Minister,

in the Liberal Party that did not heal until the mid-1920s, by which time the Labour Party had greatly increased its parliamentary representation and had become the 'alternative government' to the Conservatives. Radically-minded Liberals began to leave the party during the war years. Charles Trevelyan sat as an independent in the House of Commons from 1915. Other founders of the UDC, such as Morel and Ponsonby had joined the Labour Party by 1918. Noel Buxton had begun his own journey to the left. In the first post-war election of December 1918, he stood as 'Liberal-Labour' candidate, but he lost by 200 votes, after which he joined the Labour Party.

For Charlie, not then an MP, the transition was simpler. During the war, he went to meetings in different parts of the country to put his case for a negotiated peace and in doing so found most of those who responded and agreed with his position were socialists. He realised that he needed to collaborate with those whose economic ideas were further to the left than he then espoused[1] in order to create a united front concerning a peace policy. In the context of 1917, it was the Independent Labour Party that Charlie judged the most significant for supporting peace candidates in by-elections.

At this time the Labour Party was an umbrella organisation, which had various groups affiliated with it, including trade unions, pressure groups such as the Fabian Society and also the Independent Labour Party. Up to 1918, people would join one of the affiliated groups rather than the Labour Party itself. This federated approach produced some political anomalies. For example, after the 1918 General Election, the Labour representatives were the second largest group to take their seats[2] in the House of Commons after the overwhelmingly victorious Liberal-Conservative Coalition MPs. However, the Labour MPs did not have a formal leader until early in the 1920s and were not technically a 'party' in parliament and so did not become the 'Opposition'. Instead, one of the non-Coalition Liberal MPs (a smaller group) had to serve in the role of Leader of the Opposition.[3]

---

had made a speech in the House of Commons on 19 December.

1   It should be noted that, in later years, he claimed his move to socialism had begun when he was Principal of Morley College. 'I *started* on the road to Socialism through the rage which I felt at my Morley College friends having never had, & being never able to have, the vastly greater chances, which Fortune had heaped on me with lavish hand.' Charlie to David, 8 April 1934, BFA.

2   Sinn Fein, the party advocating Irish independence, would not take their seats in the Westminster Parliament, otherwise they would have been the official opposition to the Coalition government, as numerically they had won more seats (73) than the Labour Party (57).

3   The Labour MPs elected a 'chairman' of the Parliamentary Labour Party. This had been Arthur Henderson and then Ramsey Macdonald, but the latter had resigned

During the First World War, the Labour Party contained a very broad range of views. Some members of the ILP regarded the Labour Party as too weak on social reform and foreign policy, its radical edge diluted because of its many constituent parts. In August 1914, for example, the ILP was the only part of the Labour Party to refuse to support the War. There were individuals who were opposed, but other constituent elements of the Labour Party believed that to support the war effort was a necessary evil.

It was the ILP therefore that was closest to Charlie and Dorothy's views on the need for peace. In January 1917, Charlie decided to attend the Labour Party Conference in Manchester. He was a 'guest' and sat in the gallery of the Victoria Hall. He judged that two-thirds of the delegates were for a peace, although when the trade union block votes were used the two-thirds majority swung the other way. After meeting ILP members at the conference, Charlie was then invited to attend the National Council of the Independent Labour Party.[1] His association with them in time led to him joining as a member. It was a natural evolution from his campaigning. However, it was a transition that came because of foreign policy and peace issues, not economic policy. Although he became the ILP's Treasurer in the mid-1920s for three years, he was a moderate voice in their deliberations, still concentrating on foreign and colonial policy.

Dorothy's politics were in contrast moving far more swiftly to the left; she was to outrun Charlie by some way. By 1918, she was unequivocally a socialist and had it not been for her pacifism would have possibly called herself a communist. Two influences were prominent in this transformation. First, the work on the Notes had converted her to an internationalist outlook and approach to political problems. She saw all the working people of every nation as having far more in common than they had with the classes who ruled them. She was convinced that only cooperation across national boundaries could create a new era in which all could be included in economic progress. Only international cooperation could deliver both

in 1914 on the outbreak of the First World War because he was opposed to Britain's involvement, an opposition not shared by all Labour MPs nor the Trade Unions' leaders. Arthur Henderson (1863–1935) then resumed the leadership of the group, but resigned in 1917 after his suggestion for an international conference to end the war was rejected. Neither Macdonald nor Henderson held their seats in the 1918 general election. William Adamson (1863–1936), a former miner and MP for West Fife (1910–31), was the parliamentary leader from 1917 until 1921. Sir Donald Maclean (1864–1932), leader of the Liberal group of MPs in the House of Commons, acted as Leader of the Opposition during 1919–20, until H. H. Asquith returned to parliament in a by-election early in 1920. As the Liberal Party leader, Asquith then served as Leader of the Opposition until 1922.

1   Charlie to Dorothy, 25 January 1917, BFA.

peace and prosperity for the poorer members of society and only socialist parties appeared to advocate this approach. The Liberals and even trade unions seemed to Dorothy to be too nationalist in their attitudes.

The second influence on Dorothy's politics came from events in Russia. The Tsarist autocracy had been overthrown in a revolution in March 1917 (February 1917 in the old Russian calendar). It is hard for a modern observer to appreciate the excitement in many quarters at this extraordinary development that seemed to herald a new democratic and free society in Russia. The Labour Party had supported a special conference in Leeds in June 1917 to express solidarity with the new government, a conference at which Charlie had been a speaker. The new government, from July 1917 led by Kerensky,[1] introduced many reforms and promised democratic elections. It also offered to end the war on terms involving neither humiliations nor reparations, but the gesture came to nothing. Before many of the reforms came to fruition, in November (October in the Russian calendar) a further revolution brought the Bolsheviks to power. Few among the British left-wing of politics could then envisage the later developments of the Soviet Union or the attempt to eliminate Christianity – communism did not automatically equate with totalitarianism as it would for later generations. All that they registered in 1917 was the advent of Russian governments that promised equality and social justice with the abolition of class privileges. Any repression that followed the Bolshevik revolution seemed to be an understandable fight for survival against the many hostile forces that wished to eliminate communism before it had chance to establish itself. For Dorothy, this revolution seemed like the beginning of a new era when many of her aspirations could come true. There is no evidence that at this stage she had ever studied works by Karl Marx – her interest in the Bolsheviks came from reading their declarations not studying their political antecedents. So, for her, this Revolution was a matter of excitement and hope and she wanted to welcome the new politics. As ever, incapable of half measures, her espousal of the cause was not nuanced. She did not possess Charlie's caution and he worried that her enthusiasm would be misunderstood. When Charlie was a candidate for the Labour Party in the December 1918 election, he wrote to her before she attended a meeting with him,

> You need not suppress your Bolshevism, but let there be *love &*
> *sweetness* in it. Appeal to the idealism of those who want a state of
> society *here* which gives expression to their inmost (but generally

1   Alexander Fyodorovich Kerensky (1881–1970), Minister of Justice (February–May 1917) and then of War (May–July 1917) in the Provisional Government of Russia. Prime Minister July–October 1917.

buried) belief in brotherhood between the peoples. You can say that it had been your business for 3 years to follow the Labour & Socialist movement in every foreign country, & how it has been *concealed* from the public here; and what a tragedy it would be if the great uprising of the peoples now were to meet with no answering voice, no hand of fellowship, from ourselves.[1]

It was amidst this whirlwind of changing allegiances and new possibilities that the First World War came to an end. The Armistice of 11 November 1918 was a relief to both Charlie and Dorothy. Yet it did not mean that their work would end, but only that it changed emphasis. Dorothy had been devoted to informing people during 1914–18. After peace was declared, significant economic and political problems had to be faced. Dorothy realised that she did not need only to inform people – she needed to campaign for those left in dire need.

---

1   Charlie to Dorothy, 9 December 1918, BFA.

Chapter 5
Saving the children

Dorothy responded in both personal and political ways to the deprivations caused by the war conditions that she saw about her. On the personal level, she adopted ever more frugal patterns of life for herself than before the war in meeting her own needs for clothes and personal comforts. Indeed, her sister-in-law wrote of her that Dorothy 'spurned joy'.[1]

She used her beliefs about health to insist on open windows even in bedrooms in the cold months of the year and for there to be little or no heating.[2] She scorned the use of a hot water bottle. Water for baths was heated on the gas stove in the kitchen and an inch of water was all that was generally allowed.[3] She would wear a coat indoors if the temperature dropped too low. When she stayed indoors for three days to shake off a cold, she regarded that as 'a breach of my principles'.[4] On holiday, she liked to use a tent rather than stay at a hotel (however cheap) and would be happy to sleep in a field in the summer without any shelter.[5] She was honest enough in later years to accept that she put economy over health to her own detriment and became alarmed when her son appeared to be following her example, 'Now let me implore you not to fall into the snare which my family are sometimes too apt to think I fall into – & sacrifice health considerations to those of economy! That is the most false of economics – as you can always see so clearly in *my* case.'[6]

---

1. De Bunsen, p. 101.
2. There was an anthracite stove at 6 Erskine Hill and a fire could be lit on occasions in the living room, but never in the bedrooms. Conversation with Victoria Houghton, 4 January 2007.
3. David Buxton, autobiographical notes, BFA.
4. Dorothy to David, 5 December 1933, BFA.
5. For example, Dorothy to David, 9 September 1932, BFA. She wrote from her holiday in Cornwall of trying a night 'in the open' in a cornfield, keeping comfortable with 'sheaves under me and over me'.
6. Dorothy to David, 17 August 1932, BFA.

In other areas of life, she was on more stable ground in her abstemiousness. She became articulate about the false 'God of fashion', which she judged one of the idols that needed to be demolished.[1] In a book published in 1928, she expressed explicitly the views she came to embrace fully during the First World War:

> Take for example, the place we accord to fashion in dress. It is an absolute tyranny in our Western civilization. It causes a universal waste of money and universal waste of energy and of time. . . .
>
> It seems to us lacking in 'respect' to those who entertain us to appear in their homes dressed below a certain standard of expense and fashion; lacking in respect to the public in general, or, stranger still, lacking in self-respect, to appear in public meanly clothed; strangest of all, lacking in respect for the Almighty to attend Divine Worship in shabby clothes.
>
> Dress, in fact, is primarily for use. . . . ours is for display, and therefore what a vast waste of time, of thought, and of money it habitually represents.[2]

She discarded hats and gloves,[3] except when demanded by cold weather. Both Dorothy and her sister Eglantyne wore dark-coloured functional clothes – in fact the latter was known for wearing items mainly in brown.[4] Here they both echoed the utilitarianism and lack of adornment in dress they had observed in their Aunt Bun. Dorothy would wear smarter clothes if absolutely required, but merely dipped into her pre-1914 wardrobe. A photograph of her reproduced in election leaflets in Charlie's 1922 campaign in Accrington showed her in an elegant dress, but it was one that is of Edwardian style and she can be seen in this very same attire in photographs from her 'Devon' period 1908–11. Other photographs from the 1920s also show her in the high-necked blouses in fashion twenty years earlier. For everyday wear, her clothes were baggy and looked long and flowing on her thin figure – indeed she may have been one of the models for the old phrase about women in 'flowing Hampstead robes'. She rarely wore jewellery and never used make-up. Her clothes were often very worn and, as the years went by, her hired seamstress would complain to the housekeeper of how she was expected to patch skirts and blouses that were already threadbare.[5]

---

1. In this she echoes Charlie's comment in his 1905 Church Congress speech: 'the absurd ideal of smartness and fashionableness and elaboration in clothing'. CC1905, p. 80.
2. DRB1, pp. 24–25.
3. 'what a grotesque and clumsy device a hat is'. DRB1, p. 31.
4. Mulley, pp. 257–259.
5. Conversation with Victoria Houghton, 4 January 2007.

Dorothy in the early days of SCF,
wearing an adapted version of the dress she wore in the 1912 image previously shown
(see picture on page 70).

Skirt lengths were raised a little over the years, but otherwise Dorothy paid little attention to fashion. Charlie's sisters would pressurise him into buying a new suit from time to time, something Dorothy tolerated, but of which she did not approve.[1]

In respect to food, Dorothy abandoned dinner parties at the outset of the First World War and simplified the household's diet. As voluntary rationing was introduced early in 1917,[2] she had an excuse for her frugality, but the approach did not change once the war ended. Charlie went along with this at home, but remained 'undiscriminating about food' and would eat anything put before him when outside the home.[3] He threw many lunches and parties for political reasons, held at hotels and the like near Westminster.[4] Here the food would be more varied. Indeed, he continued to have an 'almost childish delight' in good food.[5] He was also still partial to sherry or cocktails if served to him.

Dorothy became ever narrower in comparison. She embraced vegetarianism during the war too. On the top of a short essay on nature written by David in the summer of 1918, she scribbled a note,

> As a quite small child (5 to 7?) he [David] enquired one day . . . what he was eating for dinner. When I explained it, he paused a moment & then asked 'Must I eat animals?' (He was very fond of animals). I explained about vegetarians. 'Can't I be a vegetarian?' Delighted at his independence of mind I at once decided to become one myself & have remained one myself.[6]

Food was healthy and nutritious, but became very simple in the Buxton household, mainly lentils in the form of rissoles with vegetables, sometimes raw, and with few trimmings.[7] Dorothy was especially enthusiastic about cabbage and lettuce. She was ever on the lookout for new vegetables and, for example, became keen on kohlrabi when she discovered it.[8] Special items were bought at the Pure Food Shop in Hampstead. The household had a cup of tea at 4p.m. most days, but with no cake or biscuits. Culinary

---

1. De Bunsen, pp. 102 and 123–124.
2. Gradually an element of compulsion was introduced over the following winter with ration books from mid-1918.
3. De Bunsen, p. 123.
4. De Bunsen, pp. 127–128.
5. De Bunsen, p. 102.
6. Handwritten note of Dorothy's on piece of writing about nature by David, dated circa 1918, BFA.
7. The housekeeper was allowed to cook meat for her and her daughter if they wished. Conversation with Victoria Houghton, 4 January 2007.
8. Conversation with Victoria Houghton, 4 January 2007. Kohlrabi is a cross between a cabbage and a turnip; the leaves, stem and root can be eaten, raw or cooked.

austerity meant that even the extravagances of Christmas were banished. In the early 1930s, Dorothy wrote to David that the housekeeper and her daughter would be sent off to eat turkey and plum pudding at their own relatives in Vauxhall, whilst Charlie and she and Eglantyne would have eggs. Charlie and Eglantyne went to the wider Buxton clan's traditional Boxing Day revelry of a 'sausage picnic', but Dorothy kept away.

> Here we shall spend it in our usual fashion & the 3 of us here will eat our poached eggs (somewhat overdone in the absence of y[ou]r watchful eye), & put off all attempt at jollification till the Sausage picnic. This Daddy & Egl[antyne] hope to attend & I shall have a glorious day with my papers all by myself.[1]

A year later, Dorothy wrote again of spending 'a thoroughly quiet Christmas', but that she had allowed Florence (Mrs Hawkins, the housekeeper) to put up 'paper decorations in the kitchen' and nowhere else – and then only for two days. Dorothy remained disdainful of the 'rain' of presents Florence and her daughter received and of her housekeeper's wish to be conventional in celebrating the season. She wrote of the wider Hawkins family's consumption of turkey, plum pudding, Christmas cakes, port and whiskey as the way 'such people celebrate the worship of the world & the flesh'.[2]

The Buxtons were still wealthy, even if they did not spend their income on themselves and had abandoned luxuries and comforts. Even here though, the First World War led to a further change in their situation. With MPs to be salaried,[3] Charlie did not need to safeguard as much of his income in case he won a seat in parliament again. Consequently, in 1919 Charlie and Dorothy put much of their money in a trust, the income from which they as trustees could use only for political and social projects.[4]

1. Dorothy to David, 11 December 1933, BFA.
2. Dorothy to David, 1 January 1935, BFA. Charlie's attitude to Christmas was that whilst he shared the Quaker view that celebrating the Incarnation was unnecessary, he nevertheless saw the festival as a social good. 'I've come to the conclusion that I'm a true Quaker in having no wish to keep Christmas as a religious festival. Assume that I want to dwell on the Incarnation & its significance – even in an orthodox way. The last thing I want is to set aside *one* day in the year for it. The result would be that I should feel I had then *disposed* of it, or at least that all other days would be treated as somehow *less* important than the great & special one. . . . On the other hand I see the greatest value in a social festival, a festival of joy and of family re-union – there are things you want to celebrate, but don't want to do so every day. So, Christmas now is a quite frankly Pagan affair, and I enjoy it more than ever.' Charlie to David, 26 December 1934, BFA.
3. Salaries were introduced in 1911.
4. Decades later, not long before Dorothy's death, the trust had to be sorted out in court and was deemed not 'in perpetuity' and so could be dissolved. *The Times*, 17

All of these measures were part of a puritan attitude that Dorothy had first espoused because of her experience during the First World War – although it must be noted she had argued for a 'puritan' outlook years before in a debate at Morley College, where she expressed a belief in increasing well-being rather than pursuing pleasure.[1] The wartime conditions however gave her both the courage and the opportunity to live them out as she witnessed the unimaginable hardship and famine conditions many people suffered. Suffering was not only about soldiers on the frontline, but about civilians being deprived of the basic requirements of life. Many of these civilians were children who were totally innocent of any collusion with militarism or politics or the attitudes of their adult relatives. Dorothy believed in 'going without' to increase the resources available to the destitute.

One of the most potent tools of war that Britain and its allies possessed in the First World War was not a battlefield weapon – it was a blockade of the enemy nations, depriving them of the ability to import food and necessities. Creating famine conditions was, in fact, an unspoken political and military tactic. The nations of the Central Powers had a strong agricultural sector, but they could not produce all the food that they required. Many farm workers were in the army and in a sector where technology was only just beginning to be developed, the lack of labourers on the land dented productivity on the farms. Britain and France's naval powers were used to prevent supplies reaching central Europe from the rest of the world. Germany responded with submarine warfare in the Atlantic, sinking supplies before they arrived at British ports, but this was not as comprehensive as the blockade of continental Europe. As the war continued, the blockade was like a noose that gradually tightened around the throat of Germany and Austria-Hungary in particular. By the winter of 1916–17, stockpiles were running out and journalists from neutral countries began reporting how thin and undernourished many people looked in those countries. Inevitably, it was the poorest people in these countries, not the rich and powerful, who were most affected. By 1918, some commentators saw the blockade as the reason for the swift (and to many unexpected) collapse of German military resistance in the summer of 1918 that led to the Armistice in November.

November 1962. Charlie's brother, Noel, also created a trust in 1919, which is still extant (www.noelbuxtontrust.org.uk – accessed 14 August 2014).

1. *MCM*, Vol XVI, No 6 (March1907), p. 91; 'Mrs. Buxton thought that the difference between the two parties was that while anti-Puritans desired to increase pleasure and to allow all pleasures full play, Puritans wished to increase happiness as a whole by discouraging false or vicious pleasures.'

Politically, even after the cessation of hostilities, the blockade still had a relevance – to ensure Germany and its allies adhered to the victors' terms when it came to a peace settlement. Once the blockade was lifted, it could not be re-introduced, so the Entente Powers decided to maintain it until Germany in particular had capitulated to its demands. Public opinion in Great Britain and France was in an ugly and vengeful mood; there was no appetite in the immediate post-war period for ideas of fairness or reasonableness, let alone mercy and forgiveness. That the Germans had 'caused' the war and now must 'pay' was a typical view of the ordinary British citizen. The Prime Minister, David Lloyd George, with his own political party (the Liberals) split between his group in the Coalition government and those in opposition led by his predecessor, Asquith, realised he could only remain Prime Minister if the Coalition also continued. The Conservatives, although making up a majority of the Coalition MPs, were content with this as they did not wish to fight a General Election against Lloyd George, who was immensely popular for 'winning the war'. Therefore, a few days after the Armistice, the Prime Minister called a General Election for mid-December 1918, asking for a mandate for the Coalition to continue. In each constituency, one candidate was given a 'coupon', a piece of paper confirming that the holder was the government's candidate. In most cases this candidate with 'the coupon' was a Conservative, but some were Liberals supporting the Prime Minster and a few Labour candidates had the coupon too. The Asquithian Liberals and the Labour Party both put up candidates in opposition to the government.

The campaign was very manipulative with the government using slogans such as 'Hang the Kaiser', 'Make the Germans pay' and 'Keep the Germans out'. Although women over the age of thirty voted for the very first time, the turnout was well below two-thirds, as many of the menfolk were still serving in the army overseas. In elections in the 1920s, turnout was usually well above 80%. In 1918, the Coalition swept back to power with a massive majority. Asquith and many opposition politicians lost their seats. Charlie fought as a Labour candidate for the first time in Accrington, a seat held by the Liberal Party since 1892. His moderate speeches emphasised that Britain would gain from a thriving Germany and Austria, for they would buy British goods and help the British economy and jobs. They could not do so if they were kept in ruins. But his arguments made little headway and he was howled down at public meetings. A few years later he was heard and believed, but in the emotional and vengeful turmoil of late 1918, he was dismissed. Dorothy went to the constituency for one meeting to give him support. It was a

hopeless fight and he came in third when the results were declared. The
Conservative with 'the coupon' won.[1] Dorothy wrote to her son four
years later of those difficult days.

> The last general election was 4 years ago[,] just after the war had
> ended and when the 'Peace' was about to be drawn up. Both the other
> parties took advantage of the excited war feelings & bitterness of the
> moment to appeal to the people on such cries as 'make Germany pay
> to the last farthing' and 'hang the Kaiser'. We can be proud to think
> that Daddy at that time refused to appeal to such feelings of hatred &
> revenge & stood out for a peace of *reconciliation* with Germany, and
> the resuming of trade relations with her, instead of ruining Germany
> by crushing peace terms. At the time he was abused & sneered at for
> taking such a line and called 'a friend of every country but his own',
> a 'pro-German' & all the rest of it. Since 1918 however time & bitter
> experience has shewn [*sic*] that Daddy & the people like him were in
> the right all the time.[2]

It was in this unsympathetic climate that Dorothy resolved to educate
the public to the effects of the blockade. Her translation and publication
of articles from the foreign press had alerted her to the growing concerns
about the lack of food in continental Europe from 1916. For her, this was a
major moral issue and, as ever, she advocated action as well as publicity. For
her, the challenge was how to reach the starving with food aid, especially
children. The continuation of the blockade made this impossible. Soon
after the announcement of the Armistice, Dorothy was in conversation
with her contacts at the Women's International League, a British branch
of a group founded in 1915 in The Hague in the neutral Netherlands to
lobby for an end to the First World War. She also contacted Quaker groups
who were very concerned with the suffering of war victims. Subsequently, a
group of people gathered at the house of Lord Parmoor[3] in Wilton Crescent
in London. Parmoor was a Liberal peer and a prominent Anglican layman
who was concerned that Britain's actions should be from his perspective
'morally right' and not just a matter of national self-interest. His late wife's

---

1. 1918 December General Election Accrington (electorate 42,160) 69.5% turnout:
   Major Ernest Gray (Coalition Conservative) 13,808 (47.2%); Major Harold
   Baker (Liberal) 8,378 (28.6%); C. Roden Buxton (Labour) 6,379 (21.7%); W.
   Hammond (NDP) 738 (2.5%); Coalition Conservative majority of 5,430 (18.6).
2. Dorothy to David, 17 November 1922, BFA.
3. Charles Alfred Cripps (1852–1941), Conservative MP Stroud 1895–1900,
   Stretford 1901–06, Wycombe 1910–14. 1st Baron Parmoor 1914. He became a
   Liberal peer after his ennoblement.

sister, Catherine (usually known as 'Kate') Courtney[1] had been a peace campaigner for decades and had been prominent in opposing the earlier Boer War (1899–1902) as well as the First World War. She and Dorothy were of a similar mind. She suggested the meeting of concerned individuals to her brother-in-law and he agreed to host and chair it. At this preliminary informal meeting, it was Dorothy who reported on famine conditions, as was made clear in Lord Parmoor's memoirs,[2] and she was put in charge of making the enquiries that would establish the facts concerning the ongoing deprivation. Marian Ellis[3], a Quaker colleague of Dorothy's who had campaigned for conscientious objectors during the war, volunteered for the secretarial role. However, after some weeks, Dorothy had recruited her sister Eglantyne to assist Miss Ellis.[4] Noel Buxton, Charlie's brother, became Treasurer.

The campaign group held a formal meeting on 1 January 1919, which launched the Fight the Famine Council (FFC). A further FFC meeting was held on 12 March 1919, at the Methodist Central Hall, Westminster. This second meeting was chaired by a Conservative MP, Lord Henry Cavendish-Bentinck,[5] so as to assure people of the cross-party support for the group's initiative. Their initial aim was to campaign for the repeal of the blockade whilst also supporting the USA's President Wilson and his quest to found a League of Nations. At the March meeting, Lord Parmoor argued that there was no interest in making enemies of millions of people in the defeated nations who should be friends. Two resolutions were passed:

1. Catherine Potter (1847–1929), married Leonard Courtney in 1883, and after his elevation to the peerage in 1908, she became Baroness Courtney of Penrith. One of her eight sisters, Theresa (1852–1893), had married Lord Parmoor in 1881 and one of Theresa's sons, Stafford (1889–1952), became a Labour MP and Chancellor of the Exchequer (1947–50) in the post-Second World War Labour government. Another sister of Catherine's, Beatrice (1858–1943), married Sidney Webb, and was a well-known academic and social reformer.

2. Lord Parmoor, *A Retrospect: looking back over a life of more than eighty years,* William Heinemann, London, 1936, p. 134.

3. Marian Emily Ellis (1878–1952), daughter of a radical Quaker and Liberal MP, she married Lord Parmoor as his second wife on 14 July 1919.

4. Eglantyne wrote to Tye in an undated letter (headed Monday), but probably from late 1918: 'Dorothy is at the moment at a meeting from which possibly a "Fight the Famine" organisation may begin to emerge. We are trying to settle the affairs of the universe!!! – I think I may have to leave the *C[ambridge] M[agazine]*, at any rate for a time, & devote myself entirely to the famine work.' Box 11, 7EJB/B/01/03/18, WL. This cannot refer to either 1 January 1919 or 12 March 1919 as these were Wednesdays.

5. Henry Cavendish-Bentinck (1863–1931), Conservative MP for North-West Norfolk 1886–92, and Nottingham South 1895–1906, 1910–29.

1. That the appalling conditions which exist in the famine districts impose an unquestionable duty on every person to spread a knowledge of the facts and to support, not only measures of temporary relief, but, in addition, to urge, before it is too late, a policy for permanent alleviation.

2. That the blockade should be raised, and that there should be no interference with food transport in or to the distressed districts, and that the industrial conditions in such districts should be allowed to return as soon as possible to the normal state, in order that an adequate food supply may be provided, and that commodities may be produced to pay for such supply.[1]

The FFC programme nevertheless was primarily a political one as campaigning for the ending of the blockade was part of a peace-building agenda that included economic reconstruction, including for the defeated nations. This policy of 'permanent alleviation' was controversial at a time of impassioned anti-German feeling in the country. Consequently, these resolutions did not reflect the full priorities of most of the participants.

For Dorothy, however much she whole-heartedly agreed with the wider aims, her mission was far more immediate. She wanted to 'save the children' from starvation. That could not wait until the founding of a League of Nations. Instead of lobbying to pressure for political changes, it required an immediate relief effort uncomplicated by political goals – indeed uncoupling the relief from the politics would make it easier to gain support and raise funds for shipping food to Europe. She decided to suggest the beginning of a 'sub-committee' of FFC to be called Save the Children. Writing in 1921, she gave the date of this decision as in March 1919.[2] This would have been just before she left on a trip to Switzerland for both Quaker and Women's League meetings, after which she collected photographs, as well as factual material of undernourished children for use in the publicity that she issued on her return to Britain. One of her companions on this trip was Ethel Snowden, wife of the Labour MP Philip Snowden.[3] Dorothy visited a centre in the Alps where some Austrian children were in care. During her time in Berne, she also helped organise a small *Comité Internationale de Secours aux Enfants*[4] (International Committee to Help the Children;

1. EJ120 in Box A404, BUA.
2. Dorothy to Henry Noel Brailsford, 28 October 1921, Box 13, 7EJB/B/02/06, WL.
3. Philip Snowden (1864–1937), Labour MP for Blackburn 1906–18, for Colne Valley 1922–31, National Labour Peer as Viscount Snowden from 1931, Chancellor of the Exchequer 1924 and 1929–31.
4. This is explicitly acknowledged by Eglantyne in Eglantyne to Tye, 28 September 1919, Box 8, 7EJB/B/01/02/12, WL.

CISE) and organised her first shipments of aid to Austria, using £1000 of funds that Quakers had granted her.[1] Dorothy arrived back in Britain on 6 April 1919 a month after she had started her trip, by which time she had made her mind up to start a separate Save the Children Fund. [2]

Dorothy herself proposed this at a meeting of the FFC on 15 April 1919. There were differing views. As Eglantyne would later note, some thought the SCF a good idea as 'charity promotes the right atmosphere for Governments', yet others were against as a charitable agency gave a convenient excuse 'that means governments don't have to act'.[3] From this variety of views came the decision from the former group to support the creation of the SCF, but the second body of opinion pushed that it should be fully independent. The Save the Children Fund was then officially launched on 19 May 1919 at a packed meeting held at the Royal Albert Hall. Addressing the gathering, Dorothy famously raised her arm with a tin of condensed milk and proclaimed that such a tiny item now symbolised morality and religion.[4] Dorothy was the named honorary secretary. The FFC registered the SCF as a separate charity on 22 May to confirm its total independence.[5]

The sisters were effectively left by FFC members to run the fledgling charity. The FFC carried on its own political agenda to which Dorothy still contributed. She suggested, for example, a hunger strike if the food blockade was ever re-imposed, but this idea received very little support and

1. Davidson 372, Relief Work 1919, 211, LPL: 'When Miss Jebb and I started the Save the Children Fund last May, one of our first acts was to get a consignment of milk, rice, etc., sent from Switzerland to Dr Wenckebach's clinic. He lately has been telling me that this supplied the first appropriate food he had had for I think he said – years for his patients, and he is still eking it out.' For details of the fuss to deliver the supplies, see BB1, also, Ethel Snowden, *A Political Pilgrim in Europe 1919–21*, Cassell, London, 1921, pp. 60–61. Dorothy also probably used another £1000 of her own moneys on top of the Quaker grant, BB1.
2. Dorothy to Tye, picture postcard, postmarked Hendon 6 Apr 1919, 'Just landed at Folkestone & homewards at last! Have been away exactly a month & it seems like years. Have had an extraordinary interesting time & long to tell you all about it.' Box 6, 7EJB/B/01/02/01, WL.
3. Eglantyne, memorandum, Box 8, 7EJB/B/01/02/13, WL.
4. The exact words she spoke were probably ad-libbed and sources differ as to her exact phraseology. One oft-repeated claim is that she proclaimed the tin held more morality than 'all the creeds', but it is impossible to be sure of her precise words. In 1962 Dorothy reminisced: 'In the course of my speech, I held up a tin of condensed milk and declared that it was far more important than all the theologies, this bit of nonsense evoking great enthusiasm in the audience.' Dorothy to Mrs Nelson-Smith, 12 February 1962, BFA.
5. Mahood, p. 168. SFC was formally 'incorporated' in 1921.

was dropped.[1] Eglantyne, however, withdrew completely from the FFC. She had been arrested earlier in April for distributing leaflets in Trafalgar Square advocating an end to the blockade, leaflets which had contained a picture of an emaciated Austrian baby. As the leaflet had not been vetted by the government, she had committed an offence against the Defence of the Realm Act's censorship rules. On 15 May 1919, the case was heard at Mansion House Police Court. She was found guilty and a fine of £5 was imposed. She insisted the FFC knew nothing of her leaflet or its distribution[2] and so resigned as the FFC honorary secretary, thus freeing herself to work instead wholly for the new SCF.[3]

At the beginning, both sisters were somewhat overwhelmed by what they had taken on. As Dorothy later recalled, one of the issues they faced was judging wisely the offers of help they received. In an all-volunteer organisation, the danger of the well-meaning, but incompetent, as well as the interfering and ultimately obstructive, was enormous. This was all still embarrassingly fresh in the memory for Dorothy in 1921, 'When she [Eglantyne] and I first started the SCF in March 1919, we were both idealists, with *no* experience to qualify us for dealing with *people*.' She went on to note that they had collected 'the queerest collection of *cranks*, *fools* and *vassals* (providentially only *one or two* of the latter!) which could well be imagined'. The work quickly became so great that the new charity had neither the office quarters nor competent staff to deal with it.[4]

Dorothy worked from cramped quarters at Bank Chambers, in High Holborn,[5] to provide what she termed a 'Famine Information Bureau' whilst overseeing the SCF work as she was seen as the expert on famine conditions in Europe.[6] Eglantyne was dispatched to win support from the influential and powerful wherever she could gain access. In September, Eglantyne would take on the SCF honorary secretary role, but in the middle of 1919,

---

1. Circular SCF letter from Dorothy, 1 July 1919, Box A0415, SCFL.
2. *The Times*, 16 May, 1919.
3. It should be added that both sisters had also handed the bulk of the work for the *Cambridge Magazine* on to Mosa Anderson, who ran the 'Foreign Opinion' until its cessation a year or so later. The content however still provided a valued resource to them in their information-gathering for their relief work.
4. Dorothy to Henry Noel Brailsford, 28 October 1921, Box 13, 7EJB/B/02/06 WL.
5. Room 341, 329 High Holborn.
6. William Goode, the Supreme Economic Council, British Department, based in Paris wrote to her in September 1919: 'I am impressed, I was almost going to say "astonished", by the thoroughness with which you have entered into all the problems of Relief, and I am grateful for the moral and practical support afforded by the united conference of Relief Societies.' EJ 244, Box A414, BUA.

this was not yet the case. Dorothy, herself, worked immensely hard on many different fronts and felt overwhelmed. She wrote to her mother early in July 1919,

> You sent me a very comforting letter on Whit Sunday when I was struggling to emerge from a fit of depression; & it helped me on ever so much! This work *does* seem difficult & harassing, but I daresay the toughest stage is over now that people like Curzon & Smuts have made such pronouncements. It is a great feather in Eg[lantyne']s cap that she pulled the strings to get the Curzon Appeal & it makes up for many a blank draw – I expect we shall go ahead much easier now. I have missed not seeing anything of the wonderful summer we had in May & early June; for me it had to be all spent in 'Bank Chambers' & I seldom get back here [6 Erskine Hill, her home] till 8.30p.m. or later: to leave again at 9a.m. However it is petty to count one[']s own insignificant sacrifices when one thinks of all the incredible sufferings of millions. . . . My Camb[ridge] Magazine days seem a perfect *holiday* to look back on compared to what my work is now. I keep hoping it may get easier but am very doubtful about it.[1]

Dorothy realised quickly that she would have to delegate, noting in mid-July that she hoped to hire help for the information-gathering with a gift of funds from her mother.[2] She realised she could not expedite research, as well as undertake administration duties and publicity all on her own.

> I certainly have at last been driven to a vivid realisation that achievement on at all a large scale *must* depend on being able to get other people to do at least 90% of the things which it seems indispensable that one should do oneself! I am driven to come to grips with fundamental conditions of success, – which I have put off facing for too long. The recluse instincts of my nature are always in secret revolt against anything which forces me out of a lonely furrow. But present experiences are forcing me to face facts, & recognise when one[']s real limitations come in.[3]

---

1. Dorothy to Tye, 2 July 1919, Box 6, 7EJB/B/01/02/01, WL.
2. Dorothy to Tye, 19 July 1919, JFA: 'I propose to try & annex some really cultured person who could get up the subject thoroughly & to be able to replace me or at any rate supplement me as the expert on information. At present no one has given half the time to the job I have & so no one knows so much & I feel the whole structure rests on my being able to supply reliable information. I will try & get someone started within the next week if possible.'
3. Dorothy to Tye, 26 July 1919, Box 12, 7EJB/B/01/03/23, WL.

It was this realisation that led her to handing over the role of honorary secretary (and the accompanying administration) to her sister. There was also the need for Eglantyne to have the 'official' title as she had emerged as the main contact for people with influence and power. The new honorary secretary wrote to the old one in formal terms,

Dear Mrs Buxton

The Executive instruct me to say that they cannot help feeling on their own account the greatest regret in accepting your resignation, while understanding that you yourself ought now to be released from this additional work. We are all of us so deeply grateful to you for having acted so long as our honorary secretary, as well as being the head of the Information Bureau. In the interests of our Cause you shouldered a double burden from which many people might well have shrunk. May we convey to you our heartfelt thanks for the splendid services you have rendered us and express our appreciation of the way in which you rose to the emergency, and of the courage and self-sacrifice you have constantly displayed.

We rejoice that changed circumstances enable you now to be set free for your information work, and we hope that the different branches of the movement may continue to develop in close unison and on sound constructive lines.

Yours very sincerely
Eglantyne Jebb, Hon, Sec.[1]

This was an explicit acknowledgment that Dorothy was essentially running the new charity in its early months, as well as doing the research – the noted 'double burden'. Soon after this letter was sent, the SCF moved its office on 10 September 1919 to 7 St James' Terrace, Regents Park and later Dorothy persuaded the SCF Council to appoint a salaried General Secretary to oversee the administrative side of the charity work that she had been doing on a voluntary basis.[2] The man chosen was Lewis Bernard

---

1. Eglantyne to Dorothy, September [1919], Box A1474, SCFL.
2. She certainly claimed it was her initiative in October 1921 and, given her love for her sister, it is doubtful Dorothy would have claimed to have done something that in fact Eglantyne had done. She wrote then that she, 'persuaded the Committee to take on Mr Golden as Secretary, a man who did not profess to be much of an idealist but who appeared to be honest and possessed of great business ability'. Dorothy to Henry Noel Brailsford, 28 October 1921, Box 13, 7EJB/B/02/06, WL. This means that the claim in Mulley, p. 255 that Eglantyne was responsible was not the full story. Eglantyne probably met Mr Golden first, but it was Dorothy who approached the SCF Council on the matter, as they would need persuading of the necessity to spend money on a salary, and Eglantyne was out of London.

Golden (1878–1954), who had British citizenship, but who had been born in Russia. Escaping that country at the time of the 1917 Revolution, he had experience working in continental Europe including as a foreign correspondent for the *Daily Mail*, and so had an excellent range of skills to offer the new charity. His official appointment was from 22 December 1919. He became the sisters' indispensable 'right-hand man', who carried them administratively, but also supported them in other ways, including ensuring they did not overwork themselves. As Dorothy wryly commented, 'he stands between me & all my bug bears. The only worry is he hunts me remorselessly out of the office before he will go himself!'[1]

It is clear that in these very earliest initiatives that created the Save the Children Fund, it was Dorothy who was the leader. Eglantyne herself acknowledged this in a letter in April 1920 saying that although her sister always gave her the credit, without Dorothy's 'persistent work the SCF would never have been started'.[2] Dorothy helped form the FFC before Eglantyne became involved and it was she who provided the research on famine for the meetings. It was she who helped start the CISE in Berne (the title which may have influenced her later choice of 'Save the Children')[3] and then proposed the setting up of the SCF as a separate entity, of which she served as the first honorary secretary. Yet it has often been assumed because of later developments that the initiative came principally from Eglantyne, who is therefore referred to as effectively the 'founder'.[4]

This down-playing of Dorothy's leading role was partly owing to her own desire to praise her sister after Eglantyne died. In 1924, for example, she described herself as the founder of the SCF,[5] which was recognised by

---

1. Dorothy to Tye, 6 January 1920, Box 10, 7EJB/B/01/03/07-13, WL. This letter is dated 6 January 1919, but the postmark is 1920 and the content suggests that 1920 is correct. Presumably, Dorothy made the common error when in haste of automatically using the old year at the beginning of the new.
2. Mulley, p. 348; also, Rodney Breen to David Buxton, 14 March 1994, BFA.
3. The daughter of the Buxtons' housekeeper remembered being told by Dorothy that the name 'Save the Children Fund' was something that came to her (Dorothy) whilst in the attic office room at 6 Erskine Hill. Conversation with Victoria Houghton, 4 January 2007.
4. For example, see Katherine Storr, *Excluded from the Record: Women, Refugees and Relief 1914–1929*, Peter Lang, Oxford, 2010, p. 244: 'Eglantyne Jebb is always credited with founding SCF.'
5. To her son, David, criticising him for speaking abruptly to her in public, she wrote of the reaction of any who heard: 'They would inevitably think: "Here is the lady who founded the SCF & who was so busy helping the children of foreigners that she quite neglected to teach her own child good manners!". . . .' Dorothy to David, 26 July 1924, BFA. On her trip to Sweden in November 1920, the press there described her as 'the founder' of SCF.

the SCF itself,[1] but after her sister died Dorothy wanted the SCF to be
Eglantyne's memorial. She saw how Eglantyne's less political public persona
was a more potent advocate for the success of the charity than her own
strong left-wing affiliations and more partisan image in the public eye. So
she asked for her part to be underplayed. But in her later years, she began
to feel that it should not be omitted. When Edward Fuller published *The
Rights of the Child* in 1951, Dorothy sent him an unequivocal clarification
and his reply put this succinctly,

> Thank you very much for your letter of yesterday and its interesting
> and informative comments on the foundation of the SCF. . . .
>   You are, of course, quite right in recalling that after her
> [Eglantyne's] death you made it clear to me that we should record
> her as the founder. This concession has indeed been of great help in
> crystallizing for the general public the idea of the Fund.[2]

Dorothy's role has also been neglected owing to the pattern of the
material that has survived. Dorothy's daughter admired her aunt and
kept most of her correspondence, whilst commissioning a biography that
explicitly named Eglantyne 'the Founder' in the sub-title and in the Jebb
genealogical family tree inside – there is no similar title under Dorothy's
name in the table.[3] Simultaneously Eglantyne apparently weeded and
disposed of some of her mother's letters, thereby skewing the historical
researcher's access to a full record. More significantly, two factors at the
time also contributed to Eglantyne being pushed more to the fore as the
years went by. The first was Dorothy's involvement in other political
matters, which will be dealt with elsewhere. Her political dealings meant
she distanced herself from the day-to-day work of SCF after the first
two years. The second was the fact that Eglantyne was much better at
influencing people. Dorothy had the energy and drive and persistence
to found an organisation, but Eglantyne was the superior in persuading
others to back it. Whereas Dorothy was passionate and demanding in
meetings, Eglantyne was more sympathetic and appealing. Dorothy could
be forthright and challenging in face-to-face encounters whilst her sister
was better at establishing a winning rapport. Dorothy judged Eglantyne
as the 'real soul of our movement. Everybody who comes in contact with
her gets inspired & they worship her'. Nevertheless, in the same letter to

1. SCF minutes, 45th meeting: 3 July 1925, minute C553, Box A1213, BUA.
2. Edward Fuller (PR Officer of the SCF) to Dorothy, 23 February 1953, Dorothy
   Buxton box: A1474, SCF archive, London. *The Rights of the Child: A Chapter in
   Social History* was published by Victor Gollancz, London, 1951.
3. This is the book by Francesca Wilson, see bibliography.

their mother, she made it clear this was a shared enterprise and it was the joint endeavour that thrilled Dorothy: 'I do feel it so glorious too that we should have this work *together*, – climbing the same trees like we did long ago!' [1]

In summer 1919, Charlie became concerned with Dorothy's unremitting schedule even if he himself was pre-occupied with his own work, especially attending conferences, such as the international socialist conferences in Berne in February (as an interpreter for the British delegates) and Amsterdam in late April 1919, followed by a trip to Italy with Ramsey Macdonald to visit the Italian Socialist Party in early summer.[2] However, he remained as always Dorothy's staunchest supporter. 'This agitation of yours, considering the odds you had to face at the start, has been something astounding. These are historic days, which your children's children will remember with pride & inspiration. How proud I am of you.'[3]

In August he managed to persuade her to take some time off and travel to Scotland, promising that after the first fortnight, which was to be 'time off', the holiday would be followed by a tour during which both would make speeches at meetings.[4] It was at this time that Eglantyne assumed the honorary secretaryship, but when she was away or unwell (as was frequently the case in the autumn of 1919 and early months of 1920), Dorothy took up the work again and it is she who dispatched the letters from January to March 1920 signing herself 'acting honorary secretary'.[5] This included letters concerning the receipt of funds, a task taken over by an honorary treasurer from March 1920.[6]

---

1. Dorothy to Tye, 16 July 1919, JFA.
2. Photographs of all these trips can be found in Charlie's scrapbooks, BFA. Ramsey Macdonald, out of parliament, but still one of Labour's leaders, tried to revive the 'Second International' of moderate socialists, which had been torn apart by wartime nationalism, breaking working-class links across Europe. This was to counter the communist 'Third International' established by Moscow to promote a socialist revolution.
3. Charlie to Dorothy, 28 June 1919, BFA.
4. Dorothy to Tye, 'written on train to Crewe', [no day] August 1919, Box 11, 7EJB/B/01/03/18, WL. 'We go on to Scotland on Monday & should have a clear fortnight & then 8 or 9 strenuous days of meetings got up for C[harlie] & me to address together, C[harlie] on the general situation, I myself on famine – Dundee, Edinburgh, Aberdeen, Perth, Glasgow, Kilmarnock.'
5. See Box A0411, BUA, where there is correspondence, for example, between Dorothy and the Russian Red Cross Fund (represented by Algernon Maudsley and Princess Christian).
6. Hubert Digby Watson (1869–1947), who had been for many years a civil servant in India, was appointed honorary treasurer of SCF on 15 December 1919 and remained so until 1946, serving also as Chairman 1931–46.

This sisterly double act was inevitable as Eglantyne travelled considerably. The most notable visit made by Eglantyne was to Pope Benedict XV in Rome in December 1919 to thank him for his support. The Pope had courted unpopularity amongst his own flock by taking a neutral stance throughout the First World War. At the same time, he had advocated unceasingly the need for a ceasefire and for a just peace, which annoyed some on both sides of the conflict who wanted all out victory for their nation. With the war over, the Pope's attention for all those who suffered demonstrated a continuation of this deep concern and it gave any appeal from him an authentic consistency. Benedict XV's encyclical *Paterno Iam Diu*, issued on 24 November 1919, had exhorted the faithful throughout the world to give generously in collections of alms, food and medicine on 28 December 1919 (Holy Innocents' Day).[1]

Eglantyne's major role was to bring together all the various charitable gifts and create a coherent international effort. To do this, she needed to persuade many different parties to pool their efforts into an international SCF, working to this end from Switzerland where the Red Cross was based and also where the League of Nations was being founded. The task was neatly described by her in a letter written from Paris in late September 1919:

> I think business has proceeded satisfactorily. What we shall probably do is to transform the *Comité Internationale de Secours aux Enfants* – a little committee which Dorothy helped to start in

---

1. The relevant passage is: 'We direct that on next December 28, the feast of the Holy Innocents, you should order public prayers and gather the alms of the faithful. In order to help on a larger scale so many poor children in this most noble competition of charity, in addition to money it will be necessary to gather food, medicines and clothing, all of which are so greatly wanting in these regions. We need not delay in explaining how such offerings may be conveniently divided and forwarded to their destination. This task may be confided to the committees which have been formed for this object, and may provide for it in any manner whatsoever.' The following year on 1 December 1920, he issued another encyclical, *Annus Iam Plenus*, that made a similar request, but this time explicitly naming the Save the Children Fund, the relevant quotations being: 'We cannot desist from offering a public tribute of praise to the society entitled the "Save the Children Fund," which has exerted all possible care and diligence in the collection of money, clothing, and food. . . . Accordingly it is Our wish that you forthwith announce throughout the whole of your several dioceses that a collection of alms is to be made on the twenty-eighth day of this month, the feast of the Holy Innocents, or if you prefer, on the Sunday immediately preceding, for the support of the children made needy by the way and that you particularly recommend this collection to the children in your diocese; further, that with all diligence in your power you see that the money thus collected is sent either to Us or to the "Save the Children Fund," which We have before mentioned'.

Berne in the spring, into the Central Committee for the relief of children, securing for it the official recognition of the International Red X & the league of Red Cross Societies. It is already under the official patronage of the Swiss Federal government & has all its letters & parcels carried free inside Switzerland. If strengthened and enlarged it ought to make a good central Save the Children office, but the Committee needs pins digging into them to make them really cooperate, especially with the Red Cross; & the two Red X organisations are *also* at loggerheads, & no wonder, as the League was started to supercede the international Red X, (which had committed no fault beyond that of remaining neutral) by an Allied organisation. I much hope that the arrangements I propose may be endorsed & completed with all speed.[1]

The work Eglantyne did and her achievements in creating the SCF worldwide have been amply covered elsewhere.[2] What is less understood is Dorothy's role in supporting her sister in the next stages of forging the SCF when she made two crucial interventions. The first came in November 1919. With the Pope strongly supporting donations among Roman Catholics for SCF's work, there was the prospect of an international SCF being well-funded. Many individuals and organisations competed for the expected funds: Roman Catholics were suspicious of Protestants and vice versa and both wanted to control any money that came from 'their' denomination; those who were sympathetic to Germany were faced with those who were still deeply antagonistic; the representatives from Berne did not want the SCF established in Geneva instead of their city and vice versa. Amidst the competing voices, 'saving the children' seemed to come second. Eglantyne felt some panic and confusion as to how to deal with it all – she called for 'strong support from home', but,

> No one came rushing out except Dorothy, whom I hadn't asked to come. But I might have known that she would stand by me when everyone else failed. . . .
> Dorothy's coming is a great help. When I looked out of the window yesterday & saw her walking across the street with her luggage my horizon cleared amazingly. She keeps the right thoughts.[3]

Dorothy arrived on 14 November and was able to give Eglantyne sound advice and moral support. She found many people thought Eglantyne should give up trying to create an international SCF. Dorothy would have

---

1. Eglantyne to Tye, 28 September 1919, Box 8, 7EJB/B/01/02/12, WL.
2. Most fully in the monographs by Mulley and Mahood.
3. Eglantyne to Tye, 15 November 1919, Box 8, 7EJB/B/01/02/12-16, WL.

none of it. To her, Eglantyne was the saint who would triumph against the pettiness of those who resisted. Shuttling between Berne and Geneva, Dorothy wrote a letter to her mother on the train.

> Such a kettle of fish, – such a tangle of discordant prejudices and interests I never did see or hear of! I feel we have made an unprecedented *ethical venture* in trying to unite *all* the creeds and all the parties for the saving of the child. Only to find, of course, that the saving of the child comes quite second in most minds to their personal party or religious prejudices. . . . and in the midst is our beautiful darling saint of an Eglantyne striving to follow the thread of lofty pure and disinterested purpose through a perfect jungle of intrigue, suspicion and hypocrisies. She is eating and sleeping well in spite of all, but is naturally somewhat worn from the fray. . . .
>
> It is a great struggle to keep our thoughts calm, and not to be overcome by anxiety and torn by sundry doubts and difficulty at every turn.[1]

Yet calm and resolute she remained and kept her sister so as well. Dorothy was exactly the right person to stiffen Eglantyne's resolve as she passionately instilled in her sister the rightness of what they were doing and she dismissed the idea of defeat. Eglantyne found a deputy, Suzanne Ferrière,[2] whose uncle, Frédéric, was the Swiss doctor who had reported for the Red Cross from Vienna in 1918 and had helped move the sisters to act in the first place. He also facilitated the receipt of funds by the Red Cross on SCF's behalf, which helped establish SCF's independence and indeed *bona fides*, given that it was such a new and untested charity. Having re-established her sister's morale, Dorothy returned home to 'send out a rescue party' to ensure there were no further 'wobbles' or causes for doubt.[3] This was also the time she secured the appointment of Lewis Golden.

Dorothy once more took up the honorary secretarial duties back in Britain whilst Eglantyne organised the SCF in Geneva. Money was pouring in, not just from the church collections on Holy Innocents' Day, but also

1. Eglantyne to Tye, 25 November 1919, Box 8, 7EJB/B/01/02/12-16, WL.
2. Eglantyne described her thus: 'Suzanne Ferriere has become my understudy here – she belongs to a family who for 50 years have worked in connection with the International Red Cross. They are born into the Int. Red Cross as doctors or secretaries or writers, they live in it & die in it. Suzanne is perfectly true to type, a sweet dignified young person with rather the air of a princess, & a clear head, & a strong character. She will be a great help to me. She takes up her new duties tomorrow.' Eglantyne to Tye, 30 November 1919, Box 8, 7EJB/B/01/02/12-16, WL.
3. Eglantyne to Aunt Bun, 29 November 1919, Box 6, 7EJB/B/01/02/01, WL.

from other sources. The Miners' Union had sent £10,000 of the £40,000 received in the last week of 1919, an enormous sum.[1] £40,000 was the equivalent of not far off £2 million in terms of a century later.

In February 1920, Dorothy had to step in a second time to help her sister. Eglantyne, back in London, fell ill and was unable to attend the first conference of the newly-founded International SCF in Geneva that month. In January 1920, she outlined her ideas to Dorothy of what needed to be done and who should be encouraged to speak, continuing, 'Blessings to you, my own own. The great thing now is to let God's plan develop – Every fresh development – good or bad – should suggest to us the thought – How can we make use of it to forward the Divine Will. . . . Try at the Conference that everyone should have a hearing.'[2]

Dorothy essentially stood in for her sister and guided the conference to success. Charlie was there, as was Mosa Anderson, his faithful secretary, and he wrote to his mother-in-law that Eglantyne was missed because the delegates praised her in her absence as the 'presiding genius'. He went on,

> They realize too, Dorothy's great part in the business, but more in the English than in the international sphere. I mustn't write more. I am glad Miss Anderson & I have come here, as we have succeeded in taking some small loads off Dorothy's shoulders, but all the same this is an effort for her which is almost superhuman, as she is more or less running the whole affair, & I shall be relieved when it is over.
>
> The Conference cannot (in my worldly judgment!) do all that she wants it to do. But it will do a great deal in promoting the idea of a coordinated plan of relief all over Europe.[3]

Charlie's comment on Dorothy's frustration that the gathering did not do 'all she wants it to do' reflected her concern not to 'fail' her sister. Eglantyne, however, was very appreciative and full of gratitude for her sister running the conference.

> I think you did *gloriously* at Geneva. I am so thankful you were there. The chief reason why you did not get through all you hoped lay in the nature of the circumstances, & we hear only now to proceed on the foundations laid.
>
> Next I am anxious to assure you of my conviction that all difficulties will be overruled for good. We have in hand something far bigger than we realise. Our whole civilisation is likely to undergo

1. Dorothy to Tye, 6 January 1920, Box 10, 7EJB/B/01/03/07-13, WL.
2. Eglantyne to Dorothy, Wednesday, [January 1920], Box 13, 7EJB/B/02/06, WL.
3. Charlie to Tye, 26 February 1920, Box 10, 7EFJ/B/01/02/14, WL.

vast changes in the near future, & we must try & work on our own little corner of the work in its connection with the great spiritual movement which is taking place.[1]

Further to these specific incidents, it may be helpful also to illustrate the day-to-day involvement with SCF development and policy between the two sisters by considering an example: the relationship between SCF and the Archbishop of Canterbury. Even before SCF's foundation, Eglantyne had contacted Archbishop Randall Davidson on behalf of FFC,[2] as he was both someone charged with moral leadership of the nation, as well as a person with considerable influence on governments of whatever political composition. As such, she sent him reports and correspondence. Making little headway, she then persuaded Lord Parmoor to write.[3] Undaunted by the lack of effective response, she approached the Bishop of Lichfield, who was more responsive.[4] She asked him to request a resolution in Convocation urging church people to do all in their power to help and also to produce a prayer for the relief of famine and for wisdom and courage for those who try to help.

The Bishop wrote on her behalf to the Archbishop:

> I had a long talk this morning with Miss Eglantyne Jebb who seems to me to be employing her reason as well as her emotions with regard to the subject. She says, which I think is true, that the 'Church' has not done anything officially and indeed very little unofficially to help in a cause which is undubitably Christian.

Archbishop Davidson replied sympathetically. The matter was 'vast and complicated' and concerning, but he remarked that he could do nothing immediately as his own brother had recently died and he had to deal with family matters.[5] Matters changed when it became clear that Eglantyne's written approaches to the Pope in Rome had received encouragement. Herbert Hoover,[6] the man in charge of American relief efforts, had launched

1. Eglantyne to Dorothy, 6 March 1920, Box 13, 7EJB/B/02/06, WL.
2. Eglantyne to Archbishop Davidson, 24 March 1919, Davidson 372, Relief Work 1919, 23, LPL.
3. Lord Parmoor to Archbishop Davidson, 7 May 1919, Davidson 372, Relief Work 1919, 87–88, LPL.
4. John Augustine Kempthorne (1864–1946), Suffragan Bishop of Hull 1910–13, Bishop of Lichfield 1913–37.
5. Bishop Kempthorne to Archbishop Davidson, 18 June 1919, and the Archbishop's reply 21 June 1919, Davidson 372, Relief Work 1919, 100–102, LPL.
6. Herbert Hoover (1874–1964), Chairman of the Commission for Relief in Belgium 1914–17, Director of US Food Administration 1917–18, Head of the American

a successful appeal to churches in the United States towards the end of 1918 which brought in many donations. The Pope saw this as a template that he could copy among European Roman Catholics and said he would produce an encyclical. From then on, Archbishop Davidson took the SCF more seriously and wrote himself to Pope Benedict. As a consequence, the original mid-November date for collections among Roman Catholics was put back to the Sunday after Christmas (Holy Innocents' Day, 28 December 1919). This was in response to the Archbishop's request for more time to organise the Anglican collection and the decision by both leaders that a joint appeal on the same day would be more powerful. The appeal then went out to both Roman Catholic and Anglican congregations.[1] The Archbishop had also gathered together his own group to consider the issue of famine relief.

By this time, Eglantyne was in Switzerland and it was Dorothy who had to press home the advantage. She sent the Archbishop articles, offered to introduce him to a visiting doctor from Vienna and assured him of the SCF's cooperation with other groups. He became a patron of the British SCF. He then sent an emissary to interview Dorothy and she remembered a Mr Ellison, 'coming to see me late one evening at the office when I was struggling alone with arrears of work long after office hours'. Ellison was a nephew of the Archbishop, the son of his wife's sister.[2] They discussed possible cooperation between Lambeth Palace and the SCF and Ellison told her that his uncle,

> had formed a Committee for Famine Relief and that they were considering whether to act independently or to offer to amalgamate with us. Of course I said all I could to encourage him in the latter alternative, as it clearly would be good for the work of neither body that they should exist side by side with identical objects, and the inevitable *competition* which would arise between them was odious in connection with a charitable object.[3]

Dorothy worried that the shoe-string appearance of the SCF set-up may have led Ellison to report coolly about cooperation to his uncle. However, by January 1920, the Archbishop wrote to Dorothy to confirm that he

---

Relief Association 1918–21, President of the USA 1929–33.

1. *The Times*, 24 November, 1919, p. 13.
2. Craufurd Tait Ellison (1888–1942) was the son of Agnes Sitwell Ellison (1860–88), who had died soon after Craufurd's birth. Agnes and her sister, Edith – the wife of Archbishop Davidson – were daughters of a previous Archbishop of Canterbury, Archibald Campbell Tait (1811–82). C.T. Ellison had been a career army officer before the First World War. He later fought in the war, suffered injury, and then worked for some time for his uncle.
3. Dorothy to Henry Noel Brailsford, 28 October 1921, Box 13, 7EJB/B/02/06 WL.

would send a representative to the Geneva Conference, Archdeacon Greig,[1] and she requested he be a patron of the international SCF not just the British one.[2] Mr Ellison also attended the February 1920 conference that Dorothy ran in Geneva on behalf of her sister. He enquired there if the Archbishop could communicate with the International SCF directly rather than go through SCF London,[3] which alarmed Dorothy who assumed that it might be her own pacifism and left-wing views that were the cause of this request. Eglantyne dismissed such concern, insisting that the Archbishop's Committee was, 'consciously or not . . .wanting to take a full active part in the new movement, & they feel that the existing machinery is not sufficient to enable them to do so'.[4]

Far from impeding the Archbishop's involvement, Eglantyne saw that Dorothy had been of service in creating the link. The issue was one of judging the most effective route to supporting SCF, not that they had not been convinced of the rightness of the cause. In the end, following a meeting on 12 March 1920, the Archbishop set up a separate Imperial War Famine Fund for all in need. Although it had a wider remit than SCF, any funds earmarked for children were to be sent on to SCF.[5]

The cooperation of the two sisters, backing each other up, encouraging one other when they had doubts, asking for recognition for the other, being as one in the goal they wished to achieve, is the real dynamic of the founding of SCF. Dorothy, with political interests in Britain and a family to raise, could not be at the heart of activity in Geneva and thus the international SCF became Eglantyne's work. Dorothy spent much of 1920 back and forth to Switzerland, even putting her children into school there, but with political involvement with the Labour Party increasing, including Charlie's efforts to be elected as a Labour MP, Dorothy had to make London her base. She was part of the SCF's committee on the needs in Germany and took a lead in the response of SCF to Russian children's needs during the civil war that raged there after the 1917 Revolution. She also visited Sweden to give talks and speeches for the fund in the autumn of 1920. In the summer of 1921, she became unwell and withdrew from

1. Archbishop Davidson to Dorothy, 1 January 1920, Davidson 373, Relief Work 1920–21, 2, LPL. John Greig (1865–1938), Archdeacon of Worcester 1911–21, Bishop of Gibraltar 1921–27, Bishop of Guildford 1927–34.
2. Archbishop Davidson to Dorothy, 6 January 1920, Davidson 373, Relief Work 1920–21, 6, LPL.
3. Dorothy to Henry Noel Brailsford, 28 October 1921, Box 13, 7EJB/B/02/06 WL.
4. Eglantyne to Dorothy, 6 March 1920, Box 13, 7EJB/B/02/06, WL.
5. Policy document agreed by SCF Executive Committee on June 4th 1920, Box A414, BUA. SCF had a representative on its Council and Eglantyne and two others were invited to be on the executive council.

the day-to-day work of SCF. However, she remained an active member of the Council from its formation in 1920 until 1933, when she asked to step down. This was challenged and she consented to stay on if she was not expected to be at every meeting, which was agreed.[1] She and Charlie also remained generous donors to SCF's funds for many years.

Eglantyne remained at the head of SCF and went on to work with representatives of the new League of Nations to enshrine in international law and convention the protection of children. The Geneva Declaration of the Rights of the Child, adopted by the League on 26 September 1924, which outlined the basic requirement to provide every child with food, shelter, care and education as a common standard was a landmark that owed much to her. This and the building of a lasting charity in the SCF were her achievement.

Within a few years however, her uncertain health caught up with her. The thyroid problems for which she had already had surgery during the First World War began to re-occur in 1928.[2] She required further surgery that summer. Given that she had a weak heart, the necessary procedure could not be expedited with a general anaesthetic, so she had a series of smaller operations with a local anaesthetic. In the first half of July 1928, Dorothy went out to be with her during this period and she spent the greater part of three months in Geneva. It was a worrying time for Dorothy, but she felt 'up to it'.[3] By mid-August the operations were not yet finished, but Dorothy said the 'silver lining' of it all was that the two sisters spent much time together, the first such period for some years. Dorothy noted that Eglantyne still had an active mind even in these medical circumstances and that she was 'extremely good company'.[4] Later in August, Eglantyne became 'critically ill', but by early September, she improved and Dorothy was able to travel to a place near Berne to have some holiday time with Charlie, who had joined her.[5] Then she went back to Geneva to find her sister apparently progressing very well and so returned to London in late September. The time together in retrospect was a huge blessing because on 13 December that same year, Eglantyne unexpectedly suffered a stroke and died four days later. Dorothy was ill herself and this time was unable to travel to Geneva, even to attend the subsequent funeral. Her sister's

1. SCF Council Minutes, Box A1213, BUA.
2. As early as 1920, a further small tumour had grown and Eglantyne spent three weeks in bed. This was the reason she was unable to attend the first SCF conference in Geneva in February 1920 and Dorothy went in her place. Dorothy to Emily, 17 February 1920, Box 12, 7EJB/B/01/03/26, WL.
3. Dorothy to David, 21 July 1928, BFA.
4. Dorothy to David, 13 August 1928, BFA.
5. Dorothy to David, 2 September 1928, BFA.

death was a devastating blow for her. Inevitably she began to downplay her own role in starting the SCF and to do everything to enhance her sister's reputation and legacy. She edited and published Eglantyne's poems in 1929,[1] an essay the same year[2] and contributed to a short account of her sister and SCF in 1931.[3]

Nothing in this chapter has attempted to question the esteem in which Eglantyne Jebb is held – an esteem that now has her memorialised in the liturgical calendar of the Church of England on 17 December – or deny her the deserved credit for her part in SCF. What it has attempted to correct is the idea that Dorothy was an extra in the founding of the charity. Its later development and reach were the achievement of Eglantyne, but the founding and initial impetus would not have happened without Dorothy. She was the driving force of the first year of its existence, at the heart of its foundation and crucial to its inception. Without her, Eglantyne may well have continued working with other bodies and the SCF would not have come about. Restoring sufficient credit for this to Dorothy would undoubtedly have Eglantyne's strong approval.

---

1. Eglantyne Jebb, *Post Tenebras Lux*, Weardale Press, London, 1929.
2. Eglantyne Jebb, *Save the Child*, Weardale Press, London, 1929.
3. Dorothy Buxton & Edward Fuller, *The White Flame*, Weardale Press, London, 1931.

Chapter 6
Battling the Personal

Throughout all these years of campaigning and agitating, Dorothy had also had another very important role to fulfil – that of being a mother. Her children spoke of her with great respect for all she achieved – indeed they were proud of her – but nevertheless they felt ambivalent about her role as their mother. As David would lament years after her death, Dorothy 'was hardly available as an effective mother'.[1] Like many political activists, Dorothy felt the call to serve society as strongly as her urge to care for her own children. As with many others in the heat of a political struggle, doing good for the many in the world proved a more powerful pull than doing good for the few in the home. No assessment of Dorothy could neglect the repercussions of her activities on her relationships with her children and it is important to consider her record as a parent.

That Dorothy had wanted children – and that she loved the two she had – cannot be questioned. However, her style of mothering was not typical for her generation: it could not be, given her public work and its demands. She concerned herself with the decisions that affected them: schooling and education, travel, and also health issues. Yet the practical work was often delegated to others. Dorothy did not cook and bake for them, worry about their clothes, or deal with all their everyday concerns. She had hired some help to look after her daughter Eglantyne and by the time of David's birth the nanny was a German called Frieda, who proved a great success. Dorothy wrote to her sister-in-law of how Frieda was an 'angel' with young Eglantyne and she could hear them 'laughing at all hours'.[2] This use of hired help was not in itself unusual for upper-class women and Dorothy did not attempt to transcend her class background in this area.

---

1. David Buxton, memorandum dated 16 November 1977, BFA.
2. Dorothy to Victoria, [March 1910], BFA.

Dorothy's own mother had been around in the house when she was growing up, despite servants doing the fetching and carrying. Whatever adventures she went on with Aunt Bun or her siblings, walking and riding and exploring, her mother was there when she came home. Tye wanted to know everything she had done. In the house, she encouraged little Dorothy to draw and read poetry and share her thoughts and feelings. She was a secure presence. Dorothy with her own children was not so available. Before the First World War, Charlie was away on trips to the Balkans or for election campaigns or other meetings, so that the children saw him intermittently. Dorothy was also away part of the time. She and Charlie took holidays without the children and Dorothy also took other time away, for example, to look after Aunt Bun when the latter was unwell.[1] The children stayed for periods with their grandparents or aunts and uncles, enabling them to spend time with their young cousins. Sometimes one or other of their parents were there, sometimes not. In January 1912, for example, young Eglantyne (5) and David (nearly 2) were at Cromer, their mother away and their father investigating political connexions in Norfolk. So, the children were dependent on other relatives and, of course, Nanny Frieda. As Charlie wrote on one occasion, 'I just saw Eglantyne in time to say goodnight, tonight. David came down while I was away, they say, but on discovering that Mummy and Daddy were absent, insisted (without tears but with great determination) on going back to Nanny.'[2]

At this stage the children seemed to thrive. Both were intelligent and Eglantyne in particular had an aptitude for drawing, like many in the Jebb family. She had a detailed and impressive drawing of a rabbit published in a national newspaper when she was only seven, as it was shown in an exhibition of children's drawings staged in London by the Royal Drawing Society.[3]

Frieda had succeeded Annette and then came Frau Schoene, a Swiss-German woman, who left after the First World War broke out. Other more short-term appointments followed, with the family passing on recommendations to each other. Charlie's sister Constance, for example, advised him of 'a charming French governess available for holidays'.[4] Yet by 1915, with servants in short supply because of the war,[5] the children were seen as too old to require a

1. Charlie to Dorothy, [late January or early February 1911], BFA.
2. Charlie to Dorothy, 12 January 1912, BFA.
3. *Daily Mirror*, 21 April 1914, 5, copy in BFA.
4. Charlie to Dorothy, 24 June 1916, BFA.
5. Male servants had volunteered for the armed forces whilst women had been recruited for munitions factories where they could earn higher wages and have set hours, unlike employment in a household. After the war, many would not return to roles as live-in servants and such staff became accordingly more expensive. Therefore 1914–18 was the beginning of the move away amongst the wealthy from

The Buxtons in 1912 at Kennington Terrace

nanny full-time. Trips to relatives with the children became fewer for the Buxtons, except to Tye in Crowborough, and at Christmas time. Charlie's parents had become too ill to cope with grandchildren and then they died in 1915–16.

From mid-1915, Dorothy was usually closeted in the attic of 6 Erskine Hill at work on *The Cambridge Magazine*. Charlie was often away, but when he was home he spent time taking the children out and engaging with them. Dorothy was around them far more than her husband, but was increasingly disengaged. She certainly saw Eglantyne and David in the house. However, she was generally preoccupied, more and more as the war dragged on, so that whilst they may have had her presence they had little of her attention. To her, the pattern of a demanding and mounting workload seemed the only sacrificial response when young people were dying – needlessly in Dorothy's opinion – so how could she slacken off or take longer breaks? She worked late into the night, depriving herself of sleep, which she romanticised whilst at the same time realising that it was perhaps an unhealthy routine. There was ambivalence in her description to her mother, 'I must tear myself away from my Attic where I pass so many really happy hours 'in the midnight in the silence of the sleep time' when only the wind sounds its lovely impersonal voice of all the ages'.[1]

Her sister Eglantyne at one point had to go away for a fortnight to care for their older sister Emily in Ireland, who was convalescing after a time in hospital. Eglantyne was anxious beforehand to arrange for her own translation and editing work to be covered by someone from outside. Otherwise, Dorothy would insist on covering that too and that extra work she seriously thought might 'kill her', Dorothy being so worn out already.[2] The burden never ceased and Dorothy and Charlie agreed that

large resident-staff establishments, a change led by social factors, not choice on the part of employers.
1. Dorothy to Tye, 11 March 1918, BFA.
2. Eglantyne to Ethel Sidgwick, 15 February [no year], BFA. 'Anyhow I should be away for *two* week-ends, – it is at week-ends that the Cambridge Magazine work is

if that meant 'home life' suffered so be it. He wrote from one of the by-election campaigns in which he was involved, 'Oh how I long to get home! But having put off my engagements I have no reason for doing so except family affection – & this *must* go by the board in these days. Every soldier sacrifices it – clearly then I must!'[1] And again, 'I love your noble Spartan spirit! We must be ready for the sacrifice of one another's company, when men are sacrificing all things.'[2]

For Dorothy and Charlie there was a mutual understanding and acceptance that these were exceptional times demanding exceptional sacrifices. He wrote to her in agreement, 'I am quite sure you are right about filling our short span with bold efforts.'[3] A week later, he wrote similar sentiments, 'I know what you feel & you know what I feel . . . of working together in absolute harmony and at full pressure for great ends.'[4]

However, it was one thing for the Buxtons to understand these sacrifices and feel still as one in making them, but for their children it was bewildering. Eglantyne and David had to learn at this early age to be content with their own company and be self-absorbed and self-reliant. This meant they became well-read and interested in ideas, but were far less able to make social connexions. Both suffered when at school and university in later years from a difficulty in making good friends. As children, they came to see their activities as essentially solitary occupations and did not expect to share them with others, whether study or play, even when wishing to do. Even at the very end of the First World War, they were still only twelve and eight, and were too young to grasp all that their parents were trying to do. All they felt was that in some way they were not loved as much as children seemed to be in other households. Their maternal Grannie gave them lots of attention when they were with her, why could not their mother?

By mid-1918, with war still raging, Charlie and Dorothy were both exhausted; Charlie so much so that he was advised by his doctors to take a long rest cure, which he took at Llandrindod Wells. He found it hard to follow doctor's orders, but he felt after several weeks that he was 'distinctly better' and credited this to resting and lying down much of the time. He had emotional space to think about his family too. Charlie realised he did not see enough of Dorothy even when he was at home. In a letter written during the rest cure he came as near to insisting that this should

---

heaviest, – and I do not want the whole of my share of it to fall on the top of my sister here and kill her.'
1. Charlie to Dorothy, 10 March 1917, BFA.
2. Charlie to Dorothy, 16 April 1918, BFA.
3. Charlie to Dorothy, 6 March 1917, BFA.
4. Charlie to Dorothy, 13 March 1917, BFA.

change as he could. 'I believe that you will effect such improvements in the organisation of your working life, that we shall in future see more of each other at home.'[1]

If he felt Dorothy was tied to her desk, clearly this affected the children in exactly the same way, if not more so. They understandably longed for more of their parents' attention. In 1917, Charlie, away at another by-election supporting a 'negotiated peace' candidate, had written to Dorothy asking her to explain to Eglantyne why he had to be away so long, indicating that the child must have been asking poignant questions as to why her father was not around.[2] In 1918, the Buxtons were a little 'stung' by the comments of a friend about the issue of their giving insufficient attention to their children. Charlie defended their hectic schedule as being instructive for their offspring and claimed that the friend did not have an ethic of work as they did:

> The point that emerges, as I think it over, is that the *gospel of work* seems to be entirely absent from her *Weltanshaunung* [philosophy of life]. Of course she would accept it in theory, but evidently she does not in reality. She has a blind spot at that point. Now *we* think that the world is a workshop, & that being so, we want our children to think so too. If their parents, even their mother, is seen to devote herself wholly to *them* [ie the children], they will certainly not be helped to learn this gospel.

However, he then continued by accepting that they had to do better by Eglantyne and David. Clearly Dorothy – from her husband's response here – had demanded specific examples to illustrate how she was distant from the children and this may not have been the first letter on the subject:

> I do think there's just an element of truth in what May says, but nothing more than what we both fully realise already – & what can be remedied by careful & thorough reorganisation of work. I remember one time when I came back from Wembley P[ark] with the children & they were *bursting* with information about what we had done – but you had your mind full & didn't respond so that they dried up at once, & you never did hear! (Much to my inward indignation of course). (You challenge me to produce examples of my generalisations, so here is one – which I am sure you could parallel in my case.) But this can be avoided, & will be.[3]

---

1. Charlie to Dorothy, 27 August 1918, BFA.
2. Charlie to Dorothy, 3 February 1917, BFA.
3. Charlie to Dorothy, 30 August 1918, BFA.

As the children grew up, there were signs of an emotional rebellion against the mother who was present, but effectively remote. By 1918, Eglantyne at twelve was beginning to be more self-conscious as she grew into her teenage years. This produced both a lack of self-confidence socially and also a desire to make herself pretty in how she dressed, the latter stemming naturally from the former. This, however, was not to Dorothy's liking. In her busyness, she seemed incapable of appreciating that her daughter was becoming a teenager. Dorothy could not understand why her daughter had found an interest in girlish trinkets and clothes. Both she and her own sister Eglantyne were dressing with unadorned simplicity at this stage – to Dorothy, this should have been sufficient example for the young Eglantyne to follow suit. She assumed her daughter should reflect her parents' values, as any departure from them among the younger generation would be noted outside the home and undermine their public stance. This was an understandable reaction, but failed to appreciate the need for every young person to own particular values themselves and not merely have them dictated or imposed. Dorothy must have brought the subject up with Charlie as he commented in a letter, 'You mustn't take Eglantyne *too* much to heart! As for her femininity, that is nothing; it is counterbalanced by many masculine qualities in other directions, & anyhow is a passing phase like all other phases. As for her want of confidence – if such there be that is the defect of a self-reliant character.' Dorothy also felt that her daughter took less notice of her than she did her father, a charge to which Charlie replied, 'And why shouldn't we have our specialities among our children? I never could see the objection to it. If you don't envy me my extra pull with E[glantyne], I won't envy you your extra pull with D[avid]. So that's a bargain.'[1]

In hindsight, it might be judged that Eglantyne's refusal to listen to her mother's strictures was perhaps a protest against the insufficient amount of loving attention she received. Dorothy did try to make an effort, as she did recognise her own failings. In August 1918, she took David on a seaside holiday in Cornwall after he had had an operation and then Eglantyne joined them for a further week. Dorothy's sister Eglantyne noted,

> After all the work you've done for years I do think a real break was owing to you! – & leisure to be with your children. And I am quite convinced too that their claims are reconcilable with the C[ambridge] M[agazine] & now that you've got a large staff it will be, I hope, less difficult to work this out in practice.[2]

1. Charlie to Dorothy, 30 August 1918, BFA.
2. Eglantyne to Dorothy, [August 1919], Box 13, 7EJB/B/02/01, WL.

Her sister is an important witness when considering Dorothy, as the two were so close and one cannot imagine her criticising Dorothy or commenting unfavourably without good reason. So, the fact that she believed the children had 'claims' suggested that the situation was a problem in her eyes, too.

Dorothy, a year later, admitted the problem herself in a letter to her mother in August 1919, saying how much she was looking forward to a fortnight's holiday with the children at Aunt Bun's and then in Scotland. It was the first time with her children in a relaxed setting since the Cornwall trip. She commented that it was such a,

> luxury to be together & without the feeling that I ought to rush off in 10 minutes! I have never been able to enjoy either of my children since I was in Cornwall a year ago & later with you. This will be my first visit to Lee for 2 years & as to David – I don't think Bun has seen him since he was tiny. It is an extraordinary fact to be travelling *en famille* after such a long time.[1]

But it was to be followed by a speaking tour in Scotland with Charlie that would take them in little more than a week to Dundee, Edinburgh, Aberdeen, Perth, Glasgow and Kilmarnock. So, for Dorothy, the pace of work as she helped campaign and organise the Save the Children Fund could not be mitigated.

With the war over, the obvious solution was to send the children to boarding school. When David was sent to such a school in 1919, Dorothy soon missed his presence, 'D[avi]d has returned & it is good to have a little son once more. He seems so hopelessly cut off from me at school; it is almost intolerable sometimes.'[2] This showed how Dorothy needed her children and cared about them even if she did leave them to their own devices. She did not want them far away. When she and her sister Eglantyne spent a great deal of time in Geneva, Switzerland, for their SCF work – one or other had to be there at any given time through much of 1920 – the idea of a Swiss school arose.[3] It would give the children a taste of life in another country and encourage their language skills. Yet, they could also be visited regularly by their mother and aunt. At Easter 1920, aged fourteen and ten, the two children were enrolled at Mr Reeve's school at *Chateau d'Oex* and they were schooled there for four terms until the summer of 1921. Once they were there, Dorothy wrote to her mother that the children were settled and 'very blooming' and in her judgement 'leading a very happy life'. Saturdays were for

---

1. Dorothy to Tye, August 1919, Box 11, 7EJB/B/01/03/18, WL.
2. Dorothy to Tye, 26 July, 1919, Box 12, 7EJB/B/01/03/21, WL.
3. Dorothy to Emily, 17 February 1920, Box 12, 7EJB/B/01/03/25, WL.

The Buxtons in July 1929

expeditions and Dorothy worried that they did not have enough spare time, but academically they were doing well.[1] 'Eg[lantyne] talks French beautifully & D[avi]d has a lovely accent – tho' not quite such a facility in other ways.'[2]

Away from the family home, Eglantyne seemed to do much better. Her Swiss school reported that 'all her work has been first rate'.[3] In the following years she began to shine academically whether in Switzerland or back in England.[4] By early 1924, she was doing well over the whole range of subjects. Her aunt wrote about her,

> You will have heard that Eglantyne Buxton has once more distinguished herself in examinations. What is remarkable is that she is just as good at mathematics as she is at languages & literary subjects; indeed I think that algebra & geometry are her favourite subjects after Latin, which is what she likes best of all.[5]

1. A decade and a half later, Dorothy met up with Mr Reeve once again and he reminisced that the time when the Buxton children were there was 'the golden age' of the school. Dorothy to David, 5 June 1934, BFA.
2. Dorothy to Tye, undated but probably 1920, BFA.
3. T. H. Reeve to Charlie, 26 August 1921, BFA.
4. Dorothy to Tye, 23 November 1922, BFA. She went to Sidcot School, near Winscombe in north Somerset, where one of her schoolmates was Pauline Trevelyan, a daughter of Charlie's fellow former Liberal MP and friend Charles Trevelyan. The school was an old Quaker foundation, first begun in 1699.
5. Eglantyne to Aunt Bun, 3 January 1924, Box 6, 7EJB/B/01/02/03, WL. Eglantyne

And in another letter, 'Dorothy . . . tells me that, taking Eglantyne's two examinations together, this year & last year, she has got distinction in every single subject in which she was examined, so she really has done very well.'[1]

It became apparent that young Eglantyne had the ability to read for a degree and so by the autumn of 1925 it was decided that she would apply to Oxford and she took the relevant entrance examinations.[2] She went to Somerville College in October 1926, aged twenty. Yet, during her third year (1928–29) she suffered a nervous breakdown of some kind. She recovered sufficiently enough to take her final examinations and achieved a second-class degree in PPE in June 1929, but thereafter she refused to continue any further study or pursue a career path. As it was Eglantyne who went through her mother's papers on Dorothy's death, the fact of very few letters about her difficulties having survived is perhaps not surprising. Even other members of the family were kept in ignorance of what had happened, both at the time and in later years. In subsequent years, young Eglantyne became reclusive and withdrawn and did not discuss the matter herself.

She had had health issues like many children and Charlie in 1914 recalled her having had an operation.[3] However there do not seem to have been any serious physical issues for her. It was therefore likely that the burden, on the one hand, of trying to live up to her parents' aspirations, and on the other of feeling that they did not give her sufficient personal affirmation, came to some sort of crisis in that final academic year at Oxford. The shock of the unexpected death of her revered Aunt Eglantyne late in December 1928 may have been a factor too. She also had little social self-confidence and her diffidence probably isolated her from her fellow students. In later years, it became apparent that she would have liked to have had children,[4] but in her early twenties she clearly had no sense of how to establish a romantic relationship that might have led to a long-term partnership. The emotional turmoil she carried inside led also to physical inertia and sometimes pain in

---

used the surname Buxton in this letter so as to make clear for Aunt Bun that she was speaking of Dorothy's daughter and not another niece who was also called Eglantyne but a Jebb.

1. Eglantyne to Aunt Bun, 10 January 1925, Box 6, 7EJB/B/01/02/03, WL.
2. Eglantyne to Aunt Bun, 2 October 1925, Box 6, 7EJB/B/01/02/03, WL. 'Eglantyne Buxton, I hear, is to go to Somerville Oxford. She is working up for an exam in November in French, German, Latin & European History.'
3. Charlie to Dorothy, 20 November 1914, BFA.
4. Dorothy to David, 30 April 1945, BFA. '[Eglantyne's life] *has already* been wrecked by the 16 years of illness which have made marriage impossible for her, & then satisfying of her maternal instincts which are far the strongest element I believe in her make-up . . . Egl[antyne] who would love them [children] far more I believe than anything else in the world . . .'

her limbs – and she became like her grandmother, Tye, a long-term 'semi-invalid'. Dorothy did blame herself, noting in a letter to David a decade and half after the breakdown, 'I fully realise now how little I have ever understood her (nor did D[addy]), & this was a direct & also indirect cause of her breakdown & the disruption of her life.'[1]

She spent time taking Eglantyne for treatments. In autumn 1930, for example, this was to a clinic at Champneys, near Tring in Hertfordshire. Yet, nothing seemed to come of it. She wrote to David that whilst Eglantyne claimed she felt better there, Dorothy did not see any marked improvement:

> She still suffers dreadfully & of course it is horribly lonely for her.
> She *cannot* see people as it exhausts her too much to talk even for
> a few minutes with bad after effects in the form of increased pain
> etc. I think she needs all the love & sympathy we can possibly give
> her, & we should not hesitate to give all possible expression to it.

The nervous ailment manifested itself in digestive troubles and not eating much in turn made her weak. She looked quite emaciated:

> Eg[lantyne]'s difficulty in recovering vitality is certainly owing to
> intestinal troubles. It is impossible for her to assimilate enough
> food, & in any case the processes of digestion are constantly
> accompanied by pain wh[ich] uses up much of her small store of
> vitality.[2]

This was the same trouble that affected her father on and off for the last twenty years of his life.[3] This may not have been helped by the emphasis on a 'raw food' policy that Dorothy favoured in the household, a further refinement of her vegetarianism and a way to save money as cooking was kept to a minimum. Otherwise, it may have been a nervous reaction, a sign of tension and inner stress.

Her parents did all they could to encourage her to develop some independence. In late 1933 they agreed that Eglantyne should take a trip with a Mrs Higgins to the Continent, consulting a nutrition expert

---

1. Dorothy to David, 26 February 1945, BFA.
2. Dorothy to David, 2 January 1934, BFA.
3. Ironically, outside his own home, Charlie was considered a voracious eater, who would consume anything put before him. He went regularly to visit a Labour party colleague in Hampstead, Hasting Lees-Smith, whose young son could remember this very clearly about Charlie when reminiscing years later: information from Brother Edward SSF (1921–2010), formerly Christopher Lees-Smith. The Buxton diet at home may have been 'healthy', but it was not gentle or comforting to the stomach.

in Paris, but in general to have a change of scene.[1] Mrs Higgins was to Dorothy 'experienced in just what was wanted' and was 'very sympathetic and understanding' and 'practical'. Away from her family environment, Eglantyne enjoyed Paris and Monaco and put on weight.[2] When Mrs Higgins had to return to England, Charlie's sister Mabel went out to keep her niece company.[3] When Mabel had to return, instead of going on to Evian for further treatment, Eglantyne came home.[4] So as to ensure she had the further treatment, her parents changed their plans and took her to Evian in May and June 1934, it counting as their summer holiday.[5] In the company now of her parents, perhaps it was not surprising that she did not make a 'notable advance',[6] although she had put on weight. The doctors diagnosed that there was nothing organically wrong with either Charlie or Eglantyne and it was due to 'general condition'.[7] Surely, this was a polite way of saying their symptoms were due to nervous or psychological factors? In hindsight, therefore, the digestive troubles might be judged a symptom rather than a cause.

Eglantyne's condition did improve to some extent and she did start to have an independent life from her parents. She learned to drive and bought a car.[8] Then, in early September 1934, Eglantyne went to stay at her club in central London[9] and went on to lodge during the week with a Miss Primrose, 'an old Newnham person' in Tufton Street. She took on voluntary work for Sir John Harris[10] and the Anti-Slavery Society that October.[11] Her work was well received, 'The work is interesting & Sir J[ohn] Harris is evidently delighted with what she produces. He said to Mosa quite spontaneously "I don't know how we ever got on without her."'![12] She seemed happier with a job to do. However, when she went back to 6 Erskine Hill for the

1. Dorothy to David, 5 December 1933, BFA.
2. Dorothy to David, 24 January 1934, BFA.
3. Dorothy to David, 6 February 1934 and 20 February 1934, BFA.
4. Dorothy to David, 6 March, 13 March and 20 March 1934, BFA.
5. Dorothy to David, 15 May 1934, BFA.
6. Dorothy to David, 12 June 1934, BFA.
7. Dorothy to David, 24 June 1934, BFA.
8. Eglantyne certainly had a car by Christmas 1934. On Boxing Day that year, she had trouble starting the car and Charlie told David he had urged her to buy a better one as the 'motoring is so important for her'. Charlie to David, 26 December 1934, BFA.
9. Dorothy to David, 28 August 1934, BFA.
10. Sir John Hobbis Harris (1874–1940), missionary and anti-slavery campaigner, Liberal MP for North Hackney 1923–24.
11. Dorothy to David, 25 September 1934 and 16 October 1934, BFA.
12. Dorothy to David, 29 October 1934, BFA.

weekends, she would spend most of the time lying on her bed exhausted.[1] Unfortunately, the experiment did not last and in 1935, it came to an end. '[Eglantyne] has now come home again for a period of renewed complete rest. The effort to work was evidently rather premature, tho' I think the change was worthwhile on psychological grounds.'[2]

On some deeper level, the attention that Eglantyne finally received from her parents because of her poor health may have made it less likely for her to recover full psychological fitness. When she was well and active she had had little attention. One of her general resentments was that Mosa Anderson, her father's secretary, had become a permanent member of the household and was treated like the 'eldest daughter'.[3] In some ways, she felt that a possible role she might have fulfilled, working for her father, had been usurped. She might have been better if she could somehow have escaped her parents' household – but that would have meant even less attention from them. She was never able to resolve the conundrum of her relationship with them.

Early in the Second World War Eglantyne bought herself a house in Peaslake, Surrey, called Whingate, which had been two cottages made into one larger residence. Mosa Anderson and her widowed mother lived in the village, hence the initial connexion with the place. She remained quiet and unobtrusive in her life and her lack of contribution to society upset her parents, given her obvious intellectual gifts. In the end, her father did run out of patience and in their last years he and Eglantyne could barely cope with each other.[4] Dorothy remained puzzled, but loyal to her daughter however.

Dorothy's maternal journey with David had many difficulties, too, but the path it took was different. Whilst Eglantyne shrank into herself, David became louder and more demanding. He simply refused to be ignored. This was both at school, as well as home. When sent to a 'farm school' in Wendover at the end of the First World War, his headmistress noted that his behaviour was worse when he first arrived back at school after time at home. 'His manners, particularly when he first came back to school[,] were a great disappointment. . . . He must learn to control his temper & the ugly expression of his feelings.'[5]

After four terms in Switzerland (1920–21), he was then sent to a Quaker establishment called The Downs School, located at Colwall, near Malvern. It had been founded in 1900 and by 1918 had grown to

---

1. Dorothy to David, 18 December 1934, BFA.
2. Dorothy to David, undated letter but 1935, BFA.
3. David, autobiographical notes, no date, BFA. Conversation with Mary Buxton, 11 February 2007.
4. Dorothy to David, 18 February 1945, BFA.
5. Isobel Fry to Charlie & Dorothy, Easter Term 1920 school report, BFA.

around forty pupils. The head, Geoffrey Hoyland, had married into the wealthy Downs Cadbury family, noted for their Quakerism, as well as their chocolate factories, and this had provided means by which to improve the school's facilities. It had several unusual features, such as a measure of self-government amongst the boys, so it was not a typical preparatory school. David did not thrive intellectually there. He seemed to learn best on his own and the communal aspect of school was challenging for a boy left so much to his own devices when at home. The headmaster wrote of him, 'He evidently finds the community life rather puzzling at first and one's natural criticism of him is that he is far too self-centred and thinks more of his own dreams and doings than of the community and his place in serving it.'[1]

By the end of 1923, David was struggling and had 'acquired a definite dislike for most school subjects'. From January 1924, Dorothy decided to teach him at home with private tuition.[2] However, from her perspective, his behaviour did not improve. She became very upset with what she perceived as his cheekiness and presumption. Instead of sitting him down and talking to him about the problem, where any reprimand could have been combined with affirmation and warmth, she sat down and wrote him a letter with some robust criticism of his behaviour. He was fourteen and a half and the letter wounded him deeply. He wrote on the envelope, 'Read once on receipt July 1924 but found too distressing to read again until Nov[ember] 1997, an interval of 73 years. . . . [My mother] should have realized that this was the wrong time for such an outburst. I was very sensitive & it shattered me.'[3]

She began by accusing him of 'self-satisfaction' and that he never said he was sorry for anything. Yet he was critical of others and she added, 'you sometimes adopt this attitude of superior wisdom even towards *me*'. She went on,

> It is nothing but bad manners on your part to contradict me, or to find fault with what I say, at any rate when other people are present. It is not *what* you say but the cross way in which you say it, which is such bad manners. Anyone hearing you would certainly say it must be because I have 'spoilt' you – that what you need is *school*. It is certainly true that you would never *dare* to speak to a schoolmaster the way you do to me.[4]

The letter continued in similar vein for several pages. There was a glimpse of self-observation in it, but it was soon swallowed up by further rhetoric:

---

1. Geoffrey Hoyland to Dorothy, 29 September 1921, BFA.
2. Dorothy to Mr Evans at Leighton Park School, 2 April 1925, copy in BFA.
3. On the envelope of Dorothy to David, 26 July 1924, BFA.
4. Dorothy to David, 26 July 1924, BFA.

I have learnt to realise that my voice, especially when I am tired, is apt to be unpleasant. But you often fail to realise that your own voice is often cross to the point of rudeness. It is a case once more of the mote and the beam. In this as in many other matters you are quick to criticise others where you yourself fall only too short if you only know it. Christ called those people 'hypocrites' who condemned evil in others which they were guilty of themselves.

She criticised him also for making no effort to make pleasant conversation. Grown-ups had worry and sorrow to contend with – death, disease, disappointments, poverty – and conversation with young people was a place they could find refreshment & temporary escape. She ended by expressing how she knew he did not wish to hurt her deliberately and that, 'I can imagine no greater joy in life than you have been to me.' However, she felt it imperative to teach him how to behave.

The letter was an extraordinary outburst, both in its tone and in the medium by which it was conveyed. How could David possibly respond? This was not a conversation, but a written pronouncement. Dorothy seemed to have no idea that if her son was precocious, he was seeking attention. She had a certain responsibility for that as she had been so little involved with his doings for so long. She had not spent the time with him to explain how to get along with others and her own interactions were so geared to a particular end that he had not been able to observe a range of social conduct. He witnessed political gatherings and the casual acquaintance forged in travel, but he had never been socialised in the finer arts of meeting people. Dorothy forgot that whilst she had abandoned much she associated with an upper-class background, she nevertheless had learned those conventions in her own upbringing. So she had been schooled in an awareness of what was expected and what was appropriate on whatever occasion arose. Her children were not – and if they were rude and cross in speaking to other people, from where had they learned this?

Dorothy insisted David be sent away to boarding school again because of her alarm at his demeanour and behaviour. In April 1925, her son was sent off to another Quaker school, Leighton Park, near Reading where his cousin, Bernard (one of the sons of Charlie's sister Victoria) was already a pupil. 'David from his first letters appears to like the school in spite of having to wear a starched collar!'[1] However, he was soon far less happy there. Within weeks he suffered bullying from other boys and felt very isolated.

---

1.   Eglantyne to Aunt Bun, 3 May 1925, Box 6, 7EJB/B/01/02/03, WL.

They commandeered his bicycle without asking him. His vegetarianism was laughed at and they teased him by throwing eggs about his room.[1] He was chided for refusing to join in their 'revels of destruction'.

Dorothy's reaction was to write a letter to him asking that he analyse why the other boys behaved like this. He was to cast the 'cold, dispassionate light of science' on the subject while she proceeded to insist they were reacting out of sub-conscious primitive instincts. It was all lofty analysis, yet completely inappropriate in its tone and content to a fifteen-year old in distress. There was no comfort in the letter and no practical advice on how he should deal with his tormentors. Brought up with little training in social relationships, on top of an innate tendency to be interested in things and ideas more than people, David was totally lost in his new environment. He was a serious person and found the inane fooling around of other pupils hard to tolerate.[2] David was alarmed also about unseemly behaviour in the dormitories with respect to the circulation of 'foul magazines' and 'forbidden literature',[3] and so Charlie proposed to write to the housemaster to say that whilst David had 'never complained', he had questioned him and learned 'some little information'. This information would 'horrify' the housemaster if he knew about it. However, he would insist 'that he must not take any step which would be put down' to David's intervention. Charlie continued, 'I was fuming after I got yours last night! But feel calmer after meditation this morning.'[4]

After that, Charlie provided David with private envelopes to post letters directly to him if required, so that they could communicate without his mother necessarily knowing. In the event, David did survive all that his school days threw at him, but it made him even more independent and self-reliant. Dorothy and he remained close despite their clashes and they continued to communicate, unlike Dorothy and her daughter. She continued to try to push him to her own spheres of activity. For example, when he was preparing for university, Dorothy insisted he tell his school

1. Handwritten note of Dorothy's on piece of writing about nature by David, dated circa 1918.
2. Charlie comforted him by recounting his own memories of being targeted for teasing: 'I know the kind of incredibly stupid joke which you describe. It is pathetic that people should be amused by it. I had a rather similar thing at Harrow; instead of being called Charlie Buxton[,] I was called Barley Chuxton! This was thought extraordinarily funny, & repeated all day long by one dunderhead after another, until I loathed the very sound of it, and even now could hardly hear the words spoken without an instinctive shock of disgust!' Charlie to David, 15 July 1925, BFA.
3. David to Dorothy, 24 May 1925, BFA.
4. Charlie to David, 12 July 1935, BFA.

that instead of staying there longer in order to undertake more preparation for his further studies, his parents wanted him to experience working-class life and suggested he spend the winter before going to Cambridge working for a painter and decorator.

> We of the 'educated' middle class mostly pass through life *un*educated on this most important matter of all. . . . We are a tiny minority but our influence is out of all proportion to our numbers. In the past we have used it abominably. The Bolsheviks have helped to open my eyes to this. We, the bourgeoisie, live in a little curtained off corner of the world, with cushions & padded seats. The really big things of the world are seen as *small* to us, & the small things big. That is why so many of the boys at L[eighton] P[ark] & perhaps more at other public schools, seem to have such a strange perverted point of view as regards things of real interest. It will be much the same at University. I do so want to get you away from all this, & get material for judging for yourself about those things in life which really matter most. One *can't* get it adequately second hand (unless one is a perfect genius in imaginative power).[1]

However, though only eighteen, David was sufficiently independent and confident enough to make decisions for himself. He wanted to learn Russian and he chose to travel instead. His parents were now a little chastened by their mistakes with Eglantyne and therefore allowed him his own path. He travelled to Russia on his own and became fluent in the language in a very short time.[2] He later spent time working in a peasant village. Ironically, David took his mother's injunctions on expenditure so literally that she began to worry he was taking too many risks while travelling. On hearing he went fourth class on a boat around Crimea, she exclaimed, '*A propos* of that I do think there is a limit to the amount of heat & smelliness to which it is prudent to expose yourself.'[3] Whilst glad he had experienced how the poorest have to travel, she exhorted him in another letter,

> It was a relief, I must say, to hear of you back, for the moment anyhow, in relative cleanliness, freshness & space. . . . *Having had* this experience I hope now however it may not be necessary to repeat it, as such conditions must of course be highly unhygienic especially in such hot weather.[4]

---

1. Dorothy to David, 22 November 1927, BFA.
2. Dorothy to David, 17 July 1928, BFA.
3. Dorothy to David, 21 July 1928, BFA.
4. Dorothy to David, 28 July 1928, BFA.

On his return, David went up to read natural sciences at Trinity College, Cambridge, in October 1928, a degree he completed successfully.

Dorothy certainly was aware that she had made mistakes with her children. When David was at university, his Aunt Victoria saw him deliver a lecture and wrote to Dorothy to tell her how excellent he was. 'How *false* have been all y[ou]r fears in the past. Y[ou]r regrets that you "neglected" him in the War – that you sent him to wicked schools.'[1] Victoria was acknowledging here that Dorothy must have shared her self-criticisms with her sister-in-law on occasions. Despite Victoria's assurance, the outward show did not mean that the Buxton children bore no inner emotional scars as Dorothy's treatment of her children as they grew up certainly lacked finesse and sensitivity. She was not a 'natural' parent as her first instincts were always cerebral rather than emotional. Children need to have emotional responses first. However, both Charlie and Dorothy saw their children as 'little adults' and judged them by their adult standards. They certainly wanted them to reflect their values and Dorothy in particular took this for granted. There was little room for them not to be interested in politics and reforming the social system. David had more chance to be closer to Dorothy because he instinctively shared her interest in nature, in plants and animals and insects. They could enjoy time in the garden or at the seaside or on walks in the countryside, sharing their thoughts on the natural world. Young Eglantyne did not have such commonality with her mother and she had her instincts quashed. She never had the chance to explore her feminine side and lost all confidence in herself. By the time her parents realised she needed a different approach, the psychological damage had gone too deep.

Yet, it would be unfair to judge Dorothy as a failure as a mother. Both her children were privileged in their travel all over Europe in the 1920s. They had many experiences not given to most young people. David had developed huge self-confidence to travel alone at eighteen. The children had excellent and varied educational opportunities. They lived in a stimulating milieu, full of significant people and events. They had aunts and uncles and a grandmother who cared for them and a large number of cousins. Indeed, they had a mother and father who loved them and wanted the best for them. It was just that their parents were not able to demonstrate their love in a way that could nourish them into confident adulthood with respect to relationships. David survived this predicament emotionally – but only just and with considerable scars. Eglantyne did not. For that, Dorothy must bear her share of responsibility.

It has to be added that Dorothy's somewhat abrasive and lecturing style of motherhood was influenced also by her health. Being continually overtired made her susceptible to being short-tempered and impatient. It may have

1. Victoria to Dorothy, [January 1929], BFA.

The Buxton family camping 1922

added sharpness to her judgements. The exhaustion finally caught up with her: at the age of forty she developed a serious health problem and began to have epileptic fits. In August 1921 she was due to take a holiday that she desperately needed when a telegram came from Dr Nausen at Riga. It outlined the human tragedy of children in Russia dying of starvation. 'Every minute is precious' was how he ended his telegram requesting very urgent assistance. Dorothy felt she could not do anything but drop her holiday plans and respond by addressing meetings and raising money. It proved an effort too far for her weary body. 'It was this – as events shewed [*sic*] – which caused the epileptic fits to begin.'[1]

After the first fit, the remedy seemed to be rest. She comforted herself that it might have been 'a one-off'. Then Dorothy resumed her active life. Yet further fits came and it was clear this was a concerning development. However, she did not want to take them too seriously. She believed she could will them away with positive thoughts and thereby banish any repetition. In April 1922, Charlie wrote to her after he had personally witnessed one of the fits. He cautioned that the fits must be taken seriously and he was particularly worried by the accompanying 'losses of memory'.[2] He insisted on longer breaks, trying to persuade her by saying that her having refreshment was refreshment for him too.[3] After eighteen months, the trouble remained, but Charlie, encouraging as ever, tried to rally her morale,

1. Dorothy's note on the transcription of Dr Nausen's telegram in 'Russian famine' file, BFA.
2. Charlie to Dorothy, 1 April 1922, BFA.
3. Charlie to Dorothy, 27 February 1923, BFA.

I am sure there are not many women of 42 who have such powers, intellectual *and* physical, as you. I say physical, because they *are* really wonderful, only I must add that they have to be carefully looked after. You must always have a background of strength, a reserve, & this has got seriously depleted over a long period.[1]

Their parents wanted young Eglantyne and David to keep the fact of Dorothy's affliction known only to the family and those in close proximity. Although the children were away at school for periods of time, they were quickly made aware of what was troubling their mother. David remembered on occasion having to carry her upstairs after she had had a fit and put her on her bed to recover from the attack. Eglantyne felt the secrecy was a great strain as it meant she could never ask for 'help or sympathy' from anyone outside the family circle, which 'added greatly to the burden'. She noted that, 'we had to face the burden & horror of it for 20 years'.[2]

On first being unwell, Dorothy withdrew from major SCF work and then eventually, in 1924–25, she gave in and reined in her other public commitments.[3] She could not risk being ill in public and withdrew to her desk even more. A new pattern emerged of campaigning and raising money through letters to the press and individuals instead of addressing meetings.[4] She still spoke at a few public engagements, but they were rare occasions. She still attended SCF meetings, but could send apologies on days when she felt tired. She did a minimum of socialising. She had retired like her mother to the shelter and safety of the home. But unlike her mother, she did not stop working. She changed her mode of contribution, although it did not eliminate the stress. Eglantyne (her sister) seemed to think tiredness was the root of the problem, a concern she expressed when sympathising with Dorothy after she suffered another fit while visiting her old friend Barbara Hammond:

1. Charlie to Dorothy, 2 March 1923, BFA.
2. Eglantyne junior, undated note in 'Dorothy miscellaneous personal' file, BFA.
3. Eglantyne thought this was a consequence of Aunt Bun persuading her 'to take her health in hand', no one else being able to influence her sufficiently. Eglantyne to Aunt Bun, 7 March 1925, Box 6, 7EJB/B/01/02/03, WL.
4. This included some overseas. Charlie was a great advocate for the created language of Esperanto, which he learned with some facility. In July 1927, he and Dorothy went to Danzig for the annual Esperanto conference and Dorothy made a speech. 'Today M[ummie]'s speech has been brought off – a great success! – in the first "Laborkunsido" (business session) of the Congress. . . . I got hold of several people in connexion with M[ummie]'s speech – finally the President, Dr Privat, who made it easy by calling on her & introducing her. She had a sort of desk to put the manuscript on, & delivered it with great confidence in impressive tones. It was brought in as part of a discussion on correspondence among children of various countries in Esperanto.' Charlie to David, 30 July 1927, BFA.

I am so very sorry, my own darling, to hear you have had another attack. It must have rather spoilt your visit to Barbara Hammond, & I had so much hoped that the treatment, (though I keep repeating that it was not one I wanted!) would prevent their recurrence. Do take care of your beloved self during the next few months to see whether they can be warded off just by the avoidance of fatigue.[1]

Towards the end of 1925, Dorothy suffered a double bereavement. Tye's health began to deteriorate quickly in the autumn and it was clear she was not going to recover. Dorothy decided to stay with her mother at Forest Edge, Crowborough, until she died. She wrote to her son,

I am going through one of the difficult periods of life: 'the deep waters'. Grannie has reached the end of her journey here; she may pass on any day or any moment. . . . shall stay till the end. I have never been with a person who was dying before. It teaches one a great deal.[2]

Tye lingered until early November and then she died, aged eighty, with both Eglantyne and Dorothy by her side.

Dorothy & I each held one of her dear hands, while she gave one or two little gasps in her sleep, & then in a few moments we saw that her release had come. . . . Amongst the many beautiful things Mother said during these days was, 'I leave my work for my children to carry on; I do not leave it to one more than to another. I leave it to them all.'[3]

Some weeks later, eighty-four-year old Aunt Bun died at Lee in Shropshire. It was a double blow to Dorothy to lose the two most significant women from her upbringing. She remained outwardly calm, insisting that whilst her mother's death was a 'wrench', the 'separation is much more apparent than real'. She added, 'I find myself far more equal to the occasion than I could have expected.'[4]

This was Dorothy's usual bravado, first seen when she lost Gamul nearly thirty years before. To her, there was work to be done and her mother would not have wanted Dorothy to stop merely because she (Tye) had died. After all, her parting words were to leave 'her work' to her children. For Dorothy, a period of mourning seemed quite unnecessary. Unhappiness

1. Eglantyne to Dorothy, 28 June 1925, Box 13, 7EJB/B/02/01, WL.
2. Dorothy to David, 15 October 1925, BFA.
3. Eglantyne to Aunt Bun, Box 6, 7EJB/B/01/02/03, WL.
4. Dorothy to David, 25 October 1925, BFA.

Dorothy's mother, Tye, in 1908

would be conquered by telling herself she was not unhappy and by being
absorbed in work. But Charlie, who was present and supportive to his wife
in the days after Tye's death, was not convinced and he became quite firm
that Dorothy must rest: otherwise, she might be prone to further fits.

> It is sometimes easier to *write* than talk, & I don't want to emphasise
> your 'contre-temps' – I know that is bad. In fact, I do not emphasise
> it in my own mind – I always think of you as the pure spirit with
> the bodily form corresponding to that.
>
> But I compromise so far as to take into account such facts as, in
> my opinion, cannot be ignored. Therefore I beg you to realise &
> to consider carefully the fact that the deaths of Mother, and Bun,
> have been for you a serious matter, however little you thought so at
> the time. If I can be satisfied of this being done on your part, I shall
> not worry nor talk about it. But of this I *must* be satisfied. Definite
> measures *must* follow.

He went on to suggest a rest at a boarding house with breakfast in bed
every day – and then a further consultation with a doctor.[1] But Dorothy was
not receptive and the fits continued at intervals. The cause of them would

---

1. Charlie to Dorothy, 16 December 1925, BFA.

be hard to establish after so many years, but one of the possible triggers might have been low blood sugar. Dorothy's increasingly abstemious diet may have had a role therefore.

As we have seen in the last chapter, her beloved sister Eglantyne died in December 1928. A month later her second sister, Louisa (Lill) succumbed to cancer. The oldest of all, Emily (Emm) in Ireland had a weak heart and it seemed as if she too might die in 1929.[1] She had a serious heart attack in 1934 and then died in 1935 aged sixty-two.[2] These losses were body blows to Dorothy's morale. After the first two sisters died, she suffered a significant period of depression in 1929 and later admitted how helpful her son was to her at that time. 'I had a horrid wave of depression last vac[ation] & I have not forgotten how lovely you were to me; indeed your love to me did act like a balm to a bad wound on that occasion, – & *goes on* bringing comfort & joy to me whenever I think of it.'[3]

With such emotional pressures in her life and her psychological tendency to be a workaholic, whatever form the work took, Dorothy's fits continued. Florence Hawkins, the housekeeper from 1930 onwards, claimed to be able to sense when Dorothy was going to have a fit, possibly by observing tension in her.[4] She swung in the following years between giving in and consulting doctors and then rejecting their advice and insisting she could cure herself through mental exercises, her so-called 'higher method'.[5] She tried cold baths,[6] sleeping outside on 'good hard ground',[7] homoeopathy,[8] then the drug luminol and radiotherapy.[9] Sometimes, Dorothy seemed to shake off her malady and then months later another attack would come. 'I am allright [*sic*] again now, & agree with what you say that it would be unreasonable to expect a quite sudden cessation of my malady. If I have another interval of 6 to 8 months now I shall do very well!'[10]

---

1. Dorothy to David 1 June 1929, BFA. In this letter, she wrote that the prognosis for Emm's malady was 'hopeless' and she was getting steadily weaker, with pain, discomfort and sleeplessness. Dorothy had gone to stay with her sister at Cappagh in Ireland in mid-May 1929 for about a month. In November 1929, Emily went to Teignmouth for treatment for many months and Dorothy visited her there. Dorothy to David, 14 November 1929 and 10 February 1930, BFA.
2. She suffered a fit a few days before Emm's death and to her sorrow was not able to attend the funeral, Charlie going on his own. Charlie to David, 5 June 1935, BFA.
3. Dorothy to David, 10 February 1930, BFA.
4. Conversation with Victoria Houghton, 4 January 2007.
5. Dorothy to David, 2 March 1931, BFA.
6. Dorothy to David, 11 December 1933, BFA.
7. Dorothy to David, 2 July 1934, BFA.
8. Dorothy to David, 18 December 1933, BFA.
9. Dorothy to David 17 April 1934, BFA.
10. Dorothy to David, 10 February 1930, BFA.

Charlie despaired however and wrote to David of how Dorothy would not continue with the drug treatment that had been the only successful method of preventing further fits. David responded to his father with a great deal of sympathy:

> Though you don't tell me much[,] I know how she persistently disregards the most obvious & elementary rules in dealing with herself, & how difficult it is in such circumstances to restrain oneself. She really must resume the luminol. She says it[']s bad for the brain but repeated attacks are probably *more harmful** [*in margin* * not to mention incidental dangers & the worry the whole thing involves] & there the recognised drug *does in fact prevent* as she found when taking it. Of course she is killing herself by perpetually slaving away at one stunt or another & brooding over unpleasant things. For this, I admit, there is no remedy at all, but it is otherwise with the matter of the making.[1]

During the Second World War, Dorothy ceased to have the epileptic fits, but it is not clear whether they faded away as she became older and ceased to be so pressured, or whether she had at last consented to a consistent medication regime. What can be said is that for the twenty years during which she was subject to fits, they took a toll on her own and her family's well-being. Her reactions to the problem illustrated many of the main traits of her personality: stubbornness, self-denial, mental toughness, endurance, a lack of compromise. The very virtues which made her a valiant defender and fighter for the underprivileged and disadvantaged also made her dislike accepting help and caused her to damage herself and those closest to her.

Much of her reaction to her health difficulties were a product of what she believed about God and the world. So we must now turn to her deeply-held, but complicated, religious views.

---

1. David to Charlie, 11 August 1935, BFA.

Chapter 7
Ultimate questions

Throughout the events of Dorothy's life considered so far, there has been a glimpse of her religious views over the years. However, the deaths of Tye and Bun, and then her sisters tested her faith in a profound way, so it is relevant to consider now her religious views and their evolution.

Dorothy had been brought up in a conventional 'low church' Anglican atmosphere and was confirmed in the Church of England in February 1896 just before her fifteenth birthday. Religion was embedded in her education. Her family held daily prayers and she and her siblings learned Bible passages off by heart. However, her upbringing in matters of religion was not monochrome. Dorothy was not limited to the conventional pieties and beliefs expounded in the curate's confirmation classes. As discussed in chapter one, her mother, Tye, whilst maintaining a conventional Anglican practice, had a taste for the exotic in religion and engaged with the Catholic Apostolic Church and charismatic worship. In contrast, Dorothy's Aunt Bun was unequivocally a sceptic or agnostic, although she spoke little about religion to the younger generation when they were growing up. She provided an example for Dorothy throughout her childhood of someone who did not seem to feel any need for a religious faith. Both her mother and aunt provided her with a range of religious viewpoints with which Dorothy could engage. Her future religious journey was a movement between these two points of view: the impact of religious experience and the struggle with the demands of neutral agnostic analysis. The result was a curious mixture. She certainly had a sense of God in her life, but this was not expressed in a conventionally religious way. It was as if she embraced both Tye and Bun's approaches at the same time and came back with a strange amalgamation of their positions. The spiritual journey to that point was a winding lane not a straight thoroughfare.

The element of life that most captured Dorothy's attention in childhood – beyond the love and companionship of her family – was the natural world. The phrase 'wonders of nature' might have been coined for Dorothy. She felt a sense of connexion with nature, whether birds or plants or insects, and therein found a spiritual beauty and power. After the death of her father and even more after losing her brother Gamul, she found the natural world her place to seek refuge from her overwhelming sadness, where questions about life and death, which had been aroused by her personal losses, were calmed, even if not answered. Her sense of God in adulthood consequently became deeply associated with the natural world.

It was not surprising therefore that she wanted to study science at university. If the examples of her mother (who explored faith issues) and Aunt Bun (who did not) competed for Dorothy's attention from a young age, by the time she reached university it was the sceptic position that definitely dominated. Dorothy wrote that her motive for studying science was to understand the physiological basis of human psychology; she had become convinced in the material basis of human experience.[1] For Dorothy, all could be explained by science. It was true that she was still interested in metaphysics and the spiritual dimension of life, but only in its social effect and its bearing on moral issues and ethics.

Religious practice was not significant for her as an undergraduate at Newnham and she found it easy at her college not to be involved in church. As Mary Agnes Hamilton, one of Dorothy's contemporaries in the student body, put it,

> there was no sort of official pressure, and no notice taken of whether one did not go or not. Smoking was an offence; non-attendance at church was not. It was assumed that those who stayed away, like those who went, did so in response to their own sense of right – a private matter.
>
> We did not talk about religion mainly because our belief in progress and human perfectability was sufficient; full of faith in man, we did not need faith in God.[2]

Dorothy's interest was in the mind, however, as she had been attracted from her teens to the idea that a person could have control over their thoughts, emotions and physical responses. She had worked hard at fifteen to overcome her sadness when Gamul died – she had been 'brave' according to her family – and she had concluded that a 'lack of faith' was at the root of unhappiness.[3] Yet, what kind of faith was it that could keep unhappiness at

---

1. Hamilton, p. 44: 'Dorothy Jebb (at that time a convinced and even proseletizing materialist) . . .' On p. 45: 'she was, at this stage, by way of being a convinced, and even militant, materialist.'.
2. Hamilton, pp. 60 and 61.
3. Dorothy to Eglantyne, February 1897, JFA.

bay? Was it a belief in something supernatural or else in rational explanation or was it discovering the secrets of the mind? Psychology seemed to Dorothy to promise a route to the answers. These were the early days of the field of psychology, with Freud's discovery of the unconscious being very recent. It is difficult for the twenty-first century mind to connect with a world where psychology and its insights were not commonplace, but, in Dorothy's undergraduate days, this was a new field, an area developing and expectantly awaiting further discoveries. For Dorothy, this could be a key to human life that would inform her religious views, as well as her politics.

Yet it was not study that changed her religious position so much as people whose opinions she respected. They came to bear in pulling Dorothy away from an atheist position. One influence was Eleanor Sidgwick, the Principal of Newnham College. Mary Agnes Hamilton remembered how eminent Mrs Sidgwick appeared to the students, the impression she made 'profound and lasting'.[1] 'Students were. . . . awed by a recognition of her intellectual eminence; but even those least reverent about "dons" in general, and scornful of some particular specimens (and I fear I belong to that group) had a sense of pride in association with her.'[2] Mrs Sidgwick's opinion therefore counted to students and Dorothy was no exception. In an interview with Dorothy already considered in chapter two, the Principal created doubt that the natural sciences could explain everything about human life. There were dimensions that were beyond possible analysis using the scientific method. Physiology would not explain psychology.[3] This conversation in 1903 did not change Dorothy's mind at once, but it certainly established that she needed to be open to differing views of human life and experience.

Her family were even more influential. Dorothy's mother had settled into a strong belief that there was another 'plane' where human souls resided after death. It did not mean she was a spiritualist – she had no time for séances, mediums, ectoplasm and attempted conversations with the dead, all of which were popular at the time. Yet, she did believe that through concentrated and directed prayer any person could be united with those who had died. As Tye lay dying many years later, Dorothy noted that her mother murmured several times, 'it is not *death*; it is *life*'.[4] It was all part of Tye's conviction that there were many avenues of knowledge and understanding.[5]

1. Hamilton, p. 38.
2. Hamilton, p. 40.
3. It should be noted that Mrs Sidgwick was also a member of the Psychic Research Society and she and her late husband had been convinced that such research would establish proof of immortality.
4. Dorothy to David, 25 October 1925, BFA.
5. She was for example fascinated by graphology, the interpretation of handwriting. Dorothy to David, 23 October 1934, BFA.

Yet, Tye's strong belief in another 'plane' of life would not have meant much to Dorothy if she had not seen the effect that a belief in God and another 'world' had on action in the society around her. Her dearest sister Eglantyne was a Christian and became more deeply pious in the years before the First World War. This motivated her charitable work. Her letters to Dorothy in the pre-war years especially are infused with a strong religious spirit and content. Then Dorothy found in the man she loved a deep faith that motivated his political and social concerns. Charlie was first and foremost a Christian. From his faith, all else flowed. Had he ceased to believe in God and the example of Jesus, his sense of the goodness of humanity and the need for justice in society might have been lost. His call to challenge all that was unjust and his desire to enter politics in order to change conditions in society were all the product of his religious convictions. Dorothy clearly saw when she met him that this was something very deep in his personality which motivated his political views. She soon converted to his way of thinking – as if his presence re-ignited the sense that faith was necessary, a judgement that she had abandoned in her more materialist phase. By the time she spoke to Mary Agnes Hamilton about her engagement in the spring of 1904, she did not (to her fellow student's surprise) mention any differences about religious issues which might have proved an obstacle between her and her fiancé.[1] It was clear Dorothy had modified her position. Charlie was, according to his sister Victoria, relieved about this change: 'Oh joy that all should come right.' In another letter, he wrote, 'We both feel, I think, that 'the fact of Christ' is something which we cannot get away from. We see Him . . . above all in the world around us, a powerful all prevailing personality, surrounding our being and giving life to all good causes.'[2]

This considerable turnaround was based on the issue of values. Dorothy loved nature and found a spiritual impulse from the natural world. Science allowed her to study it and understand it better. However, nature was as full of cruelty as of beauty. For every sweet sparrow she observed, there were other creatures killing each other for food. There was a brutality about the world of animals. For Dorothy, humans needed to evolve away from such savagery and struggle. She wanted a world based on justice, where resources were shared and equitably distributed. In other words, she wanted a society built upon a set of values, not one dominated by natural impulses of competition and aggression. Science, she came to believe, could give people knowledge and understanding, but it could not make them better behaved or more loving or less violent. To improve society, there had to

1. Hamilton, p. 45.
2. De Bunsen, p. 43.

be ideals and values for people to follow. Through Charlie and others, she came to believe that such a set of values could only be based on God. It was an insight that she retained for the rest of her life. It might be added here that even her sceptic non-church-going student contemporary Mary Agnes Hamilton came eventually to espouse the need for God and religion in the 1930s. Faced with the evils of European politics at the time, she found socialism and humanism too weak to counter the threat to human values that Nazism and other irreligious ideologies raised.[1]

However, to say Dorothy 'believed in God' was not the same as her adhering to a prescribed set of dogmas or repeating particular religious practices. What she believed about God changed over the years. Aunt Bun had brought her up to believe in evolution and she saw this, as many of her contemporaries did, as not purely scientific theory. Many Victorians had interpreted evolution as a social theory too and saw humanity evolving to have more and more sophisticated beliefs around religion. In this view, religious narratives that were important to help uneducated and illiterate communities understand the 'love of God' were not necessary in a more intellectually-developed context. For Dorothy, as humanity 'progressed' people would adopt 'higher' views. So whilst never considering herself a materialist or atheist again, she nevertheless was adventurous in what she came to believe or did not believe. She retained only what supported her absolute need to maintain a set of values about social and human relations.

At first, this need was conventionally met by the beliefs and practices of the Church of England. Once married, Dorothy was happy to accompany Charlie to an early morning Eucharist most days at their local church in Kennington. This routine began a daily time of prayer and meditation first thing in a morning that she continued for the rest of her life. Her church-going was accompanied by an exploration of theological and spiritual ideas. When expecting her daughter in 1906, she recorded that she read William James' *Varieties of Religious Belief*.[2] This has remained a classic text since its publication in 1902 and is still studied over a hundred years later. James argued in the book for the importance of religious experience over religious institutions (as the latter were manifestations of the former) and that religious belief was important in understanding an individual's psychology. He also defended religion as helping people live their lives more fully and productively. However, he put forward the view that religious experience was true – but only for the person who experienced it. It could not be counted as 'truth' to another, who had not experienced it. Dorothy commented

1. Hamilton, pp. 307–308.
2. William James (1842–1910), philosopher and psychologist, author of *Principles of Psychology, Essays in Radical Empiricism* and *Varieties of Religious Experience*.

on the book that it was, 'of absorbing interest, but neither was it exactly inspiring'. However, she noted that her sceptical Aunt Bun was very excited by it.[1] Despite Dorothy saying this book had not inspired her, the view of religion being personal, and the implication that everyone could make their own religious 'truth' depending on their own individual experience, was very much the direction she espoused in the following years.

Attending church daily seemed to lapse after the birth of her first child and there is no evidence of its continuation once the Buxtons moved to Devon in 1908. Their belief in religion being a vehicle for propagating their ideas of a better society had swiftly subsided in these years too, even for Charlie, in the face of the realities of their political and social campaigning. As Charlie noted in 1910, 'Politics is the great means of educating the people now – for religion, in the hands of the churches, has not the educative influence it used to have. Politics is the only thing that opens up wide horizons of any sort to the working people's minds.'[2] It was also that the Church of England's connexion with the Conservative Party, perhaps even more prominent in the country than in an urban setting, had made them uncomfortable with participating in Anglican parish life. As early as 1906, at the Church Congress, Charlie had publicly fretted about the way the Anglican bishops in the House of Lords supported the Conservative Party and the hostility they showed to their clergy who supported the Liberal or Labour parties.[3]

Yet all this did not mean the Buxtons had lost their faith. Charlie and Dorothy certainly still had their quiet time in a morning. Through her reading, Dorothy had begun to emphasise more and more the power of the mind. If prayer was to communicate with God, it was also to discipline the mind to be in control of the body and emotions. To be receptive to God, the mind had to be spiritually formed and that meant a mastery over the both the physical body and psychological emotions. Dorothy had been taught of the need to master her emotions at a young age as we saw at the time of her brother's death. She certainly felt it important to practise this. The mastery over the body was a newer element. It led her to a fascination with the practice of Christian Science.

Christian Science was one of a group of 'new' religions, based on Christianity, yet different in significant ways, that emerged from nineteenth-century America. It was founded by Mary Baker Eddy,[4] who in her writings

---

1. Dorothy, memorandum January 1907, BFA.
2. Charlie to Dorothy, 9 January 1910, BFA.
3. De Bunsen, p. 94.
4. Mary Baker Eddy (1821–1910). Her main work was *Science and Health, with Key to the Scriptures*, Christian Science Publishing Company, Boston, Mass., 1875.

put forward the view that all pain and ill-health could be conquered by the power of the mind. She preached that this was the true message of Jesus Christ, whose message had been misunderstood until her own revelations had uncovered it. For Eddy, sickness was an illusion: believe that you are not ill and your health would recover. Dorothy had little interest in the dogmatic tenets that underpinned this idea, but she was fascinated by the practice. After all, if humans could evolve spiritually to the extent that they could control their health and eliminate pain, then this would have profound implications.

When Dorothy first became aware of Christian Science ideas cannot be firmly established, but she was certainly exploring them by 1909–10. Christian Science had reached London initially in the early 1890s, first using a former Methodist Chapel in Sloane Street in London's West End, which they eventually demolished to erect a purpose-built chapel on that same site in the years 1904–07. It was dedicated in 1909, although services had been held in part of it from 1905.[1] The finished chapel could seat 1,300 people, an indication of the interest in the Christian Science movement in Edwardian London. The rapid growth of the movement and its popularity was traced with some alarm by Anglican authorities and it was discussed at conferences such as the 1905 Church Congress,[2] the London Diocesan Conference the following year,[3] the 1908 Pan-Anglican Conference[4] and the Lambeth Conference of 1908.[5] Services were not conventional worship services, but consisted of readings from Mary Baker Eddy's works with testimonies from those who had followed Eddy's instructions and felt either cured or helped without recourse to doctors and medicine. There were a few hymns and Bible readings, but the focus of the service was the testimony.

Dorothy's interest in Christian Science did not mean she abandoned conventional medicine – she was too much of a natural scientist to do that. However, she did try to learn about Christian Science approaches in parallel to her knowledge of biology. She came to have immense confidence in the power of 'auto-suggestion' to influence the brain. This was first manifest when she gave birth to her second child in February 1910, which she did

1. The chapel was closed for services in 1996 and the building sold for re-development. It is now known as Cadogan Hall, a venue for talks and concerts.
2. *The Times*, 7 October 1908.
3. *The Times*, 18 May 1908. The Diocesan conference passed a resolution: 'That this conference, while emphasizing the power of faith in healing, views the main outline of the teaching and the attitude of the Christian scientist as antagonistic both to Christianity and to science.'
4. *The Times*, 18 June 1908.
5. *The Times*, 4 July 1908.

without chloroform and relied on a Christian Science nurse instead. She seemed to think this had made a great difference, particularly in the pain levels she experienced.

> I attribute my good time mainly to C[hristian] S[cience]; as I was treated all the time. More advanced C[hristian] S[cientis]ts get even less pain, up till the most advanced of all who have painless deliveries & get help & dig the garden next morning! I am not doing anything much unusual however as since we have a doctor we think it only fair to carry out his instructions & not argue. So I shall stay in bed the fortnight he likes to prescribe.

The doctor seemed to have been tolerant of the two Christian Science practitioners present at the birth[1] and Dorothy, herself, had particular praise for the nurse who stayed on the longer of the two.

> I do like her personally very much indeed & in addition she is a most advanced C[hristian] S[cientis]t; so that I feel I should have her & I am wonderfully fortunate to have done so. She helps me enormously, & I regard this time as my great opportunity to get more understanding of C[hristian] S[cience] which is quite the first thing in life to me as I see in it the one means to realise all else I desire.
>
> In spite of being so advanced herself she is *not* a fanatic & if I follow her advice I think my path in life in trying to apply C[hristian] S[cience] will be considerably simpler & less exacting in some ways than I had made it before.[2]

Dorothy was so enthusiastic she advocated Christian Science methods to all the family. A letter from Charlie in 1911 included a reference to Dorothy encouraging her Aunt Bun to use similar techniques of auto-suggestion, the efficacy of which was not a surprise to Dorothy by this account. 'It is a very wonderful thing (not wonderful to you I know) that the power of the spirit & of right thinking should have brought about the great change for the better in Bun's condition.'[3] Another letter from Eglantyne to her sister Louisa revealed using a Christian Science practioner to help their mother, Tye. 'Mother has not been very well lately; giddy attacks again, but I asked Dorothy to send out a Chr[istian] Science lady to look after her, & she has sent a *Pearl*, who arrived last Sunday.'[4] Charlie,

---

1. Charlie to Victoria, 2 March 1910, BFA.
2. Dorothy to Victoria, March 1910, BFA.
3. Charlie to Dorothy, 'Monday', probably to be dated to February 1911, BFA
4. Eglantyne to Louisa, 14 January [no year but before 1914], Box 6, 7EJB/B/01/02/03,

himself, referred considering going to the Christian Science church for a service when staying with his parents in London, whilst at the same time showing he was still a practising Anglican. He also indicated that Dorothy was an attender of the Sloane Street chapel when in London.

> I went to St James's Piccadilly, in the meantime, in order to be able to say to the parents that I had been to a proper church!! Otherwise I should have gone to the C[hristian] S[cience] church. And I mean to go with you one day.
>
> I have read aloud a sermon of Canon Wilberforce's to Mother, which is impregnated with C[hristian] S[cience] ideas, especially about fear.

Christian Science was not an exclusive choice for the Buxtons, but an 'add-on' in the same way that they might in another era have supplemented Anglicanism with Buddhist meditation practice. Within a few years, however, the dalliance with the Christian Science Church itself waned. Perhaps as Dorothy explored the dogmatic beliefs of the movement she had come to feel less attracted to it. She later confirmed that she never contemplated joining as a full member.[1] It would have curtailed her freedom of thought far too much and she was concerned that while they had interesting ideas, they were not sufficiently active in charitable and social work. The Christian Science Church seemed to her too inward-looking and individualistic for her taste. Her ultimate judgement on the movement might have echoed a speaker at the 1905 Church Congress reported in the press,

> Christian Science left no room for works of mercy, spiritual or bodily. If this new teaching were true, there was no reason why you should feed the hungry, or minister to the sick in hospitals or homes for the dying; there was no reason why you should care for the outcast and the miserable.[2]

However, Dorothy did not distance herself from the idea of 'mind over matter'. Her belief in its relevance and power remained and she would preach to all her family and friends the value of 'auto-suggestion' for the rest of her life. This was done through the power of meditation, exercised mainly in the hour after her 7a.m. cup of tea and before breakfast. Charlie may have found this emphasis on 'auto-suggestion' a little irksome at

---

WL.
1. Dorothy to Tye, 11 March [1918], Box 10, 7EJB/B/01/03/10, WL.
2. Revd W. S. Swayne, Vicar of St Peter's, Cranley Gardens, quoted in *The Times*, 7 October 1905.

times. In 1913, when the problem with his eyes began to become more troublesome, he wrote to Dorothy of how he did not feel able to put her belief into practice.

> I hope my last letter did not suggest that I underestimate the power of meditation such as yours to influence the condition of my eyes. I do recognise it. But that is not quite the same as the ardent cooperation which is perhaps, in reality, essential. This ardour of cooperation I lack – for many reasons – I imagine, though I find it hard to say what the reasons are. One is, I think, that I feel a gift so high, & faith so effective, ought not really to be devoted to so *comparatively* small a matter as a physical defect. Ought it not to be devoted to strengthening the spiritual, or moral, or intellectual, nature, rather than the physical? Is it not otherwise thrown away in some sense? – except of course in cases of really grave physical evil (& seeming evil) affecting the whole life. I don't know.[1]

What she might have thought of his plea of lacking 'ardent cooperation' can only be imagined. He certainly maintained the outward show of times of meditation, even when not with Dorothy, although it was possible he used this as a more conventional time of prayer.[2]

Dorothy continued to follow a spiritual journey and read books by mystical writers. One she recommended to Charlie was James Rhoades,[3] largely unknown in the twenty-first century, but popular at the time and she was keen on his poem *Out of Silence*.[4] Rhoades believed that a person could achieve fulfilment by uniting with the 'Principle of Life' in a conscious union, although as is perhaps inevitable his poetic argument was not specific as to what the 'Principle of Life' was. Nevertheless, it was a piece of literature reflecting the 'new thinking' that Dorothy enthused over.

By December 1914, when Charlie wrote his appreciation of her, some of which has been quoted in earlier chapters, he commented on his wife's views,

> She has gained the power, not easily but by little slow advances, by self-mastery ever increasing, of living in the spiritual world. She has reached something like the position which the saints of Christian or

---

1. Charlie to Dorothy, 25 April 1913, BFA.
2. When Charlie was in Paris in 1919 and met up with his old friend Lawrence Hammond, the latter wrote to his wife about Charlie's morning meditations. Barbara responded by saying the thought of Charlie meditating 'made her laugh'! Barbara Hammond to Lawrence Hammond, 23 April 1919, MS Hammond 11 286, HP.
3. James Rhoades (1841–1923), a poet, mystic and translator.
4. Charlie to Dorothy, 20 November 1914, BFA.

Eastern thought have won through prayer and fasting. To reach it
while still living in the practical world of modern England, to strike
the right balance, without the self-abandonment which cuts off the
saint from the world, is infinitely hard. But she has done it. . . .

She was changed, too, by the long wave-tossed wandering, the
fearless threading of the tangled mazes of thought, which led her to
the knowledge of God.[1]

These sentiments might strike the modern reader as overblown, but what
it reflected was the amount of energy Dorothy put into religious thinking.
Her conclusions may not have been orthodox, yet her belief that God was
a necessity in her life was a major motivation in all she did. However, the
pursuit of such 'higher thinking' and her need for freedom in it could not
keep her within a conventional church setting. By the First World War,
there was no will in her to support the Church of England any more or
subscribe to its theological stance. It was probable that she stayed so long
nominally in its membership out of loyalty to her husband, for whom
being mainstream in his Christian thinking was a strong attachment.
However, when Charlie became exhausted with the Church of England's
political stance, he looked elsewhere; and, as noted earlier, the pair joined
the Quakers. For Charlie this was essentially a political move and whilst
he enrolled as a member of the Society of Friends, he did not loathe the
Church of England. In his later years, in fact, he acknowledged signs of
'broader sympathies' in the national church.[2] At his death, his funeral was
held in an Anglican church and no one thought this odd, suggesting that
his spiritual roots in the Church of England had not been completely left
behind. Many of his family had remained practising Anglicans. Charlie left
the institution, but did not reject the ecclesiastical family.

For Dorothy, becoming a Quaker was more of a religious move and
one that she only considered as a consequence of Charlie's decision. The
Quakers gave her a place in which she could have both an ecclesiastical
allegiance, yet retain complete freedom of thought. She was surprised they
would accept her with her individualistic views about faith, yet delighted
they would have her on her own terms. She wrote at length to her mother:

I have been living in an unholy rush for many weeks past or I would
not have omitted to send you a letter on C[harlie]'s & my taking
the step of going to the Society of Friends. He had been attending

1. Charlie, memorandum dated Rome, 31 December 1914, Box 10,
   7EJB/B/01/03/07-13, WL. These quotations are from section V. Copy also in
   BFA.
2. De Bunsen, p. 94.

their meetings for some time before the war so had been veering that way for some time. As for me I really never thought of it until he announced his intention of joining them whereupon it struck me that there was really no reason why I should not do so myself, & *ceteris paribus* it was undoubtedly best that in these matters we should present a united front to our *children*, & to the world!

My sympathy with C[hristian] S[cience] ideas, and Higher Thought ideas never brought me to the point of wanting to join the any [*sic*] organisations – even before the war – & since the war I was so disappointed that the apparent community of root ideas left me widely separated from so many people when it came to their applications. Whereas with the Friends I felt a community which went deeper than one merely of *ideas*; & they seemed to have the applications too which I had expected but failed to find elsewhere.

I felt doubtful beforehand as whether I would be considered sufficiently orthodox!. . . . However two most genial & unalarming people turned up, & I speedily found that the lady who adressed [*sic*] herself to me knew all about C[hristian] S[cience] ideas, & seemed to *share* most of my heresies! So the 'viva' passed off pleasantly, & in spite of our idiosyncrasies (– which were by no means the same & C[harlie] & I mutually disclaimed each others!) neither of us were 'ploughed'! I do feel very glad to belong to *something* & am particularly happy to find so congenial a spiritual *milieu*.[1]

As she said, the move to the Society of Friends above all gave Dorothy a place to belong. As her sister Eglantyne put it,

In her doubt whether they would feel or not that her views were a barrier to membership, she had not at all anticipated what it would mean to her if she did join them, but when it was settled, that 'rapt' look, which she sometimes wears, informed me at once that something very happy indeed had happened to her![2]

Becoming a Quaker, however, did not indicate what Dorothy believed – rather the opposite, it confirmed that her beliefs were still evolving and would not be considered fully Christian in the view of many Christians either then or now. Yet, she spoke and wrote much about God and we do, however, have her own explanation of the complex pattern of beliefs she embraced. They are contained in several letters written to her son, David,

1. Dorothy to Tye, 11 March [1918], Box 10, 7EJB/B/01/03/10, WL.
2. Eglantyne to Tye, 7 February [no year given but 1918], BFA.

in 1924 and 1931.[1] She made plain that she saw them not as ordinary letters, but as notes on important subjects which were 'meant to be kept & reread occasionally, perhaps on Sundays'. She said she would not be shocked 'if you said these words convey very little to you'. That raised the question as to why she wrote to him on subjects she still felt he was too young to understand. In some ways, these letters were a clarifying of her own mind as much as an encouragement for him to think about religious matters.

The underlying thrust of her argument was that religion in its traditional form was not attractive to her. She believed there were eternal truths to be discovered, but that each generation found its own way of addressing them and she saw disconnecting from traditional theological language as the first step to finding 'truth':

> Perhaps I had better tell you at once that the *language* of religion is becoming very old[-]fashioned to me. The ultimate truth of things cannot change, but man[']s apprehension of it of course is changing & developing all the time. . . .
>
> In the meantime do not let us *pass by* the Truths which lie behind the symbols of religious language. We can look for the *essence* & not allow ourselves to be put off by the very inadequate 'earthen vessel' in which really wonderful things are presented to us.

Elsewhere she reinforced this message,

> Jesus talked. . . . in the language which His followers would understand; for them it was the best channel of Truth. If this language conveys a clear impression to us – so much the better – but if not, we must find new language suited to our age.

Religion for Dorothy was important for everyone and she found it unfortunate if people were deterred from exploring matters of faith because of the way it was presented by the churches:

> The language of conventional religion still acts as a *channel* for truth to many, but to others it *blocks* the channel. If to you the *phraseology* of religion seems unreal you must try & not allow religion itself to become unreal to you; *words* must *change* – but that there *is* a tremendous Reality behind all the screen of words, & neither you nor I nor anybody, can afford to live without taking into account this the greatest – the *most real* of *all Realities*.

---

1. Dorothy to David, 27 and 28 July 1924 and 25 February 1931, BFA. The quotations in the following paragraphs are from these letters.

So what was the 'reality' for her behind the archaic language with which she had so much difficulty? What is immediately apparent is that she had taken up her mother's idea of there being a 'spiritual plane' distinct from the 'material plane' in which people lived. Human beings had a material self in the material world, but also a spiritual self, which after death would dwell in the spiritual plane. The wisdom of religious faith was to connect with that spiritual self so as to be imbued with love which, in turn, would then spill over into right relations with others. The human world was debased with evil and unhappiness, but within it one could see echoes and glimpses of the spiritual plane, which was goodness and love, because people were in touch with the spiritual self.

But, she asked, did this make God superfluous? Not according to Dorothy because God was not a 'person' but the spirit of love and goodness:

> Jesus taught that God was *Spirit* & that God was moreover our *Father*. In what sense our 'Father'? Not, surely the Father of our physical bodies, subject to disease & death; not the father of our human minds full of evil thoughts. God is Spirit, & the Father of Spirit. There is a spiritual self for each one of us, where that which is imperfectly expressed in matter, has its perfect counterpart. . . . In God is the essence of all good, & in so far as we express the good in this life & in the body, we are *expressing* the *Truth*, but that Truth belongs essentially to a non material place.

It was clear that Dorothy had left behind a materialist or atheist view of existence. There was for her a 'non-material' world. Even modern psychology would not be able to explain religious experience or the power of love. Her theology was capable too of seeing all religions as embodying some version of the 'Truth' and she had no exclusive claims for Christianity. Religion would therefore not be an exclusive way of defining a group of people, which could then be manipulated into rivalries with other groups. Instead it would be a uniting force, where all could recognise the element of 'Truth' in the others. She believed in cross-cultural and international cooperation: it could be said she had embraced an idea of a God who could represent that. Differences are banished or side-stepped if all acknowledge God as Spirit.

> All goodness, & all life, Jesus taught us, belongs to this one great source which He referred to as 'Father'. This relationship of man to a source of perfect, omnipotent life is not however peculiar to Christianity. . . . it represents a widespread conception arrived at by 'seers' in all ages & lands. All good is in God & men manifest it in so far as they are inspired by the Spirit, – or to put it another way, recognise the truth of their own spiritual selfhood.

In another passage she put the same points in a different way:

> The idea of the ultimate, creative, Life giving force, of whom
> all beauty & goodness & life are an *expression*; the idea that the
> beauty & life on the *material* plane is the 'lowest expression', of
> something which finds a somewhat 'higher' expression in the
> mind & soul of man; the idea that there are yet *higher* planes –
> perhaps *many* – but which are usually lumped together by calling
> them 'spiritual', – these ideas are simply universal & ages old.
> Man seems to arrive at them inevitably & they are embodied
> in a thousand different forms in the multitudinous religions &
> philosophies of all time – from the most ancient 'civilisations' till
> now. Perhaps the most significant fact is that it is just those people
> in all times who had the most vivid conceptions of a Supreme
> Intelligence & power, who were themselves able to make the very
> most of the material offered by life in this world; – I mean they
> became imbued with the greatest wisdom or the greatest power
> themselves.

The question then became where did Jesus fit into this approach?
Surely it meant Christ was not central to her faith? She did not refer
to the Incarnation or the Resurrection or the Ascension; such terms
were the language she found 'old-fashioned'. Dorothy did not dismiss
Jesus, however, but saw him as the supreme teacher of religious truth
and values.

> 'Prophets' and 'seers' – the geniuses of their time – see & understand
> far more than they can explain to the rank & file who are not
> 'ready' to receive truth except in its simplest form. But the prophets
> *prove* how much they understand by the extraordinary powers
> they exhibit. Jesus Himself is the supreme example. No doubt He
> could understand a great deal more than was any use His trying to
> explain; – to begin with, the language of His time would not have
> contained the *terms* necessary.

And again, elsewhere in the letters,

> In particular of course, Jesus seems to offer the supreme example
> of *love*, & of wisdom & power in the *effective* use of His love. And
> Jesus Himself, who knew how to get at such wonderful sources
> of wisdom & power attributed all good to the 'Father' & took
> no credit to Himself. To Him, in fact, the *source* of all good – the
> *Reality*, was the '*spiritual*'.

The matter that remained for Dorothy was the means to connect with the spiritual self: this could be called 'prayer'. She saw this as essentially a psychological activity as '"prayer" or "meditation", are names for important psychological processes which make "Man master of his Fate" if he will take the trouble to understand & utilise them'.

Here is where the influence of Christian Science and the concept of auto-suggestion became enmeshed with her theological position. For Dorothy, auto-suggestion was the idea that a person could influence their feelings and behaviour simply by deliberately thinking particular thoughts and focussing on them. This was how she put it:

> *What do I mean then by prayer?* Prayer is, essentially, the focussing of our will & attention in an intense *desire*. Indeed one may say that *all desire*, whether expressed or not, is a prayer. Our being is asking for something, even if our mind does not formulate the desire or turn it into a request.
>
> When we focuss [*sic*] our mind & will in conscious 'prayer' you already can understand how autosuggestion comes into play; all the more so if it is the 'prayer of faith' where we really expect the asking to be followed by God[']s granting the request. That was how 'prayer' was supposed to work. God was regarded as a *Person*, who heard the prayer & considered it, much like a human being would do. For many people that explanation is still quite satisfactory.

She noted that teachers of auto-suggestion exhorted people to affirm something in the mind and then it would become true – such as 'I am well.' It was not a matter of asking God to make you well, but of willing yourself to health and acting as 'God' to yourself. So it was possible to use auto-suggestion without any theistic belief. The popularity of this concept meant that, 'Nowadays the term autosuggestion is taking the place of that of "faith" & the whole business is carried on to a large extent quite *apart* from religion.'

But she saw the difficulty in how this created a problem if the person was not well and did not become well, despite all their mental efforts. Dorothy's answer to this was that whilst the material body could become sick, this was only a part of the self. Ultimately, it was the spiritual health of the self which mattered and she accepted that death was a part of life. You could help your physical body get well in some cases, but if it did not, this was the inevitable process of the material world. She was convinced that the discoveries of psychology, particularly the realm of the unconscious and sub-conscious, had explained rather than contradicted Christian belief:

The theory of the subconscious mind is I think a great help to accepting the Christian idea of the spiritual self. It proves that the personality of everyday expression is *not* the whole of us, apparently only a *fragment* of the real self. That we have at least two 'Is', two egos, is already established from *this* end as it were; but what we call the subconscious self is *not* the same as the spiritual self, as the former can be the channel for evil as well as or good. The 'self' is in fact an intimate affair, but that being so, I think it is easier to realise that spiritually enlightened people, like the prophets, & pre-eminently of course *Jesus*, were handling very advanced truth in the best way practicable, when they gave us this picture of a *spiritual world*, of which we are members, – or *heirs*. When we are ready to recognise the spiritual nature which is our heritage we shall enter *consciously* on life perfect & eternal.

The purpose of all faith was the impact it had on relationships with other people. It was important to love others as Christ commanded.

Love, in the sense Christ meant, is the power of seeing & believing in the 'good' – the god-like, which is in other people. We may not consciously 'see' it, we may not *think* about it at all, but the fact that we 'love' someone implies that in our souls we recognise & affirm the good which is in the soul of the other. It is a relation of confidence, of *knowing* by our own direct sense that which is loveable in the nature of the other.

For Dorothy, religion came down to values. She saw evil in the world and a belief in God was the antidote. It did not matter particularly what context in which you placed this belief or what theological propositions you used to support it. To believe in God was to believe in goodness and love and helping to make the world a better place for all human beings. That is all that mattered and it motivated people to resist evil:

religion. . . . seems to me the most important thing in life because it is concerned with *values*. I agree with Coleridge that 'He prayeth best who loveth best', i.e. that to love carries an implied 'prayer' & brings one nearer to the heart of religion than can any concepts of the *mind* when uncharged by the 'spirit wh[ich] maketh alive'. . . .

I do not myself see how this help can be dispensed with. It is of course very much the fashion to call in question any difference between good & evil, – & any need, or justification, for religion. The reality of good & evil seems, for one thing however, rooted in the simple fact that one[']s own best interest, & that of others, is so constantly, opposed to the desires of the moment. The 'love' which is 'the fulfilling of the law' means a pure, impersonal disinterestedness which is a most formidable task to achieve.[1]

Was this set of beliefs Christian? It cannot be judged they are conventionally so. They were certainly not unchristian however. It was if she held a religious view based on Christian principles, but which was not upheld by the power that derives from Christian thinking. Dorothy had excised much of the theology of God. There was no Trinity, just a spirit of goodness. Jesus became for her not the 'Son of God', but the most insightful of prophets. There was no Resurrection. There was no place for the Eucharist, instituted by Jesus, or the other sacraments. There was no concept of Church, a community of believers, except in the loosest of senses of human brotherhood. What she had thrown away was not merely the old-fashioned religious language. It could be argued she had abandoned the doctrinal framework that upheld the coherence of the whole. She wanted the flesh of Christianity without the bone structure. She ended up with just pieces of a dismantled philosophy. What was left was a belief in life after death – the 'spiritual plane' – where the spirit of goodness (God) would be found and the spiritual self would eventually dwell. There was also a means of communicating with that plane (prayerful meditation), coupled with a universal commitment to loving others, an ethical remnant of the Christian faith she had been taught as a child.

It would perhaps be true to say Dorothy retained elements of the Christian faith that reflected her social and emotional concerns. Believing in an ethics and mode of conduct based on Christian love provided motivation for her work and therefore she continued to believe in it. Whatever religious aspect that did not help her goals was left behind. So why did she retain a theistic belief? She needed an ethic of love to drive her campaigns to help those in need and that required a powerful 'spirit' of Love greater than mere human energy as its justification; an individualistic atheism could not have motivated her sacrificial life-style. She needed a spirit of goodness into which she could tap to give her the energy to continue; an agnostic approach for her would have lacked any conviction or passion. She had to believe in an afterlife as she longed for a way of communicating with those she loved who had died. She could not bear to have lost them forever. All this had to sit intellectually side-by-side with her understanding of psychology and her strong sense that humans could influence their health and behaviour through auto-suggestion. These elements forged her 'faith' and sustained her. She talked much of the Divine Will and God in years

---

1.   Dorothy to David, 25 February 1931, BFA.

to come, but they reflected her own interpretation of such words and not those of mainstream Christians. She neither read, nor was interested in traditional theology, nor its twentieth-century developments, whether radically conservative or radically modernist. Charlie loved engaging with the thought of Kierkegaard and Barth and other theologians. But for Dorothy, even innovative theologians were no longer relevant to her. She had left their field of enquiry behind.

Dorothy's might be judged by some as having a 'post-Christian' religious faith, an echo of the tradition, but a departure nonetheless. Hers was an individual set of beliefs for the beginning of the age of individualism. She would share her ideas, as she did with her children and others in her circle, but she was urging them to find an individual path. Religion was a private matter. However, she believed with conviction that she was still a follower of Christ and therefore a Christian. In letters to the press, she would describe herself as such. She was a believer in a power beyond herself and in that sense would be seen as religious and certainly not an atheist or agnostic:

> To me 'Religion' means I think, more than anything else [,] the sense of a power transcending human power (as we *know* our 'humanity'), a Power working with us, & within us, for the progressive unfolding of our gift of life. It is one & the same Power of course which drives men forward in the search for Truth, & for Beauty, but it is in the search for *Righteousness* that man becomes conscious of It. It is the sense of *conflict* within, between good & evil in oneself & in others, of a 'lower' self wh[ich] is challenged by a 'higher'; the sense of our need of help in a struggle which otherwise at times seems hopeless; – the cry of the soul for a completely understanding *love* – it is all this wh[ich] leads us to the recognition of God, & of our own spiritual nature which unites us with Him; & in the hidden root of things – with our fellow men.[1]

There was also one significant area that furthered Dorothy's religious beliefs: she saw no need for the 'church' to be the foundation of human community. Her membership of the Friends provided her with a group of like-minded people, but did not for her have the role of a congregation or a parish or being a part of the 'people of God' except in a broad sense of humanity. The Church was no longer the centre of society and this perhaps could be seen as just as great a departure from Christian tradition as her theological stance. For many on the left in politics (although not Charlie), the quest for just and loving relationships had transferred from being a

---

1. Dorothy to David, 25 February 1931, BFA.

Christian quest to a secular social one. For Dorothy too, who retained the vocabulary of a believer, God and Christianity found expression in ideas for regenerating the social order, ideas of equality and 'giving people a proper chance in life.'[1] So like some of the other socialists of her time, Dorothy kept tight hold of the Christian ethic of loving one's neighbour, but expressed it in a secular political programme not a God-focussed society.[2] For Dorothy, 'community' had become a political goal not a religious one.

And yet, can we really be dismissive of her religious position and her self-identification as a Christian? She was certainly moved by the example of Jesus Christ and saw him as her role-model. In this sense, she had taken the position of many 'liberal' Christians of the time in putting Christ first and the doctrine to one side. And it was the example of Christ that motivated her. She stood up for many oppressed or marginalised people in her life, whether those in poverty or those persecuted (such as the Jews) or unfairly represented as being complicit with a totalitarian government they had never supported (such as non-Nazi Germans). This courage came from somewhere and she would have seen this as a product of her religious position. God mattered and insisted she bore witness. Christianity for her was therefore about taking actions. So, we must now turn to her politics.

---

1. Dorothy to David, 31 October 1929, BFA. She had been to a lecture by Donald Grant at the Friends' House and he had taken such 'a line', with which Dorothy heartily concurred.
2. Famously Clement Attlee (1883–1967), Labour Prime Minister 1945–51, said he believed in the ethic of Christianity, but not in what he termed the 'mumbo-jumbo'. Kenneth Harris, *Attlee,* Weidenfeld, London, 1982, pp. 563–564. Dorothy would have understood Attlee's comment, except she would have replaced 'mumbo-jumbo' with 'old-fashioned religious language'.

Chapter 8
Exercising Influence

At the end of chapter four, we noted that Dorothy's politics had swung very much to the left of the political spectrum. If it had not been for her pacifism and her religious views, she could have considered herself a Bolshevik. It is important to put this into the context of the time, as the idea of someone being a 'communist' has been so loaded with emotion and prejudice through the twentieth century. In November 1918, a year after the Bolshevik revolution in Russia, no one knew of the coming excesses of Stalin's [1] policies or the show trials of the 1930s or of the propaganda battles of the Cold War from 1945 to 1990. For Dorothy, in 1919 to support the Bolsheviks was a way of saying that she applauded a new way of organising society, a fresh path on which the poor and disadvantaged would have access to food, shelter, education and other resources and that one small group of society would no longer be able to keep a nation's wealth principally for its own benefit and purposes. The Bolshevik revolution was an attempt at organising society very differently and this was what excited Dorothy. She loathed the violence associated with events in Russia, but she believed the First World War had 'produced a general belief in violence'. Violence was now seen as the way to power with other methods seeming 'remote and shadowy' and hence ineffective. [2]

Charlie visited the new 'Soviet Union' in May–June 1920 and his experiences were later written up into a book. [3] He travelled via Sweden and Estonia as part of a British Trade Union and Labour Party delegation. After visiting Moscow, on 31 May the group set out by boat along the Volga, stopping at villages to observe the everyday life of the inhabitants. Charlie

---

1. Joseph Vissarionovich Jughashvili, known as Stalin (1878–1953), General Secretary of the Communist Party of the Soviet Union 1922–52, Chairman of the Council of Ministers 1941–53.
2. CRB5, p. 98.
3. This book is CRB6, see bibliography.

(who could speak some Russian) decided to stay on in a particular village whilst the rest of the party continued on the river voyage. He was there for a week before being summoned back by concerned Soviet officials.[1] His technical 'arrest' was not harsh and the local Soviet representative 'expressed regret' to him over the 'misunderstanding'.[2] Nevertheless he was not allowed to stay and had to make his way back to Moscow. The week's sojourn had been illuminating for him. During his stay in the village, he observed the working of the local 'Soviet', the role of the parish priest and the school teacher, and the complex dynamic between the 'narrow village patriotism' and the 'unsympathetic centralisation' in which politics in the 'new Russia' operated.[3] He could judge for himself what was going on instead of depending on biased accounts (from both sides of the political divide) competing for his sympathies. He witnessed changes that could have developed in several different ways, with no certainty at that particular time of the final destination.

Charlie's observations were immediately available to Dorothy and these encouraged her to see the Soviet Union as an experiment with many possibilities – and indeed outcomes. This was without glossing over some of the regime's repressive policies that were clearly undemocratic, as well as the fact that it used, when required, unacceptable levels of violence and coercion.[4] She believed however that the hostility of Britain and her allies to Bolshevism – including sending troops to support the counter-revolutionary 'White Russians' and the use of economic sanctions – increased the insecurity of the Soviet government so that its actions became even more extreme. She and Charlie published a joint-authored book in 1920 entitled *The World after the War*,[5] and in this they gave a clear statement of their views on the Russian situation as well as the rest of Europe.

Dorothy advocated socialism for Britain, but not Russian-style communism. She took a line similar to that which Charlie expressed in his pamphlet 'What is Socialism?':

1. Charlie to Dorothy, 4 June & 10 June 1920, BFA. 'I *have* slipped off at Samara, & got right away into a typical country village, where I am living in a peasant's house! I am not very far from the borders of Asia. This will be a great experience, which none of the others will have had. I am not absolutely alone, because I have a young Russian with me, whom for various reasons I couldn't shake off: but he is a mild pacifist & Esperantist, etc and he talks Russian to me nearly all the time, so I am very much in the atmosphere.'

2. CRB6, p. 83.

3. CRB6, p. 56.

4. CRB5, pp. 102–109.

5. This book is CRB5, see bibliography.

We believe that there can be no lasting change which is not voluntarily adopted by the majority of the people. When the majority is persuaded there will be no need for a revolution. If Socialism were carried through by violent methods, it could bring no benefits. British Socialism is strongly and sharply opposed to Communism, on the ground that Communism wants to bring about a social and political change against the will of the majority.[1]

However, Dorothy believed that if the violent Russian version of communism was not to take hold among the working classes in Europe, then a restoration of the pre-1914 social and economic system would be dangerous. For her, it was the maintenance of vast inequalities that created the seedbed for Bolshevism and so a serious opposition to communism should also mean, in practice, reforming the capitalist structures in Europe. In other words, she believed that some development of socialism in a democratic form was required in order to prevent the spread of an authoritarian version. Equally important was transforming the way international diplomacy was expedited, as both she and Charlie wanted a sharp move away from the nationalistic rivalries that were so rife in post-War Europe. At the heart of this discussion was the 'German Question' – what to do about the starving and defeated German people. Were they to be treated as conquered enemies or helped to become future friends? Would being compassionate lead to Germany becoming a threat to peace again or would it mean a secure and stable Europe?

For Dorothy – and indeed Charlie – in 1919–21, the most pressing concern was not therefore the new Soviet regime in Russia, but the plight of Germany. She wrote an article entitled 'The German Question' for *The Contemporary Review*, the text of which initially explored the problem of lack of food. However, she went further than in her Save the Children Fund literature and drew out the political sequence that she judged was the cause of the continued suffering. First, there was the blockade, but even after that had been lifted, Germany had no funds with which to import food – and equally none to import the raw materials it required to re-start its manufacturing industries and thereby generate funds. The nation's gold reserves had been seized and it had no means therefore of providing credit or taking loans. Its currency had devalued by two-thirds. Its coal was taken as reparations payments, mainly to re-build French and Belgian houses and infrastructure, destroyed during the conflict. There were strikes amongst German miners, who resented this. Many other Germans had

---

1. Charles Roden Buxton, *What is Socialism?: A Plain Answer*, ILP, London, [c. 1922–25].

no work. Those that did were trying to work whilst malnourished and weak, so production slumped. Germany had been forced to surrender its means of transport at the Armistice, meaning there were not many trucks and lorries to move any goods that did arrive at the ports. 'The industrial difficulty destroyed the means of paying for food and the lack of food in turn fostered the industrial difficulty, and malnutrition and unemployment worked hand in hand for Bolshevism.'[1]

The effects of the blockade had now been replaced by the effects of the June 1919 Peace Treaty which had imposed reparations payments on Germany to pay for reconstruction of the parts of France and Belgium physically devastated by the war. She judged these to be punitive conditions. That they had been agreed by statesmen who were thought to have a 'liberal and democratic attitude of mind' had undermined, for Dorothy, the cause of Western democracy. Men such as President Wilson of the United States and the British Prime Minister David Lloyd George had, in her opinion, betrayed their promises and showed themselves to be weak and ineffective. They had brought into being a 'Peace' that defeated neither Militarism nor Bolshevism, but instead produced economic conditions that encouraged both.[2]

Dorothy found it incomprehensible that the Allies, who were so afraid of communism, would insist on keeping Germans in a state of degradation and need that, in turn, would foster extreme political reactions. She was clear she must use her network of contacts in Europe to provide reputable facts on conditions in Germany. She also determined to see for herself by visiting when she could. This was made easier for her because throughout 1920 she travelled for Save the Children to and from Switzerland. Late in 1920, she made a visit to Frankfurt, meeting with journalists of the famous newspaper the *Frankfurter Zeitung*, who were admirers of hers because of her *Cambridge Magazine* work during the war. She also met with statisticians and economic experts.[3]

One trip she made with Charlie in October 1920 was to the Ruhr, an industrial and mining province of Germany in the west of the country, east of the River Rhine.[4] They stayed in Essen in the home of a miner, Herr

1. Dorothy Buxton, 'The German Question', *The Contemporary Review*, No 646 (October 1919), pp. [388]–395.
2. CRB5, pp. 134–137.
3. Dorothy to Tye, [December 1920], BFA. The first page is missing but the dates in the text and the references to being just before Christmas indicated the letter was written in December 1920. She wrote about the statisticians for whom it was 'such a joyful relief to the poor dears to find an English person who *really* tries to understand & appreciate their facts & figures!'
4. Recounted in Charles Roden Buxton and Dorothy Frances Buxton, *In a German*

Heinz, who lived in a modest three-room flat, accommodation specifically for those engaged in the mining industry. He was around thirty years old and lived with his wife and two children. The Buxtons insisted they live as their hosts did, eating the same food as the family, predominantly potatoes with peas or cabbage, some black bread and an occasional slice of sausage. Milk was rationed and available only for the children. The Buxtons met a range of people, not only collecting prices and factual material, but gaining impressions as well. They went down a mine, donning khaki clothes and stiff leather caps.[1] They noted that Germany still had a small class of rich people, some who profiteered from the shortages, but that the majority of the population lived on very little. Herr Heinz commented with honesty that the German ruling class would have imposed similarly harsh peace conditions on the Allies had they won, but that ordinary Germans like him had little or no influence on such matters.

In December 1920, Dorothy tried to make a similar trip to Silesia, another mining district, but in the east of Germany in an area that was soon to hold a plebiscite on whether to remain part of Germany. The eventual result was that some of 'upper' Silesia was transferred to Poland and a small section to Czechoslovakia, but the whole territory still counted as Germany when Dorothy attempted to visit. Although she made plans to lodge with a miner and his family, she did not reach her intended destination. The French authorities controlling the area insisted she leave immediately and refused to give any explanation, but it may have been because of the impending plebiscite. They apparently refused even to pass on letters sent to her as she noted to her mother,

> One of her [Eglantyne's] letters to me arrived at Berlin on Dec 9th just after I left for Upper Silesia & was forwarded to me there. It reached the office of my friends at the miners' union who sent it back to Berlin, but the French authorities who were on the war path after me by that time – appear to have kept it, (along with some of my children[']s letters! & no doubt [they] are busy trying to read meanings into these various communications![2]

Dorothy's writings on these issues were a small part of the general protests in newspapers and political meetings about the policies implemented by the Allies. Sympathy for her point of view was much wider than merely

---

Miner's Home, ILP pamphlet, New series No 41, Independent Labour Party, London, 1921.
1. Dorothy to David, 29 October 1920, BFA. This letter is written from Berlin, Charlie & Dorothy's destination immediately after leaving Essen.
2. Dorothy to Tye, [December 1920], BFA.

some left-wing circles. Many on the right of British politics also saw the need to treat Germany differently, but the French position remained much less sympathetic and would lead in time to French troops not only maintaining their occupation of western parts of the Rhineland allowed in the 1919 Peace Treaty,[1] but in extending the area it controlled. They took over three towns, including Dusseldorf, on the east bank of the Rhine in the first half of 1921 and then in January 1923, along with Belgian troops, they occupied the whole of the Ruhr industrial and mining district, so as to enforce reparation payments. This behaviour was one factor in creating a mood in German public opinion that would be prey in the next decade to populist interpretations of history that portrayed Germany as a 'victim' nation.

The importance of Dorothy's approach in the debates after the First World War was that she (and Charlie) wished to gather reliable factual information. They could then speak (and write) from personal experience. In this sense, they were able to have an authority that those purely commentating from political standpoints could not. 'Notes from the Foreign Press' had been started by Dorothy because of the need to provide accurate information. Her famine work had begun by doing the same, so that action could be advocated with confidence. Now in the field of foreign policy, she endeavoured to repeat that process. Her many letters to newspapers and periodicals were her means of spreading her message using the factual material she had gathered.

Yet hers was one voice and she understood that she needed to be part of something larger, a group that had a wider reach and influence, especially as Dorothy wished to influence policy in the party political arena. The obvious place was the Labour Party, for which her husband Charlie remained a parliamentary candidate. Charlie, with his foreign policy interests and expertise, had been invited before the end of the First World War to join an advisory committee on international and imperial questions – indeed he was to chair it. In 1919, it split into two: the 'imperial questions' – mainly about how to deal with problems that arose in the British colonial territories – and the 'international questions' on other foreign affairs.[2] Both

---

1. It should be noted that the USA maintained some troops in a northern area of the Rhineland until January 1923, whilst British troops remained in a small sector until 1929. However, the majority of the German territory was under French control.
2. The Imperial Questions committee was chaired first by Charlie, but then in time he handed the task to Sir John Maynard. Herbert John Maynard (1865–1943) had been a civil servant in India and joined the Labour Party after his retirement in 1927. He had travelled to Russia in the 1890s, but then made further journeys in the 1930s and published a well-received book entitled *The Russian Peasant* in 1942. Charlie chaired the International Questions Committee until 1937 when he

had Charlie as chair at first, with Leonard Woolf[1] as secretary, but it was the Advisory Committee on International Questions (ACIQ) that would interest Dorothy, as it dealt with Germany and Russia, reparations, famine relief and the like.

These advisory committees had no political power. Their role was to write papers and proffer advice to the Labour Party's National Executive Committee, the place where any decisions on policy could be made. They were created because the Labour Party realised that if it were to become a national party offering to provide an alternative government, it needed to develop serious policies in all areas. At that time, its emphasis was mainly industrial relations and issues that affected the British working-class, such as housing, schooling and health. Most Labour MPs and Trade Union leaders were not expert in foreign affairs – indeed there was almost an expectation that the mainly working-class Labour MPs would not be interested in such matters. For quite a number that was true, as the needs of working people in Britain were their passionate motivation – and the fate of miners in Germany, say, was not their concern. To counter that perspective, Dorothy and Charlie argued that a revival of German industry would increase markets for British goods and thereby safeguard and augment British jobs. Helping to create relationships with other nations that would prevent further wars would benefit British workers too. Solidarity with the working-class of other nations would give strength to socialist initiatives at home. Therefore, they argued, foreign affairs had a direct impact on what happened in the British economy and to the lives of the poor at home. It was not peripheral to the problems of British workers and the unemployed, but a significant factor in alleviating those troubles.

With the influx of ex-Liberals, such as Charlie and his brother Noel, to the Labour Party after 1916, there was a pool of new members who were very knowledgeable on foreign policy matters and who pushed this different perspective. The mainly working-class MPs and officials in the Labour Party were suspicious of these newcomers, so different in background and education to themselves, and they were not willing yet to allow them much power. They perhaps feared these well-travelled and educated recruits would try to dominate the party and, as such, the working-class representatives felt they had to be on their guard. So, when in 1917 the Labour Conference

resigned because he wished to maintain a 'pacifist' position. Woolf4, pp. 245–246.

1. Leonard Sidney Woolf (1880–1969) was an author, publisher and for some years before 1911 a colonial administrator in Ceylon. His wife was the noted novelist and critic, Virginia Woolf, and they both became part of the so-called 'Bloomsbury Group', an intellectual and social circle, the members of which were united by a belief in the importance of the arts and a rejection of convention.

proposed to set up various committees as part of its new constitutional arrangements, its leadership ensured that they were 'advisory'. For some, this was a frustration. Leonard Woolf noted in his autobiography that those with remarkable knowledge and experience who put in a great deal of work 'were habitually disappointed by the results of their labours' as the National Executive Committee would note their advice, but then not act. Yet he judged, 'we did influence the Party occasionally in important ways and – what was even more significant – a small number of Labour M.P.'s regularly attended our meetings and gradually became real experts on foreign or imperial affairs and policies.'[1]

As already noted, Charlie, as one of the new intake of upper middle-class ex-Liberals, was asked to lead the foreign affairs group. It met several times a month throughout most of the year in a committee room at the House of Commons or else at Labour Party headquarters in Eccleston Square. Matters were discussed and position papers written. For Charlie, this was a significant opportunity to influence as he waited for another chance to stand again for parliament. It was a committee with a fluid membership – that is, experts in certain fields were brought in on particular subjects – but by the early 1920s, Charlie and Dorothy, as well as Charlie's brother, Noel, were regular members. Whether the issue was famine conditions, Russian matters or the situation in Germany, Charlie knew that one of the most knowledgeable contributors would be Dorothy. She became a regular attender of the committee, researching and writing papers, and for a period in 1923 was 'acting secretary' in place of Leonard Woolf. When she 'retired' from the committee in 1924, because of the concerns about her health, Woolf wrote her a warm letter of appreciation:

> I was extremely sorry to get your letter and to see from it that you must resign from the Committee. As far as I personally am concerned, I should like to thank you very much for all you have given me as secretary and for the immense amount of work you have done for the Committee. I hope that as soon as your health permits – and that it will be soon – you will return to the Committee.[2]

In the event, she did not return – although it may be fairly assumed she gave informal advice to Charlie who continued on the committee until the late 1930s. In the years she had served ACIQ, her contribution was not inconsiderable. Woolf would hardly have written as he did if she had been an occasional 'extra' to the deliberations and the work of ACIQ. Yet she has been ignored by many who have written on the development of

1. Woolf3, pp. 227–228. Also Woolf4, p. 238 for a similar lament.
2. Leonard Woolf to Dorothy, May 1924, BFA.

the Labour Party's foreign policy in the 1920s, not even being mentioned in the text let alone discussed, and the emphasis has been on Charlie, with an unexpressed assumption that Dorothy was a mere appendage, being the chair's wife.[1]

Her serious involvement, however cannot be doubted. In the Buxton papers, there is a memorandum in Dorothy's hand listing her work in the period October 1921–May 1922. Under the heading 'On reparations', she wrote:

1. Drawing up of a memorandum on Labour policy to be submitted to Lloyd George [then Prime Minister] by the Labour Party, Dec 16, 1921.
2. Drawing up of a Draft Memorandum on Labour's Foreign Policy to be used as a pamphlet for election purposes, dealing with Reparation, Russia, Austria, Inter-allied Debts etc. (circulated by the Advisory Committee, Nov. 1, 1921).
3. Compilation and distribution of dossiers (several editions of each) dealing with various aspects of the reparation question (unemployment, effect on different trades, dislocation of the exchanges, creation of insecurity etc.)
4. Drawing up of a memorandum ('The Threat of Renewed War') for the 'Fight the Famine' Council, May 1922.
5. Work connected with the Fight the Famine Conference (October 1921), the meetings of the Economic Committee of the Fight the Famine Council and the Advisory Committee on International Questions of the Labour Party.
6. Article in 'Labour Leader', Jan 5, 1922: 'America & the Rescue'.

There are then similar lists under the heading 'Upper Silesia', 'Conditions in Germany', 'Russia' and 'Miscellaneous'. They contain further mentions of the ACIQ, as well as work for the FFC and the SCF, which included giving speeches, for example at the Spring 1922 Labour Women's Conference in north London. Official documentation backs up the claims of these lists.

---

1. See for example: Henry Winkler, *Paths not Taken: British Labour and International Policy in the 1920s*, University of North Carolina Press, Chapel Hill, NC, 1994; Henry Winkler, *British Labour seeks a Foreign Policy, 1900–1940*, Transaction Publishers, New Brunswick, NJ, 2005; Caspar Sylvest, '"A Commanding Group"? Labour's Advisory Committee on International Questions 1918–31', in Paul Corthorn and Jonathan Davis (editors), *The British Labour Party and the Wider World: Domestic Politics, Internationalism and Foreign Policy*, Tauris, London, 2008. None mention Dorothy or record that she was an active member and drafter of documents. Leonard Woolf's autobiographical volumes discuss Charlie and his contribution, but do not mention Dorothy (Woolf3 and Woolf4).

The lists covered just eight months of a membership of several years on ACIQ so a complete catalogue of her contribution would be much longer.

What these lists reveal is, firstly, the interconnexion between Dorothy's work on famine relief and her political lobbying. She saw no difference between charitable action and political pressure: the two went hand in hand. So the information she garnered to appeal for public funds was the same she used to try to influence policy among the politicians. Second, the work for the ACIQ was a considerable part of her workload. The committee minutes reflect this, for example, on 9 November 1921, Dorothy was the proposer of the first motion 'to suggest to the Executive that a campaign of meetings be organised from headquarters to emphasize the effect on unemployment of 1. the Russian situation and 2. the reparation payments demanded from Germany'. The second resolution was 'to suggest to the Policy Committee that they consider the advisability of the party immediately sending a deputation to the Prime Minister on the questions of reparations and Russia'. This was proposed by Ben Spoor MP,[1] but the minutes add the words 'after urging by Mrs Buxton'[2] and this led to the memorandum that Dorothy wrote and which was presented to the Prime Minister on 16 December. Two of the remaining three resolutions of the meeting also mention Dorothy,[3] all indicating she was a powerful and respected presence on the committee.[4]

Her concerns were those already noted in this chapter regarding Germany, Dorothy wanting the Labour Party to commit to a revision of the punitive clauses of the 1919 Versailles Peace Treaty. The situation deteriorated there once again in 1923. Claiming reparations were not being paid, the French and Belgians decided to pressure their former enemy even further by militarily occupying the coal-producing area of the Ruhr. The resulting economic disruption helped to provoke hyperinflation. The German population responded with passive resistance. For the occupiers, much of the reparations they extracted through this military response to non-payment had to go towards maintaining their own troops, so they gained very little. The ACIQ helped shape the Labour party's response to the crisis throughout 1923 and appointed Dorothy to a sub-committee that drafted papers and leaflets, using information she gleaned from her

---

1. ACIQ minutes, copy in BFA.
2. Benjamin Charles Spoor (1878–1928), Labour MP for Bishop Auckland 1918–28.
3. 'Resolved that the Sub-Committee [Mrs Buxton, Beresford & Woolf] go on preparing the pamphlet. Resolved to consider a draft manifesto on reparations, etc., by Mrs Buxton at the next meeting.'
4. There were fifteen members present, of whom six were MPs. Dorothy was one of two women present, the other being Susan Lawrence, a Labour MP in later years.

many contacts.[1] The ACIQ's position, based on Dorothy's papers, was to recommend that the Rhineland be de-militarised under the control of the League of Nations, a body to which it was recommended Germany should now be invited to join.[2] This was what happened over the next few years.

At this stage, Charlie was back in the House of Commons. He had courted the Accrington constituency following his defeat there in 1918. He visited the area and listened to the difficulties of the working people, making specific gestures to significant groups of electors, such as going down one of the constituency's coal mines to learn more of the conditions faced by the miners.[3] Although many of the working-class male electors had been away in the army and not at home to vote at the time of the 1918 election, with a larger turnout expected at the next election, Charlie was expected to poll better in 1922. In the event, the turnout at the election was up at 88%, which helped him. He faced strong opposition from both the sitting Conservative MP and the Liberal who had been the MP before 1918, nevertheless, this meant the 'anti-Labour' vote would be split, which gave Charlie a further advantage. His win at the 1922 general election was not therefore a complete surprise, but the scale of it was. Charlie's triumph was considerable, with a majority of more than 5,000. He had increased his vote from 6,000 to 16,000 votes, with the Conservative losing 2,000. He had taken votes from his main rival, as well as benefitting from an increased presence of Labour-voting men.[4] This was despite his opponents calling him a 'dangerous' socialist. Dorothy had been a strong part of the campaign. Leaflets containing a personal message from her, with a photograph of her taken with her children, were distributed. One of her distinct messages was to invite the women voters to make up their own minds. 'Remember that you have the right and the duty to think for yourself; put your cross as you think best, not only as your husband, or your employer, or your wealthy canvassers think best.'[5] She was keen to show how the reparations policy towards Germany had reduced demand for cotton goods manufactured in the constituency and thereby reduced jobs and incomes among the women workers. To spread this message, she held small meetings for women, sometimes in ordinary houses, where she put the case for voting Labour:

1. ACIQ minutes, 10 October 1923, copy in BFA. A copy of her report for the ACIQ of March 1923 on the situation is also in BFA.
2. This was Dorothy's suggestion for an addition to party policy in the report for the ACIQ of March 1923, copy in BFA.
3. Charlie to Eglantyne, 19 November 1920, BFA.
4. 1922 November general election, Accrington (electorate 41,960), 88.7% turnout: C. Roden Buxton (Labour) 16,462 (44.3%); Ernest Gray (Conservative) 11,408 (30.6%); Harold Baker (Liberal) 9,395 (25.1%), Labour majority 5,054 (13.7%).
5. Advert in the *Accrington Labour News,* 14 November 1922, copy in BFA.

Mrs Buxton started cottage meetings before the election, & she has been carrying them on since, right up to last night, to keep up interest & enthusiasm among the women & to educate them as to the aims of the Labour Party. They were extraordinarily successful & the women admired & loved Mrs Buxton so much, & were so pleased that she should come among them in such a friendly way. . . .

Mrs Buxton had some splendid meetings & as then polling day drew near they became steadily more crowded & enthusiastic, but I think no one expected such a great majority as 5,000. It was a wonderful moment when we heard the results. . . . Both Mr & Mrs Buxton made most inspired speeches, having only prepared one to make if defeated![1]

Charlie was concerned about Dorothy overworking herself given her health concerns and sent her on a holiday to Devon immediately after the election, from where she wrote to her mother with more details of her campaigning:

When I arrived in Acc[rington] 3 weeks ago no special efforts were being directed at the women, so here a big field lay open to me. . . . We called a special women's meeting & at this meeting asked for invitations to hold informal little meetings in people's kitchens. Between 20 & 30 of these 'cottage meetings' were fixed up. Women slipped in to these little gatherings, often with their shawls over their heads, straight from 'the Mills', who w[ou]ld never attend public meetings at all. Soon we had a big *stir on* & everyone now admits that the women played an important part in securing our 5000 majority! As to me I found it a great education myself to attend these little meetings. Sitting round a cosy kitchen fire, with no male creatures present, the women would soon get to feel at home, & would start asking questions & relating their own experiences in a way which made the circumstances of their lives far more real & living to one. . . . We love all our miners & weavers & it is beautiful how they seem to love *us*. At any rate over & over again I heard them talking about Charlie in a way which made my heart swell with pride & joy. There is now undoubtedly a large nucleus of men & women who really seem to understand & to appreciate him. This does *not* mean of course that all the 16000 people who voted for us will remain with us. I am under no such pleasant illusion! It will I think be almost inevitable that there will be a swing back of the pendulum. I am certain that quite a large

1. Violet Taylor to Tye, 22 November 1922, BFA.

number of people were quite undecided up to the last few days which party they were going to vote for, & many probably were carried along simply by the *wave* in our favour which seemed to sweep the Division at the 11th hour![1]

Dorothy's caution about the future was well-judged. The two parties decided to maximise the chance of defeating 'the socialist' and in the following general elections held in Autumn 1923 and 1924, Charlie lost to a Liberal candidate,[2] the Conservatives having decided not to contest the seat.[3] In both those two elections, Dorothy played very little part, unlike 1922, and it is impossible to judge whether her intervention would have made much difference. Without her presence Charlie still increased his personal vote each time, but he was unable to capture a majority of the vote in a two-way fight.

With Charlie out of parliament again after just over a year, he concentrated on the ACIQ and his policy role in the Labour Party. With Germany led by Gustav Stresemann,[4] who was first Chancellor then Foreign Minister, agreements were reached on both economic and political issues to calm the situation in Germany. The Dawes plan concerning reparations was agreed in the summer of 1924. The decisions reached at the Locarno summit in October 1925 settled the questions of Germany's Western borders, its admission to the League of Nations and the withdrawal over the following five years of Allied troops from German soil. Economic conditions began to improve and the 'German question' was no longer the dominant political issue in foreign affairs (for a few years, at least).

Dorothy turned her attention back to the Soviet Union. The famine in Russia had led her to campaign both for food aid via SCF and for political responses that brought the new Soviet Union in from the diplomatic

---

1. Dorothy to Tye 22 November 1922, BFA.
2. [John] Hugh Edwards (1869–1945) had been a Welsh Liberal MP, representing Mid-Glamorgan 1910–18 and then Neath 1918–22. In 1922 he had been defeated by a Labour candidate. In 1923 he was then adopted for the Accrington constituency as a 'Constitutionalist' candidate, representing both Liberal and Conservative parties. However, in the House of Commons he took the Liberal whip. He lost the Accrington constituency in 1929 to another Labour candidate, who had succeeded Charlie.
3. 1923 December general election, Accrington (electorate 42,507), 86.5% turnout: J. Hugh Edwards (Liberal) 19,981 (54.3%); C. Roden Buxton (Labour) 16,793 (45.7%); Liberal majority 3,188 (8.6%). 1924 October general election, Accrington (electorate 42,786), 90.1% turnout: J. Hugh Edwards (Liberal) 20,981 (52.9%); C. Roden Buxton (Labour) 18,148 (47.1%); Liberal majority 2,243 (5.8%).
4. Gustav Stresemann (1868–1929), Chancellor of Germany Aug–Nov 1923, Foreign Minister 1923–29.

Dorothy & Charlie in the 1922 Accrington election campaign

isolation imposed on it by the international community. In Dorothy's view, fear of communism was not sufficient reason for shunning the Russian people. She pushed with others in the ACIQ for British recognition of the Soviet government and the opening of trade links. Just as relations with Germany should be 'normalised', in the same spirit, relations with the Soviet Union should be. This became Labour Party policy.

In January 1924, as a consequence of the inconclusive general election of the previous month, the first Labour government took office. It was a minority administration, dependent on Liberal MPs for any majority in votes in the House of Commons. Ramsey Macdonald was determined to be a moderate, reassuring the Prime Minister in this situation. Yet one of his bold measures was to implement the recognition of the Soviet government. This was rescinded by the subsequent Conservative government in 1927, but relations were restored at ambassadorial level in 1929 when the Labour Party formed a second administration. Charlie was possibly a candidate considered for the new post of British ambassador to Moscow.[1] Given his knowledge of both the history and language of the country and his long interest in the Soviet experiment, he would have had much to commend him. However, in the end, the government chose a career diplomat and Charlie was left disappointed.[2]

He had visited Russia again in 1927 and this time his wife and both children went with him. Ever since his trip down the Volga in 1920, Dorothy had hankered to go and see what was happening herself. The political and economic situation in Soviet territory was filtered through a haze of propaganda, from both sympathisers and opponents, and only a personal visit could provide more accurate information – and accurate information was Dorothy's aim in all she did. In 1927, therefore, the Buxtons arranged a visit, following which she wrote a book *The Challenge of Bolshevism*, both to tell of her journey and also to share her political and social arguments inspired by what she had seen.

The visit was over twenty-four days during August and September, with time in both Moscow and Leningrad, two provincial towns and a period living in the home of a village school teacher in Sokolishchi near the Volga.[3] What impressed her, as she stated at the very beginning of her book, was the 'moral advance' she witnessed. She deplored the means by which the state had created the new order, but she wanted her readers to ponder on the objective. Russia had experienced a repressive and violent government before the Revolution, as well as after it, and the repressive measures resembled those used in many non-communist states in Europe, such as Italy under Mussolini, Hungary and Rumania. Those countries were not scrutinised and found 'wanting' as the Soviet Union was.

For her, it was therefore important to look at the vision and goal of the Soviet system – and here she saw something of great value. It was for her the working out of her Christian principles: everyone received according to their needs and gave according to their powers, based on a re-distribution of

1. Wright, p. 343, quoting the *Sunday Despatch*, 13 October 1929. There was similar speculation in other newspapers, for example, *The Yorkshire Post*, 3 October 1929 and 14 October 1929.

2. 'The dream is over, for today the appointment is announced of Sir Ernest Overy, whose name I've never heard of before, but who appears to have much experience of Mexico, Persia & other places.' Charlie to David, 13 November 1929, BFA. Dorothy confirmed that Charlie was disappointed, but she was of the opinion that his work in Britain was of greater importance. Dorothy to David, 14 November 1929, BFA.

3. DFB1, p. 7; Bunsen, p. 117.

wealth so all could have equal opportunity to thrive. She could be accused of missing the point that the 'end' does not justify the 'means'. If the 'means' are unsavoury, the 'end' will be distorted and not what was originally intended. Dorothy knew, however, that even a small criticism would be seized upon by anti-Bolshevists to 'prove' their own arguments and so she was reticent to criticise at all. It was easier, too, for her to look favourably on the communist experiment in 1927 because it was an untypical phase in the regime's relentless drive to destroy the old and build a new society.

Dorothy visited Russia in what might be described as a slowdown in the revolutionary trajectory. After the excesses of 'war communism' during the civil war of 1919–21, Lenin[1] had introduced a 'New Economic Policy' which had allowed some freedom for the peasants (the vast majority of Russia's then population) to sell their excess produce and keep the proceeds. In other words, the Soviet government had allowed a certain measure of capitalism to function whilst the country recovered some stability after the war years. This was opposed by some Russian communists, but was generally accepted as a discordant yet necessary measure and remained in place until 1929. Food supplies recovered and the Russian countryside began to prosper. In 1927, when Dorothy visited, the peasants had re-established a reasonable life for themselves under this policy. They were certainly better off than they had been under the Tsars and they had a hopeful outlook for the future. As Dorothy put it, the people were under a political tyranny – no different than before – but the new 'tyranny' 'does not affect the working conditions of daily life nor the management of a very great deal in local affairs. The peasants are at last in actual, if not nominal, possession of the land, and this age-long desire of their hearts is fulfilled.'[2]

It was not just material benefit that Dorothy saw – she recognised a benefit in social relationships. She spent many pages of her book extolling aspects of life she saw in the Soviet Union: the simplicity of dress, the abolition of fashion, the equality of greeting everyone as comrades instead of a self-conscious class-ridden set of responses, the seriousness of publications compared with the triviality of Western magazines, the praising of people's work ethic rather than the accumulation of possessions, the opening up of cultural resources to all. She saw this as a moral approach that would, through the education of the next generation, create a superior society to that of the 'bourgeois' democracies. It was this 'changes of values' that she most applauded in all that she saw.[3] Of course, as a woman who voluntarily

---

1. Vladimir Ilyich Ulyanov, known as Lenin (1870–1924), leader of Russia (later Soviet Union) 1917–24.
2. DFB1, pp. 17–18.
3. DRB1, p. 71.

spurned many of life's treats and comforts herself, she was naturally attracted to a society that had abolished them for most of the people she met. Many of her readers would not agree with her attitude and would accordingly see her commentary in a different light, but for Dorothy a life of simplicity was a paradise. So, she ignored the compulsion and repression that was used to create the new Soviet Union and extolled the result instead.

She was not totally in denial however. In her book she did condemn the communist use of violence. 'The cruelties belong to a policy inspiring Fear, which, by arousing the hostility of many who might otherwise be wholly friendly, demonstrates one of the ways in which Force defeats its own purposes.'[1] However, she saw this as 'a transition stage'.[2] In 1927, she was convinced that communism could evolve into a peaceful political force once the strain of establishing such a new system had died away. This might seem hopelessly naïve to many who know the subsequent history of Soviet communism, but it was not certain how things would develop at the time of Dorothy's visit and her book chronicled a moment in history where the idealist could still be genuinely excited that a new kind of society was coming into being.

Then there was religion. She seemed unaware of the pressures being exerted on Christianity in the new Russia because in 1927 the wholescale closing of churches and elimination of the bishops and priests had not yet begun. David's daily journal of the trip included a passage in which he noted that, whilst there were anti-religious posters, the churches were still open. He added a passage which might well have expressed his mother's view of the Russian Orthodox Church at the time:

> In the evening we paid our first visit to one of the churches, where a service was in progress. The magnificence of the gold ornamentation, the beauty of the singing, and the priests in their gorgeous robes, made a strong impression. As is the case with many churches, the outside looked dirty & dilapidated, but the inside had passed unchanged through the revolution: it was part of the old order living on, a different world from the new Moscow outside. There can be no question as to the tyranny of the church. It is a remnant of the old régime, & it taught people to tolerate the old régime. It is a dangerous influence, which will gradually, but probably very gradually, disappear and better religion will spring up, & no propaganda will prevent it. Apart from propaganda, the communists have done nothing against the church. . . . We went

---

1. DRB1, p. 54.
2. DRB1, p. 49.

into a great many churches at different times, frequently services were in progress, but the congregations were not large. Very few churches were closed.[1]

Dorothy, as a Quaker with 'higher views', looked at religious ceremony and ritual with a certain impatience, so David's comments about such practice fading away and being replaced by something 'better' was in line with her attitude. As for the idea of the Russian Church having not been subject to anything more than propaganda, such a view was misguided. Many priests and church people had lost their lives at the hands of revolutionaries during the civil war. The Patriarch had been harassed and put under house arrest. When he died in 1925, the Church was not allowed to elect a successor. The communist government had expropriated the Church's property and tried to use economic restriction to undermine its work. The Russian Orthodox Church in 1927 was not free and many were afraid to be seen going to church in case there were repercussions in other areas of their life. These were not factors that could be ascertained by the fleeting glance of a visitor.

Dorothy's religious views made her prioritise action over worship and she recognised a contrast between communism in Russia and Christianity in Britain. She saw the latter as too passive and inert in the face of human suffering and want. She regarded Bolshevism, therefore, as a fundamental challenge to what she judged was a version of Christianity that was too complacent. She ended her book, 'Passivity becomes complicity. If the Communist is not to put the Christian to shame, no sacrifice short of complete devotion of life and wealth can avail.'[2]

Dorothy had visited Russia just in time to retain her sense of hope about the new regime; within eighteen months, the situation in the Soviet Union began to change radically. With Lenin dead and Trotsky[3] exiled, Stalin took full control of both party and government. Economic and social policy changed dramatically. A five-year plan for rapid industrialisation was instituted, but it required more grain to feed the increased number of industrial workers it would create. The peasants were resistant to the demands of central government and so a policy known as the collectivisation of the peasants was announced. The ordinary people were forcibly deprived of their individual plots of land and removed to large collective farms, the richer ones (termed 'kulaks') were eliminated by killing or imprisonment, and the traditional agricultural ways of life of Russia and its culture were destroyed.

1. David Buxton, travel journal no 8, 13 August 1927, pp. 61–62, BFA.
2. DRB1, p. 95.
3. Leon Trotsky (1879–1940), member of the Russian/Soviet Politburo 1917–26.

The peasants' beloved Orthodox religion was banned and persecuted with ruthless intent. The relative 'good times' of the 1920s observed by Dorothy were over. The result was upheaval on a massive scale. Those who resisted the policy were killed. Those who did not were rendered impotent to resist by being reduced to workers in a centralised state enterprise. The disruption of agriculture led quickly to severe food shortages, leading to widespread famine which reached its height in 1932–33. Many ordinary Soviet citizens (estimated in the millions) starved to death. It was 1918–21 all over again, but on a larger scale. Political policy was repeating the hardship previously brought by war and it was an avoidable human tragedy on a massive scale. Through the 1930s, Stalin ruthlessly suppressed all internal dissent with show trials, condemning many innocent opponents to death. Other people disappeared or were exiled to labour camps in inhospitable regions of the Soviet Union.

For Dorothy this must have been heart-breaking. Her son David went to Russia again in 1928 and made a subsequent visit in 1932. His particular aim was to visit and photograph the ancient wooden churches of Russia[1] rather than political observation, but he was able to inform his mother of the deterioration in conditions and atmosphere in the country since their 1927 visit. All her hopes that a new society would emerge from the Russian experiment were shattered. Dorothy never tried to visit the Soviet Union again. Her book was soon hopelessly out of touch with the reality of Soviet life. Whilst still clinging to a left-wing vision of the future, she retreated further from the Soviet version of communism. She regularly advocated courses of action so that communism would not be spread.[2] However, her belief in the spirit of what she would have seen as 'true' Bolshevism remained. This was a combination of certain communist values linked with Christian pacifism. In the early years of the Second World War, she was even exploring whether *The Challenge of Bolshevism* could be reissued.[3]

---

1. This was a subject in which he became a great expert and on which he published articles and monographs.
2. For example, she complained about the high salaries given to public servants in a letter to the *Manchester Guardian*: 'If we "Christians" are not to continue promoting atheism and Communism at a great rate, if we are not to go on making our Christian professions a matter of derision to Communists and others, surely part of the "immediate action" for which we should enlist the Divine help is on behalf of a widespread reduction of public salaries and in general of stricter limitation of luxurious private incomes.' *Manchester Guardian*, 15 August 1934.
3. Dorothy to Stanley Unwin, 13 November 1941 & Stanley Unwin to Dorothy 19 November 1941, BFA. The request to reprint was turned down by Unwin, as he said the text would need some changes and in any case they were short of paper, which was rationed during the Second World War.

In the early 1930s, she looked again to Germany and became concerned by the political chaos that had followed the onset of the economic depression. German industry had become dependent on American finance in the late 1920s and so the collapse of the US stock market in 1929 led to a rapid rise in job losses in Germany. This led ordinary Germans to panic and they reacted electorally by voting for the more extreme parties on both right and left. Eventually, the turmoil led to the appointment of Adolf Hitler as Chancellor in January 1933. He and his Nazi party soon extinguished democracy and its institutions and crushed all opposition. A new dictatorship had taken hold in the heart of Europe, just as Charlie had feared in his prophetic writings in the early months of the First World War.

Dorothy loved the German people and she was alarmed at these developments. She could legitimately have been accused in the 1920s of always seeing the good side and making excuses to explain away the violent actions of the Soviet regime. In the 1930s, it was others who fell into this mistake with the Nazi regime in Germany. Many in Britain fell into the trap of seeing the new Chancellor as the 'saviour' of Germany after the chaos of the post-1929 economic depression. In contrast to these apologists, Dorothy saw the dangers immediately and became an early campaigner to expose the underlying viciousness of Nazi policies hidden beneath a formidable propaganda machine. She was particularly concerned about the Jews, who were almost immediately targeted by the Nazis once they were in power. Long before the official laws that made Jews into second-class and then non-citizens – and thereby a state-sanctioned target for discrimination and harassment – Dorothy was campaigning to alert the British public to what was going on.

Concentration camps for those who opposed the Nazi regime were set up early in Hitler's time in power. Originally, they were not 'extermination camps' as they became during the Second World War, but instead harsh prisons where inmates were denied much contact with outside. People died of punishments and torture handed out there. Dorothy soon received reports of this ill-treatment of prisoners and started a campaign to make the British public aware of the terrible conditions and activities in these camps. As with her other campaigns however, Dorothy wanted to contact those who might have influence, as well as write letters to the newspapers and articles for journals. As a consequence of the activities during the founding of the Save the Children Fund, she had a Swedish contact: Countess Fanny von Wilamowitz-Moellendorf.[1] Fanny had had a younger

---

1. Fanny von Hock (1882–1956) was the daughter of Colonel Karl von Fock and his Anglo-Irish wife, Huldine Beamish and the widow of Count Wichard Heinning von Wilamowitz-Moellendorff (1871–1916). Her sister Carin (1888–1931) was

sister, Carin, who had married a German airman in 1922 called Hermann Göring.[1] Hermann and Carin lived in Germany after their marriage and soon became enthusiastic Nazis. Carin died of heart failure in 1931, but Fanny retained a connection with her brother-in-law, who within a short time had risen to prominence near the very top of the new Nazi regime.

Dorothy decided to re-ignite this lapsed contact in order to see if she could reach the Nazi leaders. She accordingly wrote to Fanny in February 1934, reminding her of Eglantyne and their Save the Children connection. She noted how she still felt that peace was the great aim to work for and thus she had become alarmed at events in Germany. She attached an article that she had written about the issues and asked Fanny if she could get it published in Sweden. She was quite explicit in the letter too:

> The outlawing and persecution of the Jews and of political minorities has caused horror through the length and breadth of England. It has resulted in a most terrible revulsion of feeling against Germany – a return to the suspicion and dislike which recreates the war feeling. A most dangerous position is thus being created.
>
> If only the Concentration Camps could be brought to an end and the horrors to which Jewish and political prisoners are exposed no longer allowed, there might be some hope of the animosity in England dying down before it is too late.
>
> The situation is heartbreaking to people like myself who worked hard against the atrocity campaign during the war. Present atrocities have been confirmed for us by people who have always been and remain friendly to Germany.[2]

Fanny was not convinced and insisted that in her recent visit to Germany, she had been impressed by the atmosphere and it was her own observations she trusted not the stories in newspapers. During her visit in July–September 1933 she had visited a concentration camp (at Sonneburg), towns in Silesia and Bavaria, as well as Berlin. She insisted that in the whole visit she had not heard or saw 'an unkind or rude word or deed against the Jews'. Hitler for her was an idealist.[3] This was not encouraging for Dorothy, but she saw Fanny as someone who could potentially be convinced of the darker truth

the first wife of Hermann Göring.

1. Hermann Göring (1893–1946), Minister for Aviation in the Nazi government 1933–45 and Hitler's deputy 1941–45.
2. Dorothy to Fanny von Wilamowitz-Moellendorff, 12 February 1934, copy in BFA.
3. Fanny von Wilamowitz-Moellendorff to Dorothy, 19 February 1934 and 20 February 1934, BFA.

of what was happening in Nazi Germany. If she were so convinced, her change of attitude might lead her to lobby her brother-in-law to soften the German government's approach.

Therefore, when Fanny was visiting Britain in April–May 1934, Dorothy arranged for her to meet with George Bell, Bishop of Chichester,[1] a bishop who had been very active in the ecumenical movement and therefore knew personally many leaders of the Protestant churches in Germany. These leaders were genuinely alarmed at both the Nazi regime's attitude to religion and its anti-Semitism. Bell became a prominent supporter of the Confessing Church in Germany, that is, the Protestants who rejected government control and who had launched themselves as a distinct Christian witness by the 1934 Barmen Declaration, a statement of principles to which Bishop Bell also attached his signature. At Dorothy's urging, Fanny saw Bishop Bell, although Dorothy warned the bishop that Fanny was not sympathetic. 'At present her attitude is one of extreme scepticism as to the frequency of "atrocities" – and in so far as rough handling may occur, she attributes it in great part to "former communists" now in Nazi service.'[2]

However, Dorothy believed that Fanny, who was very religious, was a trustworthy and disinterested person, anxious to help and someone also who would keep confidences if asked to do so. Dorothy hoped the bishop could change Fanny's opinions. Nothing came of the meeting however:

> I am sorry to say I have been greatly disappointed with what she has been able to do since. She left England full of good intentions as to what she might be able to do in connection with the question of Concentration Camps etc, but I rather fear her brother-in-law must have been too discouraging.[3]

Presumably, Fanny, once she was home, felt too diffident to take the matter up after all or else after contacting her brother-in-law, Göring waved her concerns aside with shallow reassurances. There was nothing for it, Dorothy believed, but to try to visit the Nazi minister herself.[4]

By January 1935 she had made up her mind:

---

1. George Bell (1883–1958), Bishop of Chichester 1929 "1958.
2. Dorothy to George Bell, [25] April 1934, BFA.
3. Dorothy to George Bell, 31 January 1935, Bell 7, Item 63-64, LPL.
4. She noted to her son: 'A year ago I felt that nothing could ever bring me to go to Germany, far less to shake hands with its present rulers. But I came to the conclusion that this was a cowardly attitude, & that nothing but practical utility sh[ou]ld decide such a question.' Dorothy to David, no date but almost certainly March 1935, BFA.

I have continued to study this question of the treatment of prisoners, and in the last few months have tried to find someone who might visit Germany with a view to having talks with some of the religious leaders, both of the Protestant and of the Catholic Churches. Many others like myself believe that they cannot really be in possession of the facts, which are far more accessible to people *outside* Germany. Failing nobody better, I have at last come to the conclusion that I had better have a try myself. I therefore intend visiting Germany in a fortnight's time.[1]

The bishop responded with interest, but warned her that her visit was unlikely to succeed in stirring up opinion in Germany because of the political repression there:

I was talking to a German Pastor who has been spending the week-end in this house about conditions in Germany, and the possibility of getting information – not about concentration camps but about other matters, if a few Englishmen were to go with a particular purpose – and he said that people are extraordinarily unwilling to give information, as the externals and the internals are so often so different, and people are very very reserved. So I confess to being dubious as to the amount of information you will obtain, or even expression of opinion, from people whom you are meeting for the first time.[2]

He did however recommend her to the Anglican Chaplain in Berlin, Roland Cragg,[3] and sent her a letter of introduction.[4] Dorothy's intentions were very clear, 'The object of my visit is not so much as to gain information about the Camps etc, as I feel I have this very fully, but rather to try and impart it to some of the religious leaders, who in all probability know very little about the conditions of prisoners.'[5]

---

1. Dorothy to George Bell, 31 January 1935, Bell 7, Item 63-64, LPL.
2. George Bell to Dorothy, 4 February 1935, Bell 7, Item 69, LPL.
3. Roland Herbert Cragg (1882–1951). He later became a Canon of Gibraltar Cathedral and ended his clerical career as Vicar of St Peter's, Tandridge, in Surrey. He was a chaplain at St George's Anglican Church in Berlin in the early 1930s. The day after Hitler's appointment as Chancellor in January 1933, it was said a waiter approached Cragg at his table and said: 'Heil Hitler! What would you like for breakfast?'! Cragg quickly replied: 'God save the King! Bacon and eggs.' This anecdote was retold in Vernon McKenzie, *Through Turbulent Years*, McBride & Co, New York, 1938, p, 42.
4. George Bell to Roland H. Cragg, 6 February 1935, Bell 7, Item 73, LPL; enclosed with George Bell to Dorothy, Bell 7, Item 72, LPL.
5. Dorothy to George Bell, 5 February 1935, Bell 7, Item 70-71, LPL.

It was somewhat presumptuous of Dorothy to assume that the leaders of the churches in Germany were unaware of the illegal and repressive actions of their own government and it seemed not to have occurred to her how threatening it would be for Germans to talk to foreigners, especially those who would write about their experiences once home. Charlie tried in vain to persuade Dorothy of the inadvisability of the trip, but she was immovable. As he put it to his son, Dorothy, 'absolutely resolved that she must go to Germany to stir up the leaders of the Churches (especially the protestant dissentients) about political prisoners. I thought it a wild goose chase, but what was to be done?'.[1] In the end, he decided he had to accompany her.[2] Perhaps her determination had been strengthened because she had persuaded Fanny to arrange a meeting for her with Göring himself. Fanny assumed Dorothy wanted to see her brother-in-law in order to have a friendly conversation, encouraging to both sides. Dorothy's intention was very different.

She was clearly nervous about the trip. First, they went to Cologne, where she met some people who gave her a letter of introduction to Cardinal Faulhaber[3] of Munich, so she and Charlie travelled on there. Then calamity struck – she suffered an epileptic fit in her hotel room, which meant in her own phrase she was 'in very bad form'.[4] Charlie described it to David, 'on the first morning after arriving in Munich,

---

1. Charlie to David, 5 March 1935, BFA.
2. Bunsen 160-161. Charlie noted to his son, 'Either Mosa, or I, must go too. I decided to go myself, as having more power to prevent the wildest excesses of "overdoing it" – also I felt I should certainly incidentally learn a good deal.' Charlie to David, 5 March 1935, BFA. Charlie did not agree with Dorothy's emphasis. He thought the regime's anti-Semitism was a more serious problem than the horrors of prison camps. Ironically, it was the concentration camps that would develop into the most sinister locations for the horrific mass murder of Jewish people. (In this respect, Dorothy proved more prophetic than her husband.) 'I was really *mis*representing my own attitude. I agree that the persecution of political prisoners is horrible, & that though M[ummie] may here & there exaggerate, the facts remain abominable. But this business doesn't occupy the same place in my perspective as in hers – but a much smaller place. The avowed distortion of the Courts of Justice, & the avowed racial discriminations, are far worse to me than "atrocities". And even taking all that into account, I am still for closer relations with the German state, better understanding, cordial cooperation, etc. etc. general political grounds. The danger they are said to be to world peace, I regard as much exaggerated, tho[ugh] I abominate their dictatorship.' Charlie to David, 10 March 1935, BFA.
3. Michael von Faulhaber (1869–1952), Archbishop of Munich 1917–52.
4. 'My visit to Germany was less useful than it might have been because I had one of my collapses within 2 days of arriving there, & this impaired my efficiency for the whole time.' Dorothy to David, no date but almost certainly March 1935, BFA.

occurred an "attack". Fortunately in a comfortable pension. But oh! You can imagine my feelings. My worst anticipations realised.'[1] Everything then fell on Charlie's shoulders:

> As I was bound to be back within a fortnight, & wouldn't hear of M[ummie] staying on alone (which of course she urged) I was in the unpleasant situation of having to work like a slave to arrange interviews as rapidly as possible – & at a time when in *my* opinion she ought still to have been in bed, she was undertaking unique & exceptional efforts, struggling against failure of memory & a general sense of dazedness. Anybody else would have thrown up the sponge. It was an amazing – & indeed inspiring example of sticking to a task in the face of odds. She did manage to go through with it, without giving the impression of being all at sea. . . .
>
> The thing was rendered more of a struggle from my point of view by the fact that I had to do endless telephoning in a foreign language – & at the same time being discreet, because all telephone conversations are tapped by the Geheime Staatspolizei – known for short as 'Gestapo' – that the telephone was on a different floor to ours, & I was perpetually dashing down in the middle of meals – & finally that M[ummie] couldn't remember an engagement very often, & I had to be telling it over again. All this was more or less external, but the psychical strain of carrying on under these conditions made it anything but pleasant.[2]

Dorothy was not able to see Faulhaber, only the Dean of the cathedral in Munich. Then it was on to Berlin to see Confessional Church leaders, including Praeses Koch,[3] but he was the only Protestant leader who would engage with her concerns. 'Apart from Praeses Koch, I cannot say I received much encouragement from the Confessional Church. Herr Diestel,[4] for instance, seemed perfectly satisfied that Camps and Prisons are not the business of the Church, and he did not seem the least concerned at what I tried to tell him.'[5]

The interview with Göring proved pointless. Charlie had accompanied her as far as the door, but then she was on her own. She called it 'one of the most unpleasant episodes in my life!'[6] They spent half an hour together,

1. Charlie to David, 5 March 1935, BFA.
2. Charlie to David, 10 March 1935, BFA.
3. (Jakob Emil) Karl Koch (1876–1951), one of the leaders of the Confessing Church, President (Praeses) of the Westphalian Synod.
4. Max Diestel (1872–1949).
5. Dorothy's report on her visit, 2 March 1935, copy in BFA and also Bell 7, Item 111-114, LPL.
6. Dorothy to David, no date but almost certainly March 1935, BFA.

but he would not listen to her concerns (predictably) and harangued her for most of the meeting, denying the veracity of the information she had. She was upset to find he took so much pleasure from those in Britain who were sympathetic to Nazism. This made her realise that the German government did notice what was said in other countries about them:

> I had half an hour's talk with him, or rather he talked at me for most of the half hour, and at any rate made every show of not believing what I had to tell him, either as to the evils of the Camps etc., or the bad effect the knowledge of it made on English opinion. The best I can hope is that perhaps what he heard from me may carry more weight with him when similar evidence may reach him from other quarters; and everything possible should certainly be done to get other people to try and interview him too.[1]

When the Countess Wilamowitz-Moellendorf heard about the interview, she was indignant.[2] There is no evidence Fanny contacted Dorothy again. Charlie tried to put a positive gloss on the encounter. 'The Göring interview was a heroic affair. From what I can hear, it's the first time the tyrant has been told the truth to his face – & by a woman too! He was evidently perfectly furious – & a regular brute anyhow.'[3]

Dorothy arrived home from her trip on 1 March 1935 and saw Bell personally in the middle of the month. She continued to send him and other bishops material that she received from her German contacts, as well as articles she wrote.[4] The correspondence file in the Buxton papers has letters from many bishops, theologians and theological college principals thanking her for what she had sent them. She published material as well.[5]

---

1. Dorothy's report on her visit, 2 March 1935, copy in BFA and also Bell 7, Item 111-114, LPL.
2. On a photograph of the Countess in the BFA, dated 1921, Dorothy wrote after 1935: 'She gave me the introduction to Goering – but didn't realise my *object*! . . . When I met her in Berlin in 1935 she was acting as [a] *lecturer* for *Nazis throughout Germany*! & thought I intended to get tips & encouragement from him!!'
3. Charlie to David, 10 March 1935, BFA.
4. Her own collection of materials was given to LPL in 1961, Geoffrey Bill (Librarian) to Dorothy, 10 July 1961, BFA. The papers are catalogued as Buxton MS 2551-MS 2555, LPL. They consist principally of items relating to the persecution of the churches in German, the persecution of the Jews and of statements by Nazi leaders on these matters. Many are her translations of German texts.
5. For example, An English Protestant [Dorothy Buxton], *The Church Struggle in Germany: A Survey of Four Years, March 1933–July 1937*, Kulturkampf Association, London, [1937]. A second enlarged edition was produced later.

Dorothy in 1935

Dorothy had perhaps learned some of the limits of her influence from her February 1935 trip, but she did come away with the belief that she had to challenge those who were giving the Nazis 'the benefit of the doubt'. She would do her best to take away Göring's self-satisfaction over his British 'supporters'. One of her targets was the Bishop of Gloucester, Arthur Headlam.[1] He was the chair of the Church of England's Foreign Relations Committee 1933–45. One reason he was given this role was because he was a leading Anglican participant in the ecumenical contacts that had increased after the First World War. As a consequence, his considerable range of contacts included many German Protestant leaders. After the rise of Hitler, he supported the Nazi-created Protestant Reich Church and was critical of the breakaway Confessing Church. Dorothy wrote to him on several occasions either asking him to use his contacts or else to push him to justify his position on German matters. In March 1937, for example, she asked him to intervene after the supposed 'suicide' of Friedrich Weissler,[2] a lawyer who had acted for the Confessing Church.[3] Dorothy was convinced, and we now know she was right, that Weissler had been killed at Sachsenhausen concentration camp. He had been taken there some months after his detention by the Gestapo (German police) for supposedly leaking to the foreign press a Confessing Church memorandum critical of the Nazi regime. He was tortured for nearly a week before he died on 19 February 1937. Although he was an evangelical Christian, baptised

1. Arthur Cayley Headlam (1862–1947), Regius Professor of Divinity, University of Oxford, 1918–23, Bishop of Gloucester 1923–45.
2. Friedrich Wiessler (1891–1937). He was dismissed as a judge soon after the Nazis took power and then became a leading lawyer working for the opposition and for the executive of the Confessing Church. He was arrested on 7 October 1936 and taken to the concentration camp the following February where he was murdered.
3. Dorothy to Arthur Headlam, 1 March 1937, Headlam MS 2643, Item 209, LPL.

as a child, his parents were Jews. It was almost certainly this Jewish ethnicity that was a significant factor in his murder as the non-Jews arrested with him were eventually released.

Dorothy's letter to Bishop Headlam prompted him to write to his German contacts and she thanked him in a subsequent letter sending him further material to read. Whether Headlam's intervention helped save the lives of the other detainees cannot be established. What can be stated is that Headlam was given evidence by Dorothy that his lenient attitude to Nazi Germany was not justified by the information coming out of Germany at the time. When Headlam wrote a preface to a book in mid-1937 indicating that he believed things were improving in Germany, that police interference had ceased and Christians had greater freedom, she quickly wrote to question him:

> I am puzzled as to the meaning you must attach to the term 'freedom of the Church'. The severity of the *regular* restrictions on the Church press, public meetings, etc has not been diminished, but increased, since 1935. Last year no less than three Theological Seminaries were closed by the Police. I have beside me lists of names of Pastors in prison or in Concentration Camps; lists of others not allowed to preach. The events of the last few days simply represent a more open and drastic stage in the persecution which has gone on without cessation. · · · ·
>
> There is no doubt that Hitler is anxious for the good opinion of the leaders of the Church of England, and some authorities believe that in the past this has acted as a restraining influence upon him. Your Preface may now, I fear, have been taken to mean that the Church of England accepts the National-Socialist meaning of 'freedom' as applied to Church affairs. In the Führer's mind, and in the minds of Herr Kerrl, Dr Fabricius, etc., there is nothing inconsistent between 'freedom' and the use of force against those who refuse to allow the control of the Church to pass into the hands of persons who repudiate the divinity of Christ, (Herr Kerrl himself does so); who advocate the persecution of Jews and who encourage the circulation of a degraded, obscene paper (the *Stürmer*) which week by week must serve as an indictment to the grossest acts of brutality. · · · ·
>
> May I beg you, my dear Bishop, to use your undoubted powers of influence with authorities in Germany, that the persecution may be mitigated?[1]

---

1. Dorothy to Arthur Headlam, 17 June 1937, Headlam MS 2643, Item 238, LPL.

Headlam did not respond. Dorothy in full passionate form in this letter confronted Headlam with the truth of the matter just as she had Göring two years before. She then tried to organise a joint letter from all the bishops of the Church of England to *The Times* to support the Confessing Church. She felt the one place from which she ought to receive strong support was from Christian leaders in Britain who should surely speak out for the harassed leaders of other churches?[1] To her shock, most of the bishops refused to sign, those that gave a reason stating that they had not followed the arguments among German Protestants and were therefore too unfamiliar with the issues to make a judgement. George Bell, Bishop of Chichester, refused to sign the letter (and advised others not to do) because he felt the tone of Dorothy's letter was so emotional that it could do more harm than good.[2] The Church of England bishops were mostly not pacifists, but they generally supported the British government's policy of 'appeasement' of Germany in the mid to late 1930s, believing that once Germany had reunited all German-speaking people in one state, the territorial ambitions of Hitler would be sated. So the annexations of Austria and the Sudentenland of Czechoslavakia in 1938 were acceptable adjustments to Europe's borders in the minds of those who supported 'appeasement'.

Dorothy could only feel exasperation at this benign and naïve interpretation, about which she could do very little. She would ensure, however, that any blatant 'white-washing' of German policy would not go unchallenged. When Headlam – the most 'pro-appeasement' of all the bishops – visited Germany in the middle of 1938, he returned and wrote a benign account of his ten days there, refuting those Anglican clergy who were standing up for the Confessing Church. Headlam insisted the German clergy were free to do their work. He insisted that there were only arrests of those who used the pulpit for political purposes. Such pastors had 'broken the law' and could be free if they refrained from politics. He felt British church people should encourage the Confessing Church to rejoin the Nazi-controlled Reich church. His final argument was that for

---

1. By 1939, Dorothy would finally accept that she had to stop fretting about Anglican bishops: 'I would do well to take them more coolly. There are *very* few from whom I have had any real satisfaction. In any case I feel more independent of them now as I am gradually getting more recognised as an authority.' Dorothy to David, 9 March 1939, BFA.

2. Owen Chadwick, 'The English Bishops and the Nazis', in *Friends of Lambeth Palace, Annual Report 1973*, pp. 10–11, quoting letters in Bell 9, LPL. The letter was finally published with a very few episcopal signatures in *The Times* on 20 December 1937. The bishops of Bristol, Chelmsford, St Edmundsbury & Ipswich, Lichfield and Salisbury signed, plus H. Martyn Gooch, a prominent member of the Evangelical Alliance. The Archbishop of York sent a separate letter of his own published in the newspaper the same day.

many Germans the Nazis had brought 'order and self-respect and good government'. He urged people to understand the regime and abstain from continuous scolding.[1]

The letter produced a debate with correspondents both for and against. The Bishop of Gloucester wrote again and advised that it was 'wise' to be 'courteous even to dictators' and again said the Confessing Church should refrain from criticising the Nazis.[2] His third letter, to respond to his critics, deplored the anti-Nazi resolutions passed at church congresses:

> What I want to suggest is a more excellent way. . . . Would it not be wiser and more Christian if we were to attempt to show good will instead of indulging in a continuous and often unfair criticism, which seems so often dictated by political animosity, and is expressed in language which is neither diplomatic nor charitable?[3]

Dorothy wrote in response the same day and her letter was published the following week, 'Some of us who have devoted a great part of our lives to working for friendship with Germany and can look back to the time when it was far less popular to do so than it is now, can feel nothing but deep surprise and pain at the Bishop of Gloucester's letter.' She went on to point out that he had contacts with the 'official' Germany and not the Germans who were suffering and whose voices were muzzled. They were hidden from British travellers. She went on to warn, 'To speak the truth in Germany may land the speaker in a concentration camp. But if the British people fail to realize the truth it will again be the case that one catastrophe will lead to another.'[4]

The importance of this exchange is that it serves as an illustration of the denial amongst some senior clergy of the reality of the Nazi regime. It will appear extraordinary given all that we know now of what went on in Germany in the years 1933–45, yet such attitudes were not uncommon, especially given the British government's political appeasement of Germany. It also demonstrates Dorothy's courage, persistence and energy in the face of what she considered collusion with evil forces.[5] It would be easy to dismiss her activities as mere gestures that achieved very little. Yet, none of the people concerned could claim in years to come that they 'did not know'

---

1. *The Times,* 14 July 1938.
2. *The Times,* 20 July 1938.
3. *The Times,* 6 August 1938.
4. *The Times,* 10 August 1938.
5. For another treatment of this campaign of Dorothy's, see 'Church and Politics: Dorothy Buxton and the German Church Struggle', in Keith Robbins, *History, Religion and identity in Modern Britain,* Hambledon Press, London, 1993, pp. 183–194.

or had not been provided with the facts. Just as she had in the First World War, Dorothy had sought to publicise political activity as it was. If she had displayed a blind spot in her early writings on the Soviet Union, the same cannot be said about her work on Nazi Germany.

She published a small book in 1938, a translation of a set of letters and extracts from letters written by German pastors from their prison cells.[1] It was reprinted four times in the first five months after initial publication. As the influx of Jewish refugees from Germany began to increase, she countered those who would not welcome the innocent victims of anti-Semitism by co-authoring a book that tried to demolish the argument that refugees were an economic burden.[2] She called on the government to help the private charities working in this area.

Whilst Dorothy had become a campaigner and lobbyist for the oppressed, she had distanced herself from specific party politics. Through the 1930s, however, Charlie had remained working for the Labour Party. He had re-entered parliament in 1929, successfully fighting the Yorkshire seat of Elland in the general election.[3] The Labour Party formed its second administration afterwards, being the largest party, and some thought Charlie might be selected for a government post. However, Prime Minister Macdonald remained cautious as, like in 1924, he was dependent on Liberal MPs for a majority in the House of Commons. Charlie, whilst liked as a person by many on different sides of the political spectrum, was thought perhaps too 'left-wing' to be a 'safe' choice as, for example, Colonial Secretary. So he was left on the back benches in parliament. He continued to inform policy on foreign and colonial affairs and went on several long trips, including to some of the British territories in Africa.[4]

1. Dorothy F. Buxton (editor), *I was in Prison: Letters from German Pastors*, SCM Press, London, 1938.

2. Norman Angell and Dorothy Frances Buxton, *You and the Refugee: The Morals and Economics of the Problem*, Penguin, Harmondsworth, 1939.

3. 1929 May general election, Elland (electorate 46,499), 83.6% turnout: C. Roden Buxton (Labour) 17,012 (43.7%); Sam Howard (Conservative) 11,150 (28.7%), William Haughton Sessions (Liberal) 10,734 (27.6%) Labour majority 5,862 (15.0%). This had been the Liberal seat of his old friend Charles Trevelyan in the years before the First World War. Trevelyan had decided to sit as an independent MP in 1915, but came a poor fourth in the 1918 general election behind the three main parties. The Coalition Conservative had won that time in a tight contest. However, the seat was natural Labour Party territory and had been won by their candidate in 1924. Nevertheless, as that MP was retiring in 1929, Charlie had been chosen as the new candidate.

4. Charlie went to eastern Africa on a three-month trip in 1932, leaving Britain in late May, with two weeks in Lisbon (1–13 June), then Ceuta (15 June), Palma (Majorca) (18 June), Port Said (23 June) before setting off through the Suez Canal

The financial crisis of the summer of 1931 led to Ramsey Macdonald forming a coalition 'national' government with the other parties – to an outcry from most of his Labour parliamentary party. In the subsequent general election, the 'national' government (made up mainly of Conservatives) won a huge majority and most Labour MPs including Charlie were defeated.[1] He would never sit as an MP again. He did fight one last election – in Elland once more – in 1935, slashing his opponent's majority considerably, but was still unsuccessful.[2] Dorothy had little involvement in these campaigns.

Dorothy's politics had evolved in the 1930s from idealistic socialism in the 1920s to being a trenchant campaigner for any 'underdog' whose cause to her was righteous. She wanted to be a voice for the persecuted, whether Jews, refugees, prisoners or any other distressed group. In her early discussions with Charlie during their courtship, he had defended the need for political parties whilst she had argued for none. As she grew older, party affiliation meant less and less to her. What mattered to her were causes and individuals in need of support and she was never short of issues to raise and so letters to write and articles to publish. Her lobbying and writing were therefore unremitting. It was 'her work' and she would never shirk it.

For Charlie, however, the political and Westminster world was his milieu. As the 1930s went on, his Labour Party colleagues began to question positions that Charlie held as sacrosanct. For Charlie, the need for peace was paramount – nothing could be achieved for the poor or the oppressed if there were wars raging. He therefore believed that a deal with Hitler was preferable to another war. The Labour Party, however, lost its pacifist leader George Lansbury[3] in 1935 after a savage attack at the party conference by Trade Union leader Ernest Bevin[4] on this issue. By 1937, all the main

(27 June). He arrived in Mombasa, Kenya (11 July), and then travelled through Kenya and Uganda for six weeks, leaving Mombasa for home on 5 September. He reached London at the end of September. He went to western Africa, principally to the Gold Coast (now Ghana) in 1934, setting out on 26 September and returning on 23 November.

1. 1931 October general election, Elland (electorate 47,210), 82.5% turnout: Thomas Levy (Conservative) 25,378 (65.2%); C. Roden Buxton (Labour) 13,563 (34.8%); Conservative majority 11,815 (30.4%).

2. 1935 November general election, Elland (electorate 48,396), 77.2% turnout: Thomas Levy (Conservative) 19,498 (52.2%); C. Roden Buxton (Labour) 17,856 (47.8%); Conservative majority 1,642 (4.4%).

3. George Lansbury (1859–1940), Labour MP for Bromley and Bow 1910–12, 1922–40, Leader of the Labour Party 1932–35.

4. Ernest Bevin (1881–1951), General Secretary of the Transport and General Workers' Union 1922–45, Labour MP for Wandsworth Central 1940–50 and for Woolwich East 1950–51.

members of the Advisory Committees had come to believe rearmament was a necessary evil. Charlie could not agree and resigned the chairmanship of ACIQ. There seemed to be nowhere for him to go in the face of the Nazi threat and almost inevitable war. He could not accept the fact that Hitler was not going to keep to an agreement unless it suited him. Unfortunately, there was no political deal of any lasting worth available in the late 1930s. However, Charlie could never quite bring himself to believe that. He had entered a political cul-de-sac, unable to go forward, unwilling to go back. The truth of what was happening left him feeling drained and depressed.

Dorothy was more realistic – and was more optimistic as a result. She had no false hopes about the Nazi regime, nor had she any solutions to the threat that hovered over Europe. What she knew was that she had to keep seeking the truth and publicising it. She had never feared the truth, as she reflected in a letter after the Second World War broke out:

> I have . . . often experienced a satisfaction which seemed rather *queer* to me, in getting to know *the facts – however ugly* they might be in themselves. The reason for it is no doubt the sense one gains of putting one[']s theories to the test – of again reviewing one['] s *Weltanschaung* [philosophy of life] in the light of everything that turns up – in the light of the *worst* as well as the best that this world[']s experience can give.

Being under pressure and living in uncertain times made her appreciate life and all its joys. Instead of being depressed she felt exhilarated and life had a meaning, 'But anyhow for the present, & allowing for the possibility of . . . disasters, I nonetheless feel *more* alive, *more* able to appreciate common things, & aware of a certain *new* source of inspiration & stimulus deriving from the sense of the tremendous nature of present upheavals & disruptions.'[1]

The deteriorating international situation of the 1930s left her and Charlie then with the same serious questions, but in very different moods. How were they to react to the outbreak of another world war?

---

1. Dorothy to David, 28 January 1941, BFA.

Chapter 9
To face loss again

The year 1939 did not begin well for Dorothy as she suffered another 'episode' in January and she had to take a fortnight's holiday in mid-February at a friend's cottage near Harlech in Wales.[1] Further, although the formal declarations that began the Second World War for Britain did not happen until 3 September 1939, in the years leading up to them, conflict and aggression pointed to the events to come: the Japanese invaded parts of China in 1937; the Germans intensified their internal war against their own Jewish citizens particularly from November 1938 onwards; in 1938 they also marched into Austria and the remaining territory of Czechoslovakia a year later; the Italians invaded Albania in April 1939 (after their annexation of Ethiopia in 1936); and the fighting in the three-year Spanish Civil War did not end until March 1939. All these situations produced a number of refugees and much suffering, both of which intensified once the Second World War began. Thus, despite health issues, Dorothy was determined to continue lobbying for Jewish and other refugees and for the Confessing Church in Germany as in her view, it seemed the world was already at war: 'One can[']t be as careful & prudent as one w[ou]ld *like* to be when there is *war* going on; and apart from all the wars (Spain is unspeakable), in the received sense the situation in Germany really amounts to a *war*, of a new species, but a real war in most of its features.'[2]

For Dorothy, war was about the conflict between good and evil. Those who were religious and 'spiritual', who thought there was reason to love and be charitable in the creation, were opposed to those who loved power and saw destruction and force as the way to seize and maintain it. Declarations of war were legalities: the struggle had already begun. Despite her unusual theological views, Dorothy unquestionably lined up with the forces of faith against godless ideologies. The Nazis and the Communists alike

1. Dorothy to David, 2 February 1939, BFA.
2. Dorothy to David, 2 February 1939, BFA.

were attacking religion and trying to destroy faith. That Germany and the Soviet Union signed a pact in August 1939 was not a surprise to her for the ideologies had much in common in methodology if not in ultimate aims.

Anti-Semitism was evil and for her it was an attack on all religion. Her article in the May 1939 edition of the monthly publication of the Student Christian Movement contained the kernel of her argument and appeal. Addressing a Christian audience, she put this in religious terms as a response to the barbarity of anti-Semitism:

> For one thing it was not sufficiently realised that that the attack on the Jews meant equally an attack on Christianity. There is hardly an aspect of Christianity which is not directly and bitterly challenged by the new Religion of Race intended to replace it. . . . To the protagonists of this faith all ideas of the spiritual world, as taught by Christ, and the cult of love and the gentler virtues appear simply as foolishness and weakness. . . .
>
> The attack upon Christianity can only be met by a reassertion of Christian truth at some of the points where the attack is most fierce. The spirit which denies any worth or rights to certain human beings on account of their 'blood'. . . . can only be overcome by the spirit which opens the door to them, and is ready to share all things with them in the name of Christ. For the awful outpouring of hatred there can only be one remedy, i.e., the active demonstration of the opposite.[1]

Dorothy, believing the war had already started, agitated for government spending on refugees and felt she was contributing vigourously in the battle for the soul of Europe especially. She continued to publish documents on the struggle of the German Church much as she had through the 1930s.[2] She had wanted to hold the Nazis to account since 1934, which resulted in a divergence of political opinion with her husband. Her love of Germany meant she wished to see Germany freed from Nazism; Charlie's resulted in him stubbornly wanting to cooperate with the Hitler regime, despite his despising it:

> M[ummie] & I have much controversy over the question whether a conciliatory policy towards Germany should be pursued or not. She would (I think) admit that it should, but thinks that on *every* occasion we should say 'your government is bad, & we shall not do

---

1. *The Student Movement*, Vol XLI, No 8 (May 1939), pp. 200–202.
2. Dorothy F. Buxton, *Christendom on Trial: Documents of the German Church Struggle 1938–29*, Friends of Europe, London, [1940]. Dorothy's foreword is dated December 1939.

this or that until you reform it.' In my opinion, in the rough & ready ways of diplomacy, you have to *ride one horse or the other*. If you are not *broadly* friendly, you will be broadly hostile & cooperate more constantly with avowed enemies of Germany. There it is. Besides, what strengthens Hitler *most* is *to have legitimate grievances*.[1]

Dorothy was not Charlie's only opposition: as early as 1935, his sister, Victoria, also argued with him and he felt himself sometimes under feminine attack:

> I'm concerned (like everybody else) about Germany. People are getting nervy & fanatical. Many things Hitler does or allows are enough to make them so. But I insist on distinguishing between the internal condition of Germany, which is horrible, and their position in international relations. I still think it is necessary to keep on reminding people of the Versailles Treaty: they forget how atrocious it was, & what its consequences have been. 'We' prophesied that it *must* bring its Nemesis. We are paying the price of it now. I don't think there is anything they are doing which we should not have done in their case. (I mean *vis-à-vis* foreign countries.) In arguing with the females, I find the real issue between us seems to be – is Hitler a man *you can deal with*? I still contend that he is. The characteristically *English* thing at times like this is to keep our heads & remain objective. I altogether refuse to think that war is inevitable.[2]

In March 1939, he acknowledged a shift might be needed in his view. When the Nazis took over the remaining territory of Czechoslovakia in March 1939, he wrote a confidential memorandum for the Labour parliamentarians saying that 'everybody must be prepared to *revise their opinions*, however deep their convictions may be'. He admitted that 'an unresisted Hitler domination' might now be worse than a world war as Hitler might be 'insane'. Nevertheless, he still insisted his approach had been 'perfectly right' until that point. He also wanted to seize the first opportunity of resuming a policy of negotiation and conciliation, if such a chance arose.[3]

He clung to this view and soon returned to his belief in the possibility of an agreement. Dorothy had to watch as her husband became obsessed with stopping any outbreak of fighting involving British troops. He was

1. Charlie to David, 26 June 1935, BFA.
2. Charlie to David, 4 May 1935, BFA.
3. Charlie, memorandum on the international situation, 17 and 24 March 1939, copy in BFA.

convinced a deal could be done with Hitler, something Dorothy not only felt was impossible, but would also be immoral as it would give the Nazis free rein to continue their inhuman policies. For many months in 1939, Charlie travelled backwards and forwards in Europe to try and broker an agreement. It was all in vain; politicians or officials he met believed either that it would not be to their country's advantage or else that such a deal was not possible even if it were. Many listened to the earnest pacifist without altering their opinion. One trip in June/July 1939 took him to Berlin (23 June), then Danzig (28 June), Warsaw (30 June) and Katowice (3 July) in Poland, Breslau (5 July) and then back to Berlin (8 July).[1] He did not find it easy: 'each interview, each journey (especially flying!) each new country, etc looms up in prospect as an unbearable burden in which one may completely make a mess of it'.[2]

It cannot have helped his morale that Dorothy was not at all sympathetic to his actions or his point of view.[3] His last trip was in late August and he only just managed to leave Germany before the Nazis invaded Poland. Even back in Britain, he had interviews at the German Embassy and, astonishingly, tried to put forward a secret plan to give 'spheres of influence' in Europe to the Nazis and other powers.[4] It was all reminiscent of the language and methods of the pre-1914 diplomatic world that he had always so deplored. But such was his desperation to avoid war that, whilst being true to his principles, he had lost his political judgement. He was now the emotional idealist and Dorothy the more realistic partner in the political arena.

The outbreak of the Second World War broke him. His sister expressed it as 'an impenetrable darkness' descending on the world for him.[5] Dorothy said it was a 'sword to his heart'.[6] He continued, as his health permitted, to represent his view that a negotiated settlement was still possible. This included giving speeches at public meetings in the autumn of 1939. He resigned his non-salaried role as Parliamentary Adviser to the Labour Party in a letter to the party leader of 29 September 1939, although remaining a member of the party.[7] He did this because most Labour members of both Houses had no more sympathy with his view of a 'deal' with the

1. Charlie to Dorothy, 24 June 1939 and 26 June 1939, BFA.
2. Charlie to Dorothy, 26 June 1939, BFA. Charlie was so distracted that he put '1938' as the year for this letter, but it was undoubtedly from 1939 because of the content.
3. Bunsen, pp. 158–159.
4. For a fuller treatment of this story, see Wright, pp. 346–348.
5. Bunsen, p. 165.
6. 'knowing all he did, & *had* known for so long, & his sensitiveness to all the horrors, – it was a sword to his heart'. Dorothy to David, 17 December 1942, BFA.
7. Bunsen, p. 163.

Charlie in July 1942

Nazis than Dorothy did and official Labour Party policy reflected this. He wanted to be free to advocate for what he believed. In years to come, his fruitless pursuit of the politically impossible because of his principles would be admired, yet pitied as hopelessly naive.[1]

Charlie was sixty-four in the November after the war broke out, but he was already looking frail and old beyond his years. In the press, he was described as 'tall, thin, stooping and bespectacled'.[2] He had a persistent cough and was noted for his frequent need to put a handkerchief to his mouth. He had suffered digestive problems for twenty years,[3] regularly causing worry to his family,[4] and had tried many remedies, even giving up his beloved cup of coffee. However, he did not take the one step that might have improved his general health considerably: to stop smoking cigarettes, cigars and puffing his pipe. Medical science only began to establish firmly the link between smoking and lung disease in the years immediately after the Second World War.[5] Charlie smoked a great deal and, given how one of his lungs had already been irrevocably damaged by a bullet in 1914, this was a habit that was life-threatening.[6] In the spring of

1. When his sister's biography of him was published in 1948, one reviewer noted that 'Victorian idealists' like Charlie were 'at once the glory and the embarrassment of our public life'. *Aberdeen Press and Journal,* 19 June 1948.
2. *Lancashire Evening Post,* 31 October 1939.
3. Bunsen, p. 140.
4. For example, Eglantyne to Charlie 19 January 1928, Box 14, 7EJB/B/02/09, WL. '*Your relations & friends* keep telling you that you do not look very well. Perhaps it is only the worn appearance of middle age & incessant work on very little food, & may not matter at all. But you would make us all much happier if you would consent to be thoroughly overhauled by some expert. This could not possibly do any harm; & it might do some good.'
5. As early as 1912, smoking was seen as one possible cause in the increasing cases of lung cancer (once a very rare disease), but the first definitive study did not emerge until 1939 (Munich) and in Britain post-1945.
6. The family did not realise the danger. David bought him a fancy cigarette case for Christmas 1940, Charlie to David, 26 December 1940, BFA. Eglantyne gave him

1940, he suffered a prolonged chest infection, thought at the time to be a type of influenza, and that left him permanently weaker.[1] By this time, his public life was over.

The autumn of 1939 has been sometimes referred to as the 'phoney war' because there was comparatively little fighting in that period that affected the British population. Many children so hastily evacuated from urban centres in the early part of September 1939 returned to their families at Christmastime and stayed put. The attack by the Nazis on the Low Countries and France in May 1940, alongside the start of intensive bombing raids on London and other cities, meant the war became far more disruptive for British citizens. When the bombing of London began in earnest during the 'Blitz' of 1940, the Buxtons made the scullery at 6 Erskine Hill into their 'bomb shelter' as required, but they 'kept calm and carried on' as the contemporary slogans encouraged.

> The siren for the warning here just resumed its screech. . . . and we don't take very much notice, though this doesn't mean that we haven't worked out everything & adapted a regular routine. We continue sitting in the garden or inside – or lying in bed if at night – until there is an indication of something relatively near, when we resort to the scullery. I lost count of the warnings yesterday, there were so many.[2]

Dorothy was alarmed that (in her absence) Mosa (Charlie's secretary) had approved a hole being cut in the beech hedge in their garden to allow the neighbours to come quickly from their house to share the Buxtons' makeshift shelter. She fretted about whether the hedge would ever grow properly again![3] However, the scullery did become a necessity for them all on 30 August 1940, when a house nearby was demolished by enemy action. When 12 Erskine Hill was burnt out by an incendiary bomb,[4] Dorothy realised that she had to move Charlie to a quieter, safer place. Eglantyne and Charlie, however, did not want to move. 'You may wonder why we don't go away somewhere. The fact is the whole thing is such a gamble – you *may* (or may not) get into trouble anywhere. And the arguments against are considerable. Eglantyne is strongly opposed.'

Charlie particularly valued living near his sister, Victoria, who visited him most days, and his brother Noel, who came regularly too. Both he and Dorothy were also concerned not to leave Florence and her daughter behind. Any scheme for moving had to involve them as well, especially

cigars for his birthday in November 1941, Charlie to David, 29 November 1941, BFA.
1. Bunsen, p. 165.
2. Charlie to David, 1 September 1940, BFA.
3. Charlie to David, [no day] May 1940, BFA.
4. Charlie to David, no date, but headed 'Humours of Erskine Hill', BFA.

as the Hawkins women were 'very good companions, & sociability is promoted'.[1] Dorothy was however determined to reside somewhere else and take the whole household with her – and her view prevailed. Very soon after therefore, Charlie wrote that a scheme to move was in mind.[2]

The three Buxtons, Florence and her daughter, a temporary secretary (a Danish woman called Mrs Larsen) and the housekeeper's cat ('Old Nin') arrived at The Lyth in rural Shropshire on 26 September 1940. Dorothy's brother (Dick Jebb) had agreed to them moving there for a while; but at the door, Charlie was bemused to find that Ethel (Dick's wife) had two 'prohibitions': no foreigners and no cats. Charlie used all his diplomatic skills to find a solution and Ethel eventually relented about the Danish secretary, but Old Nin was despatched to an outhouse. Charlie noted with amusement that it was the first time he had ever known people hate cats more than foreigners.[3] Meanwhile the Erskine Hill house was used by refugees as it had been in the First World War.[4] In the event, The Lyth proved too remote for the family to bear, far from contacts and the political milieu which was so important to Dorothy and Charlie. Consequently, they soon moved again and went to Peaslake in Surrey.[5] Eglantyne had already made moves to buy a house there (Whingate) from her friends the Rinders, something in negotiation before they left London.[6] For a short time, Charlie and Dorothy lodged with Mosa Anderson and her mother at Charlton Cottage as Whingate was having alterations.[7] In December 1940, Eglantyne welcomed the whole household to live with her at Whingate. This was not an arrangement without some ongoing tension, but at least the house belonged to the daughter and the parents were sufficiently sensitive enough to understand they were guests. Eglantyne was gracious – even allowing them to bring a huge desk, which Charlie had originally given to his sister Victoria on her wedding in 1904. She now lent it back to

---

1. Charlie to David, 1 September 1940, BFA.
2. Charlie to David, 11 September 1940, BFA.
3. Charlie to David, no date, but headed 'Humours of Erskine Hill', BFA.
4. From 1941 to 1953, it was put at the disposal of the German pastor and congregation of St Mary-le-Savoy's Lutheran Church (located in Sandwich Street) and became a vicarage and centre for their work. Gerhard Puritz (Chair of the St Mary's Lutheran Church Council) to Dorothy, 3 November 1953, BFA. The Lutheran Church of St Mary is still operating from Sandwich Street in 2016.
5. According to Charlie the move from The Lyth was to be expedited on 7 November 1940, Charlie to David, 29 October 1940, BFA.
6. Charlie to David, 1 September 1940, BFA, in which Charlie notes that the 'new house' had been 'virtually acquired' although 'there may be slips even now'.
7. Conversation with Victoria Houghton, 4 January 2007. Eglantyne junior to David, 22 November 1940, BFA.

him, but, once it had been manoeuvred with great difficulty into the 'back-sitting room', Charlie insisted it be used 'solely' by his wife.[1] The days of desks made from orange boxes and planks of wood were over for Dorothy.

Purchasing the house had been an act of independence for Eglantyne and part of her may have aspired to be separate from her parents. Yet, in practice she was not yet ready to live alone and Dorothy and Charlie brought the comfort of a housekeeper, Florence, with them. Dorothy would also be a tremendous asset in helping transform the garden. Arranging the house and garden to her own designs was a stimulating occupation for Eglantyne and her parents, it seems, were careful not to interfere, but instead were supportive, 'All continues to go well. I really think Eglantyne is getting something profound & permanent out of her absorption in the house and, still more, the garden.'[2]

Their son David was in contrast a world away from them. After graduating with a natural sciences degree from Cambridge, he had sought a career overseas using his knowledge and training as an entomologist. He went to advise on the growing of crops in British colonies in Africa, especially with respect to the problems caused by insects and pests such as locusts. He went first to east Africa, leaving on 19 November 1933. His mother and sister faked cheerfulness until the taxi, taking him to begin his journey south, drove away from 6 Erskine Hill when they were left feeling bereft. For Dorothy, the house was empty with her son gone[3] and there was little chance of a visit home for some time. One of the bright spots of 1939 for her was, therefore, David coming back for a 'furlough' or extended leave, something all colonial civil servants were entitled to do on a cyclical basis every few years. Whilst back in London, he met through his sister, Eglantyne,[4] a vivacious young woman, Annelore Albers, and a romance quickly developed. Many men who came back on 'furlough' realised that this was their opportunity to 'find a wife',[5] even if only subconsciously, and

1. Charlie to David, 26 December 1940, BFA, and Dorothy to David, 4 February 1941, BFA.
2. Charlie to David, 21 May 1941, BFA. Later Charlie would write, 'E[glantyne] is getting real pleasure, I think, out of the garden – unable to deny that her labours, (& much more, M[ummie]'s, of course) have gone far to make the place a delight. . . . She is so ingenious – she planted a row of Iceland poppies, so that, looking from the veranda, you see it against the apple-green shadows of the stems of the orchard.' Charlie to David, 24 June 1942, BFA.
3. Dorothy to David, 25 November 1922, BFA.
4. 'Eglantyne had a great share in bringing you and Annelore together. Perhaps the whole idea of this marriage was initiated by her.' Arnold Gerstl to David, 4 February/10 March 1945, copy in BFA.
5. Before his first three-yearly leave at the end of 1936, his father had written to him: 'I feel you ought to take advantage of your time at home to get more society – Your range was necessarily very limited in East Africa. I especially refer to marriageable women. . . . You have your own openings, but I don't know if you've exploited them

David in 1942

David, with his return to Africa looming, must have realised that he either had to propose marriage to his new girlfriend or else let her go. His next leave would not be for a number of years – even more given the threat of world war – and his opportunities to meet eligible young women where he worked were few. So, he proposed marriage and the young Annelore accepted. She was nineteen, a decade younger than him. She had arrived in Britain from Germany in 1934 aged fourteen with her mother and step-father, the family fleeing the Nazis. Her stepfather, Arnold Gerstl, (whose surname she sometimes used) was Jewish and originally a Czech citizen from Prague, who had served as an officer in the Austro-Hungarian army during the First World War. After 1918, he had worked in Germany. He was a talented artist,[1] in the German Expressionist school, whose most prized paintings are of figures in both oils and watercolours. Gretel, his wife, ten years younger, was a dressmaker and designer. They had established themselves in London and, at this time, lodged in a house in England's Lane, a street in the Belsize Park area, with a friend called Hilda Smith.[2] In the summer of 1939 the Gerstl family became naturalised British citizens.

---

enough. Then it is also legitimate to take full advantage of any openings that *we* can provide through our acquaintance.' Charlie to David, 7 November 1936, BFA. David travelled home via visits to Germany and Czechoslovakia.

1. Works by Arnold Gerstl (1888–1957) can be seen in the New Walk Museum and Art Gallery in Leicester, including perhaps his most famous painting: 'The Violinists'. One of the works housed there is a pencil drawing that Gerstl did of David in the summer of 1939. He also painted a portrait of Dorothy in 1940, Charlie to David, [no day] May 1940, BFA. This portrait is kept at Newnham College, Cambridge.

2. Hilda Mabel Smith (1890–1976). In 1958, she married Sidney A. Bill (1884–1964). Hilda moved from London early in the Second World War to a flat on Instow's seafront in north Devon. The Gerstls moved to a bungalow near Torrington in north Devon at the same time.

For Dorothy, her son's quick romance must have come as something of a shock. It would be hard for any devoted mother to judge a young woman as 'good enough' for her son and Dorothy could not escape that tendency. However, her criteria for any future daughter-in-law were somewhat different to the average mother's. In some ways, Annelore's background was not a matter for Dorothy's concern. She loved Germans and was very sympathetic to the Jews. These facts about David's choice only worried her from the point of view of a couple taking time to build an innate sympathy. The speed of the decision seemed unwise to her as she was aware that coming from different cultures more time would have been needed for the two to be able to understand each other fully. What was more immediately important to Dorothy was that David's future wife should, if possible, share some of her interests and her politics – above all her seriousness about life. She preferred no frivolousness or lapses into 'bourgeois pre-occupations'. Annelore was serious enough to pursue study at the London School of Economics, which was a plus for Dorothy, but the young woman also liked fashion and style,[1] interests that held no value in Dorothy's eyes and which she had suppressed in her own daughter. Therefore, when Annelore arrived for the first meeting at 6 Erskine Hill in red high-heeled shoes, the housekeeper's daughter (an eagle-eyed thirteen-year old) remembered a distinct frostiness descended on proceedings. The young woman was far more than her colourful shoes, but it was not the best way to make a first impression on the abstemious Dorothy.[2]

No written remarks on Dorothy's initial reaction to Annelore have survived in the Buxton archives, but there is a record of an earlier maternal reaction on a similar theme, for Dorothy had not found it easy to like David's first female friend, when he was an undergraduate at Cambridge, a young woman called Hilda. On their meeting she had found her too 'modern':

> She is v[ery] interesting to talk to but I don't feel I know the least
> *where I am with her*. . . . She is of a very modern *type* with wh[ich]
> so far I have had little opportunity of direct contact. The fact that

---

1. 'She is a true Eve, & loves pretty things and jewels especially . . . . ' Hilda Smith to David, 10 December 1944, copy in BFA.
2. Charlie was in continental Europe for much of the summer of 1939 so he may not have been present on this occasion. His own initial views on Annelore have not been recorded, but later he would write to a cousin, 'I'm so glad you are in touch with David & Annelore. She is a *dear* – we love her.' Charlie to Clarence, 25 October 1942, BFA. Annelore seemed to like Dorothy and Charlie: 'Darling, I have got such nice parents-in-law! I hope I shall never disappoint them. . . . ' Annelore to David, 8 February 1940, copy in BFA.

her outlook on some of the things wh[ich] mean most to me, is different, *need* not create a barrier, but it naturally calls for a greater effort in understanding & adjustment than with people between whom a great deal can be taken for granted.

The young woman had lent David the novel by D.H. Lawrence called *Women in Love*, as well as James Joyce's *Ulysses*. This upset Dorothy as she disapproved of such 'modern' literature. She had not read the books herself, but judged them from reviews and commentators she had seen:

> Those books contain a glorification of the physical wh[ich] to me is *evil* because it is incompatible with giving to the spiritual the place wh[ich] is required for man's higher development & therefore for his most real happiness. . . .
>
> It is the glorification of the physical wh[ich] leads to the practise of 'free love'. I am very glad that you can tell me that Hilda is *not* in agreement. . . .
>
> I am also so glad to know from you that altho[ugh] your friendship is so intimate (& I suppose you are fond of each other to the degree wh[ich] some people anyhow w[ou]ld call being 'in love') you have no intention of marriage. My chief reason for this is that I think marriage between people of different nationality, highly different upbringing, traditions, environment etc are extremely risky. All these factors create deep seated differences in the *subconscious*, wh[ich] only come to the surface as life goes on & at times especially of particular stresses & strains, just when a deep[-] seated sympathy is the most specially required. There is a vast amount wh[ich] we tend to *take for granted* in people, quite unconsciously. This applies to all loves & friendships & one sees in it the rocks on wh[ich] no end of relationships split. The risk is least with persons who have emanated from fairly similar worlds, & in all cases it is *reduced* by a long engagement.[1]

The friendship with Hilda did not progress much further as a romance, but it did reveal Dorothy's attitudes towards her son being romantically involved. It might be judged unlikely that Dorothy's approach would differ very much eight years later as she weighed up David's choice of bride. Annelore was of a different background and experience to David and for his mother it should have suggested, at least, a 'long engagement', which was clearly not possible under the circumstances. Whatever the parental doubts, the young couple married in September 1939 and, after a brief

---

1. Dorothy to David, 25 May 1931, BFA.

David & Annelore in Sierra Leone

honeymoon at the Thors Hill Hotel in Haslemere, David set off for Sierra Leone, where his latest posting was. Annelore stayed on in London, studying for her economics degree at LSE, an institution which for a time was evacuated to Cambridge. By spring 1940, however, she missed her new husband too much and did not feel confident about taking examinations,[1] so she decided to put the studies on hold and join David overseas. She managed to take the last possible ship to join her husband, arriving in Freetown, Sierra Leone, in mid-1940.[2] Dorothy would not see them again until the end of the war.

Dorothy and Charlie settled down at Peaslake the following winter as Charlie's condition deteriorated bit by bit. They loved the garden, as well as the house and what Dorothy termed 'congenial' neighbours[3] – which almost certainly meant in 'Dorothy-speak' that they were friendly, but not over-attentive, and they would not call round uninvited, thereby 'interrupting her work'![4] The housekeeper, Florence, was with them to

1. Annelore to David, 8 February 1940, copy in BFA.
2. Charlie to David, 24 July 1940, BFA.
3. Dorothy to David & Annelore, 17 December 1942, BFA.
4. Dorothy wrote for example: 'I suppose for the majority of mankind a social hurly burly in home life is amusing & welcome. But personally I simply can[']t stand too much company. I soon get to the point when I feel about human beings: "Well, on the whole I like *birds* best – if not *beetles*!" That is nonsense of course, but reflects a mood which readily asserts itself & becomes acute.' Dorothy to David, 8 April

care for their household needs, and her teenage daughter, too, who had finished school and eventually went on to study at Guildford Technical College.

The doctors began to think Charlie had tuberculosis, as well as pleurisy. His cough, however, they insisted was from the 'stomach troubles' that had plagued him for years and were the reason for his increased emaciation. Early in December 1942, an X-ray was taken that revealed that the real cause of his symptoms was lung cancer and he had probably had this for at least six months. As there was little that could be done, he was not removed to hospital, but Dorothy kept him at home so he could die there, although she did not reveal to him the actual diagnosis.

Dorothy had to do more and more for Charlie as his health declined, and she did almost all of the nursing herself until three weeks before he died. They enjoyed each other's company, regularly reading to each other and discussing issues. He still followed politics. His devoted secretary, Mosa Anderson, was able to visit most days, and she read to him from *The Times* and *The Manchester Guardian*.[1] Charlie turned also to his first love: classics and literature. He had written and published in 1929 a book of essays on literary topics from Shakespeare's comedies to the 'meaning' of poetry.[2] In 1940–42, he began writing a book on four great poets – Virgil, Dante, Milton and Goethe – a study he was to call 'Prophets of Heaven and Hell'. He managed to distract his mind entirely when working on this book and was, thereby, able to push aside his misery at his declining physical condition.[3] Dorothy did all she could to support him in this and in 1941–42, she did not go away for more than a day or two at a time as she did not like to leave him.[4]

Charlie's 'greatest joy for a long time past' was the news of the birth of his grandson, Roden, in July 1942. Annelore and David had moved on from Sierra Leone to Nigeria,[5] but in late 1941 they had taken some leave in South Africa. There Annelore found herself pregnant and returning to a bush house in Nigeria seemed inappropriate. She therefore stayed on in South Africa, whilst David returned to his posting, with the intention of

---

1943, BFA.

1. Charlie to David, 2 May 1942, BFA.
2. Charles Roden Buxton, *A Politician plays Truant: Essays in English Literature*, Christophers, London, 1929.
3. Charlie to David, 2 May 1942, BFA.
4. Dorothy to David, 8 April 1943, BFA.
5. The exigencies of war had meant David was at times seconded to non-scientific jobs like working in the customs office and standing in for a few weeks as head teacher at a school.

returning to join her later in 1942 when a longer leave was due.[1] In May, however, David learned he was to be seconded to Abysinnia (Ethiopia), recently liberated from the Italians, and so he visited Annelore in June in Grahamstown before travelling on to his new job. Left alone once again, Annelore gave birth and it was a considerable time before David saw his son. The three eventually met up in Kenya at the end of 1942[2] at the home of a cousin (Clarence Buxton),[3] David taking leave until the end of January. Annelore then joined him early in April 1943 in Addis Ababa, capital of Ethiopia.[4]

On 15 December 1942, photographs of Roden arrived in the post, sent by Annelore, and gave Charlie 'real delight'. One of baby Roden with a 'determined look upon his face' and his 'little fist clenched' especially pleased him 'and he exclaimed: "Oh! What an infant Hercules!"'[5] He had visitors[6] later that day and then Mosa read to him. Dorothy spent the evening reading some of Emily Brontë's *Wuthering Heights* aloud, and they discussed it until after 9p.m. As had become her custom, she rose at

1. The original plan was for her to stay in South Africa for two years. Annelore to David, 25 February [1942], copy in BFA.
2. David noted that he arrived late (a few days after Christmas) because of transport problems, David to Dorothy, 3 January 1943, BFA.
3. Clarence Edward Victor Buxton (1892–1967) was one of the sons of Charlie's older brother Sir Victor Buxton (1865–1919). His father had bought a farm in Kenya in 1902 and Clarence first went there in 1912. After service in the First World War, where he attained the rank of Major, he returned to Kenya and lived there for the rest of his life. He worked in the Colonial Service as well from 1919–40, serving as a District Commissioner and at one time acting Provincial Commissioner.
4. David had arrived there in March 1943, having travelled 1700 miles by road from Nairobi, setting out on 1 February, whilst Annelore was delayed by travel complications before arriving by plane early in April. Dorothy to David, 5 March 1943 and 8 April 1943, BFA.
5. Dorothy to David & Annelore, 17 December 1942, BFA.
6. One was 'Linnet' Howell, a cousin: Rosalind Howell, née Buxton (1879–1968), widow of Brigadier-General Philip Howell (1877–1916). She lived in Upshire in Essex, not far from Charlie's sister, Victoria de Bunsen. The other visitor was Arthur Rinder (1885–1958). Rinder was one of Eglantyne's few friends, a painter of flowers and landscapes, with whom she used to share singing practice. A bachelor, he lived locally with his unmarried sister Winifred (1882–1965). It was the Rinder siblings who lived in Whingate before Eglantyne bought it. In 1939, realising the war would prevent the 1941 census being planned and executed, the government produced a hasty 'register' like a mini-census. This did not have the 100-year rule on it like regular censuses and so is available online with those born less than 100 years ago blocked out. In the September 1939 Register the Rinders had a German-born Jewish refugee, the contralto Herta Gluckmann (later Cohen), staying with them. She sang concerts during 1939 to raise funds for other refugees.

4 a.m. on 16 December to check on him and, if required, give him a hot drink with a sleeping tablet. She found him coughing and speaking in 'a strange incoherent way'. He slipped into unconsciousness just before 6 a.m. Dorothy summoned the nurse who had been helping out for the previous three weeks and she arrived half an hour later. Charlie died peacefully about 6.50 a.m. He was sixty-seven.

On the outside, Dorothy took the loss of her soul mate with great equanimity. The housekeeper's daughter remembered clearly that Dorothy came into her bedroom to wake her that morning. She calmly and gently told her of 'Mr Buxton's passing' without any tears or emotional drama.[1] Dorothy had suffered to see him so ill and in many ways Charlie's death was in her mind a release. She wrote to her son, David, who had been told the news via a telegram sent by his sister Eglantyne, that he should not be worried for her. She noted how happy she and Charlie had been for thirty-eight and a half years and that they 'had "fought the good fight" in unity of mind & purpose'. Charlie had made her life 'most rich & blessed'. Her only shading to this was her fear that 'his public work' was 'little recognised', although she could not believe its value would be 'really lost'.[2] Her daughter Eglantyne was more openly anguished, the housekeeper noting that she had completely broken down when first she heard the news.[3] Dorothy wrote that the shock of the death had affected her daughter 'physically'.[4] She noted that Eglantyne had borne up well at first, but then the effects of the shock were 'very marked'. 'To be roused from her sleep to have a last look at her father before he passed from us for ever – on this plane – could not be anything but a severe shock.'[5]

The funeral was swiftly arranged for 18 December at the Anglican parish church in Peaslake. The local clergyman[6] was most accommodating and he suggested that the service should include a Quaker silence and that a Quaker should give the eulogy. The speaker chosen was Corder Catchpool.[7]

---

1. Conversation with Victoria Houghton, 4 January 2007.
2. Dorothy to David & Annelore, 17 December 1942, BFA.
3. Florence to David, 21 January 1943, BFA.
4. Dorothy to David, 13 January 1943, BFA.
5. Dorothy to David, no date as first page missing, but from early Spring 1943, BFA.
6. John Edward Penney (1912–98), Curate in charge of Peaslake 1938–43. He left Peaslake soon afterwards, in January 1943, to become Vicar of St Paul's, South Harrow.
7. Thomas 'Corder' Pettifor Catchpool (1883–1952) was a leading Quaker in relief campaigns, especially in Germany after both World Wars. He had been imprisoned for conscientious objection in the First World War. Whilst based in Berlin 1931–36, he worked for victims of Nazi oppression after Hitler came to power, suffering at one point arrest and detention by the Gestapo. In the 1950s, he died in a

He described Charlie as the 'perfect type of Christian gentleman' who had brought his religion of life into politics.[1] The lesson was read by Dr Harold Moody,[2] who ran the League of Coloured Peoples. The burial was at the cemetery high on the hillside to which the funeral procession walked. Close family and friends from London attended, but the war made travel difficult and so many who would have liked to have attended could not: indeed Dorothy discouraged them, especially with arranging the funeral so swiftly. Dorothy received over 250 letters and replied personally to them all,[3] some of them amusing her, as alongside those praising his political work, others commended him for accomplishments, such as 'fearlessness of leadership in the hunting field'.[4] She insisted she was 'surprised at her own cheerfulness' and she was 'really happy', the chief reason being 'my conviction as to life in another plane is *so vivid*. She declared that the funeral service had not upset her at all.[5]

Behind the public façade, however, Dorothy was not as composed. We do have another witness, close at hand, in Florence Hawkins, the housekeeper. She had proved a stalwart support through Charlie's illness as Eglantyne wrote to David. She had kept everyone supplied with comforting cups of tea, arranged the flowers on the coffin, and coped with many of the questions put by the undertakers so as to save Dorothy any upset.[6] Florence wrote of Dorothy that, 'The first few days I found her on more than one occasion just bowed down with grief.'[7] Even as late as May she wrote again about Dorothy, 'She seldom shows her grief, but I can see how much she missed Mr. Buxton. . . . I see her sometimes walking in the garden at night-fall, with her head uplifted and I know of whom she is thinking.'[8] In May 1943, six months after his death, Charlie's things were still 'lying around': pipes in the bedroom, coat in the hall, razor strop in the

---

mountaineering accident.

1. *Surrey Advertiser*, 26 December 1942.
2. Harold Arundel Moody (1882–1947). He was a medical doctor, who had trained in London in the Edwardian period, but as a black Jamaican had faced racial discrimination and so had had to set up his own practice in Peckham, London. He founded the League of Coloured Peoples in 1931 to campaign for racial equality. Dorothy wrote that Moody 'read the lesson in a superb way – *such* a wonderful voice, & such conviction – as if the thoughts were his own'. Dorothy to David, 28 December 1942, BFA.
3. Eglantyne junior to David, 10 February 1943, BFA.
4. Dorothy to David, 13 January 1943, BFA. The compliment came from one of Charlie's friends from his Devon period when he had been part of the local hunt.
5. Dorothy to David, 28 December 1942, BFA.
6. Eglantyne junior to David, 10 February 1943, BFA.
7. Florence to David, 21 January 1943, BFA.
8. Florence to David, 3 May 1943, BFA.

bathroom. Dorothy was convinced he was still there. In early April 1943, she awoke suddenly one day because she heard Charlie calling out to her, 'It sounded so vigorous, cheerful & eager. I suppose nearly everyone would say I *dreamt* it. But I had not been dreaming anything whatsoever; & it seemed loud enough to cause me to wake. I think he hit on this way of letting me know he was there.'[1]

To cope with her inner grief, Dorothy returned to gardening, particularly digging manure into the vegetable patch, which she tried to do for one hour every day.[2] She laughed at herself as a 'land girl' at the age of sixty-two.[3] Her other solace was her work. She started once again to go occasionally to gatherings: for example, in April 1943 to the annual conference in Leeds of regional refugee organisations, as she was a representative for her area of the country.[4] She went up to London regularly and stayed for the odd night at 6 Erskine Hill, though Florence noted that Dorothy always said she was pleased to return.[5] One significant initiative that stemmed from her refugee work was to do with those who were termed 'aliens', not being British citizens, and yet who wished to fight with British forces against the Nazis and Fascists who had so persecuted them and their loved ones. She corresponded with many of them. She systematically sent questionnaires to the relevant groups, analysed the responses and then sent requests based on this gathered information to government departments, MPs and the newspapers. She finally succeeded in convincing the relevant authorities and the way was cleared for these soldiers to participate in the armed forces. One writer on the refugee soldiers wrote that to the individual people involved, she 'restored a belief, threatened by frustration, in the honesty, fairplay and kindliness of the British people. She helped the War Office to understand the ways of the aliens, and the Pioneers to understand the ways of the British official. By 1943 most hesitations and misgivings were removed.' His overall judgement was that Dorothy was the 'most indefatigable of all the fighters for the alien'.[6]

Apart from this campaigning, one writing project that Dorothy felt was paramount was completing Charlie's book. He had wanted two chapters re-written and then there were parts not written at all. He had worried just before he died that he would never complete it, so Dorothy made an extraordinary offer:

1. Dorothy to David, 8 April, 1943, BFA.
2. Florence to David, 3 May 1943, BFA.
3. Dorothy to David, no date as first page missing, but from early spring 1943, BFA.
4. Dorothy to David, 8 April, 1943, BFA.
5. Florence to David, 3 May 1943, BFA.
6. Norman Bentwich, *I Understand the Risks: The Story of the Refugees from Nazi Oppression who Fought in the British Forces in World War,* Victor Gollancz, London, 1950, p. 73.

So I thought it over & the next day told him that I had decided
to give up my work for refugees & devote myself to helping him
to finish the book. He received this with real joy & brightened up
immensely. I myself of course had no idea that the end would come
so suddenly & I still hoped he might have intervals of feeling better
& be able to do something at the book.[1]

With Charlie's death, the task became much more difficult as Dorothy
was not a specialist in the area, but she did what she could from his notes.
Finally, in early October 1944, she sent the manuscript to Cambridge
University Press who accepted it for publication a week later.[2] The proofs
came back for checking in January[3] and it was published later in 1945.[4]

Once the book was essentially done, Charlie's literary work was complete
and Dorothy felt she no longer required the services of his devoted secretary,
Mosa. Her own work was very different to that of Charlie and so Dorothy
felt she did not require a 'political' secretary. She must have communicated
this decision with some abruptness because Mosa was deeply offended, as
Dorothy explained in a letter:

> I never thought it possible we should 'quarrel', but she seemed quite
> determined to quarrel with me. The cause of it lay in the awful shock
> to her when D[addy] died so suddenly. Her whole life had been
> bound up in the work she did for him & with him. For some years[,]
> she had hardly had anything to do with my work – which was on
> quite different lines to his, & not directly political. However[,] when
> I told her she must look for a new post she was terribly offended.
> No doubt I must have been at fault *in the way I did* it; – but there
> was no real cause for great offence as I was as fond of her & valued
> her as much as ever. I was quite bewildered by the way she treated
> me; – it seemed so out of keeping with her real self . . . the difficulty
> I mention blew over, & our relations now are as happy as ever.[5]

Although it appeared Dorothy retrieved the situation, her daughter
Eglantyne refused to do so, not even being civil, and so Mosa stayed away
from the house. Dorothy was in general a genial and smiling person to be
around, but she had no intuitive sense of how an 'announcement' might
hurt or shock someone else. Later in the same letter, she mused,

1. Dorothy to David, 3 February 1945, BFA.
2. Dorothy to David 29 October 1944, BFA.
3. Dorothy to David 14 January 1945, BFA.
4. Charles Roden Buxton, *Prophets of Heaven and Hell: Virgil, Dante, Milton, Goethe,
   An Introductory Essay*, CUP, Cambridge, 1945.
5. Dorothy to David, 17 March 1945, BFA.

I only tell you all these rather unpleasant facts because they illustrate the extraordinary difficulty of human relations, even between people of whom one would expect *the best*. Looking back[,] I feel as if I had been a child all my life in such matters, & have only recently acquired some glimmerings of knowledge.[1]

In one area of very great family sensitivity, however, she proved more understanding and behaved with greater diplomacy and feeling. In the summer of 1944, Dorothy was saddened to hear that Annelore had said she did not want to have any more children. Her stated reasons were simply that she had little support in Addis Ababa to care for one child let alone for another. There was no family there to back her up and David was regularly away for long stretches for his professional work.[2] Annelore had found it difficult to adjust to the altitude and climate, and then broke her ankle in a riding accident,[3] before suffering a bout of jaundice.[4] Although she built a social life in the Ethiopian capital and was very keen on riding, there was a considerable turnover of British personnel, which made it hard to establish longer-term friendships.[5] She taught English to both Ethiopians and non-British residents, helped at the library at

---

1. Dorothy to David, 17 March 1945, BFA.
2. The time he spends at home always seems so much shorter than the time he is away. Our life seems to consist of separations and reunions.' Annelore to Dorothy, 8 May 1944, copy in BFA. In 1943 for example, the couple were together in January in Kenya and then David returned to Ethiopia. Annelore finally joined him in early April in Addis Ababa. David was away from early May to late June working on the Somali border (David to Dorothy, 25 June 1943, BFA). After three weeks at home, he then set off on another trek to the south of the country (David to Dorothy, 5 July 1943, BFA). Late in July1943, he set off to Kenya to attend a conference on locusts in Nairobi and did not return until early September (David to Dorothy, 3 September 1943, BFA). He was then away for the seven weeks up to 25 November in the south of Ethiopia (David to Eglantyne junior, 6 December 1943). The couple therefore spent barely four months together in 1943. This was after spending almost all of 1942 apart, when even letters would take weeks to arrive. For example, David did not receive any letters from Annelore for many weeks and then nine arrived all together (David to Dorothy, 12 March 1942, BFA).
3. Annelore to Dorothy and Eglantyne junior, 18 February 1944, copy BFA.
4. Annelore to Dorothy, 26 July 1944, copy in BFA. Dorothy to David, 7 January 1945, BFA.
5. For example, in mid-1944, she noted, 'We do seem to lose a lot of friends.' She named Avis Bayley (who taught her to sew and whose husband worked for the Arabian Trading Company), Captain & Mrs Temple (he was chief of Addis Police and they lent Annelore horses to ride) and Hussey, an educational adviser, as people she had come to know well who were leaving Ethiopia soon. Annelore to Dorothy, 11 July 1944, copy in BFA.

the British Council and got involved with the local ex-pat community.[1] Another pregnancy would disrupt those contacts and make her more isolated.

Later in the year, David confided to his sister that the marriage was in difficulties in a broader sense too. He did not tell his mother initially, probably because he worried she might either write with a lofty 'I knew this would happen' approach or else bombard him with letters telling him what to do. When Eglantyne hinted at the difficulties, Dorothy did not respond in the way her son may have feared. In fact, her letters from December 1944 through to the spring of 1945 were full of wisdom and support. This was a very different Dorothy to the mother who had scolded and lectured him in his teens. Dorothy wrote to both Annelore and David through this period. In her first letter on the matter written on Christmas Day 1944, she immediately declared her neutrality:

> Egl[antyne] has not told me much; I do not even know whether you told her other relevant factors; I only know of some degree of rift, & (I presume) that the basis of it must be that A[nnelore]'s feelings for you are not quite what she herself had expected them to be – or to remain. For her too this situation must be one of pain & difficulty. Emotion of course is not obedient to the *will*, & the conflict *may* be really agonising.
>
> I will try to make A[nnelore] understand that whatever happens I shall not adopt a harsh attitude. I believe in that French saying (origin?) 'tout comprendre c'est tout pardonner'. [To understand all is to forgive all.] (In this truth science & religion definitely meet, & under the wing of the highest (completest) truth there need be no conflicting loyalties.) Therefore however urgently my sympathies are enlisted on your behalf, however much *easier* it is for me to see your side of the case than hers[,] I shall not cease to *try* & understand hers.[2]

In her next letter, she wisely noted that emotional life must not be allowed to overwhelm all else, especially a person's work. Keeping busy was an antidote to emotional misery:

> perhaps you are afraid of upsetting or worrying me[?] But, as I said in my last letter, you need have no fear of that sort. For a long time past life has seemed to me like a battlefield where one's

---

1. Annelore to Dorothy, 4 January 1944, 9 April 1944 and 8 May 1944, copies in BFA.
2. Dorothy to David, 25 December 1944, BFA.

job is to fight & struggle. Even tho[ugh] one's nearest & dearest comrades may fall by one's side[,] one's primary duty is to push on with the task one is called upon to do, & so one simply cannot & must not allow one[']s own working powers to be impaired by personal misfortune or grief. One may do a certain amount for the wounded friend but the major part of one[']s thought & energy must be devoted to fighting the battle in which the fate of countless other suffering human beings is involved. The fact that one[']s mind is then *perforce* so much occupied forbids one[']s own natural emotions gaining mastery over one. I never allow myself to *dwell* on sorrow, & find it a grievous mistake in some of my friends who seem to make a sort of cult of their own emotions – whether happy or unhappy![3]

In later letters, we can read Dorothy's take on 'modern' society. Despite her radicalism in politics, her views on personal life were quite conservative. She would never have called herself a 'feminist' and still clung to the traditional roles of men and women in society, despite her not having adhered exclusively to them in her own life. She worried that the emancipation of women had had the downside of weakening the 'maternal instinct' and detaching sexual intercourse from the desire to have children.[4] As she was not herself a woman who prioritised emotions, and because she had found an exceptional husband who encouraged her to have her own sphere of work, she failed to perceive how many women were 'trapped' by marriage. Issues explored in 'modern novels' were beyond her:

A[nnelore] is so *clever*, & also in some ways so mature for her years (she has had such hard experiences in childhood & adolescence) that one easily forgets how *young* she is. For one thing I am pretty sure that she fails to realise how terribly one[']s emotions get exaggerated & one[']s impatience etc[.] exacerbated under certain adverse physical conditions. She is not in a position to get *outside* herself, or to know how much of her present ideas & feelings belong to her more enduring self – are nearer related to the 'real' self. So I do greatly hope that you will be successful in getting her to come home [i.e., return to Britain].

I am sure she has been torn in two between her desire to be *sincere* & not to play a part, & reluctance to hurt someone so terribly whom she *does* love *in a sense*, tho[ugh] not apparently in the sense which marriage – to be at all ideal – requires. It has helped to

---

3. Dorothy to David, 31 December 1944, BFA.
4. Dorothy to David, 30 April 1945, BFA.

reduce her nerves to the state of tension when any degree of 'letting go' brings on a much worse explosion than the realities warrant. I have had some experience of how *quarrels work* – tho[ugh] not in my own family. . . .

We have to learn to forgive others & *also* ourselves. You are in the bottom of the pit just now but you may be certain, time will lead you out again, sooner perhaps than you would think possible.[1]

As in her political life her underlying argument was to accept life as it was, face the facts and try to understand why the events had happened:

I realise how difficult it must be for you to maintain any pleasure & interest in all these subjects of which you normally feel the attraction. I am certain however that it is most important to *go on* with your normal interests & occupations, however much it may all seem to have turned to ashes; & however difficult the effort of attention must be. In the end[,] you will come through much better if, by unremitting exercise of will, you can keep things going outwardly as near as possible as before. What you say about hardly knowing what you are doing or who you are makes one realise very vividly how shattering this business is for you, – how *awful* the shock of discovering how much had gone wrong. I think you share a trait which characterised myself & some members of my own family, & also Daddy to a strong degree, i.e. a capacity for interest in outside things, in literature, science, politics – or whatever it might be which gave us an independent & satisfying life apart from what the 'social world' has to offer. People of more usual type (especially among women) may or may not have such interests, but the central thing – the basic thing in life for them is found in human relationships; it is this which occupies their thoughts & claims their emotions to a degree which we of the other type find it hard to imagine. It is not that we are *lacking* in human feeling (it *may* be much stronger) but we do not in any way make a cult of our own emotions, nor do we study the emotional susceptibilities of other people, – it does not occur to us to be interested in them, & we are therefore hardly *aware* of them even. . . .

I suppose A[nnelore] feels that you do not & cannot understand her. That in itself of course is *not* a good reason for interrupting married life; it happens in a large proportion of cases; but *my* generation of women were brought up (for the most part) with the now 'old fashioned' idea that there was 'nothing to be done about

1. Dorothy to David, 11 February 1945, BFA.

it' (the marriage tie being 'sacred' etc etc), & countless women who found some degree of incompatibility with their husbands continued to have children & built up their happiness around *them*. But alas! the 'modern' young woman is so intensely self-conscious about her own susceptibilities & emotional reactions, & the trend of the times encourages her to take them *so seriously* that she gets caught in a net of her own fabrication from which escape is very difficult. *Till now* I have actually given extremely little thought to such matters at all (&, as you know, I never read the modern novels which make so much of the complexities of emotional life) but this may not necessarily prevent me now from seeing the broad lines of things fairly correctly, and I do think it is easier to *face* things, as well as perhaps to find some correctives for them, if one can see the *causes*: '*felix qui potuit rerum cognoscere causas* [Fortunate is the one who was able to know the causes of things].'[1]

Dorothy went to stay for three days with Annelore's mother and stepfather, who had moved from London to Devon early in the war, so as to hear their views of the matter.[2] Charlie's sister, Victoria, came with her husband for a week in early April and Dorothy confided in her about her son's marital situation (the only member of the wider family with whom she shared this information, as her sister-in-law was so 'knowledgeable' and 'sympathetic').[3]

Annelore, with little Roden, travelled back to Britain in April 1945 leaving David in Ethiopia. Arriving via Glasgow, she went first to Eglantyne and Dorothy for eleven days before going on to her parents in Devon. Dorothy was enchanted with her grandson, especially his curiosity about mechanical things. She also remained restrained and did not quiz her daughter-in-law:

I have been able to carry out my intention of behaving in a calm & natural manner with A[nnelore]. Before she leaves I will explain to her that I have avoided any direct discussion of what has happened, because it seemed to me best that she sh[ou]ld *first* have a period of quiet when she can review things calmly from a distance. I do not want her to feel that I am trying to force the pace of her decisions.[4]

Eventually, after David came home and it was decided he and Annelore would divorce, Dorothy felt she had to take her son's side out of loyalty to him. She decided to stop writing to her daughter-in-law, which was

1. Dorothy to David, 18 February 1945, BFA. The final quotation is from Virgil, *The Georgics*, Book 2.
2. Dorothy to David, 25 March 1945, BFA.
3. Dorothy to David, 1 April 1945, BFA.
4. Dorothy to David, 30 April 1945, BFA.

hurtful to Annelore,[1] but in the circumstances, may have been Dorothy's only choice if she were to demonstrate her support to her son. This phase did not last for long, however, and the two women became not only friendly, but would confide in each other in later years. Dorothy would write to Annelore as 'My dearest' and sign her letters with 'much love'.[2] They would also meet when Annelore took her son Roden to see his grandmother.[3]

Throughout this family crisis, the war in Europe had been drawing to a close. Dorothy was irritated that she had been ignored in the 1930s and yet now the government was showing even children the horrors of the concentration camps in cinema newsreel:

> To me it is difficult to avoid some rather bitter thoughts when I remember my visit to Goering just 10 years ago to protest about the Concentration Camps & to warn him of the menace they might be to *Anglo-British* [*sic*, she meant Anglo-German] *relations*; – & the failure I experienced both before & after that visit to arouse *any* extensive or acute interest in the horrors (the *same* as those revealed now tho[ugh] not yet on so large a scale); & the refusal of the F[oreign] O[ffice] to do anything but pigeonhole the atrocity stories with which I provided them until years later when some of them appeared in the White Paper issued for propaganda purposes just after war was declared. And now every cinema in the country has the horrors of the camps on the News Reel & they serve to convince the whole population not only that the Germans are a sub human people, but that the refugees here, being 'German' too – cannot be tolerated!! – & this even tho[ugh] 9 out of 10 are Jewish.[4]

She wrote letters off to newspapers and longed to be able to act for the displaced and hungry. She felt the whole situation was different from 1918 and a private organisation like SCF was 'practically disallowed'. It was, she

---

1. 'Your mother does not write any more to Annelore. Whatever her motive is, it expresses enmity, punishment and all the other negative things. That is certainly wrong. In the future it will make things more or less difficult. Perhaps Dorothy will not be able to change her attitude but I think it a duty to mention it. . . . I admire Dorothy deeply and I hope she will see things not so one-sided & intolerant.' Arnold Gerstl to David, 4 February/10 March 1945, copy in BFA.
2. Dorothy to Annelore, undated letters but from the late 1950s or early 1960s, BFA.
3. Annelore would take Roden to visit with his grandmother, leaving him there for part of a day. Conversation with Roden Buxton, 28 January 2017.
4. Dorothy to David, 19 May 1945, BFA.

bemoaned, 'actually illegal to send food abroad'.[1] 'How I wish I could start a brand new SCF! But private enterprise is very much shackled. . . . One is not even allowed to give one[']s personal *rations* away.'![2]

The Second World War was a time of change for Dorothy, not just that her beloved husband had died, but that she had found a way of being more settled in herself. She had been brought up in a world where an individual with contacts and funds would have the confidence to intervene and believe she or he could make a difference. The translation work in the First World War and with the SCF had been her supreme efforts. But the world changed after 1918 as people saw power and influence achieved more through organisations and mass movements, whether of the political right or left, instead of through individual action. So, even as the individual became more important with the development of psychology and in areas such as advertising and the arts, in the political arena the power resided in groups. In dictatorships, the forced involvement of the masses in staged rallies and party organisations ensured most people gained their political identity from a group, not their own thinking. In such a society, the individual could only make an impact as the head of a powerful movement. Dorothy, however, continued to operate with the old assumptions even in the 1930s, for example in thinking she could influence Göring through a half-hour conversation. She had found that she could make little effect. By 1945, we see in her personal and public life, a greater acceptance of her limitations and that a gentler, less abrasive, side of her nature had developed.

---

1. Dorothy to David, 11 March 1945, BFA.
2. Dorothy to David, 15 April 1945, BFA.

Chapter 10
Obedient to the end

When David finally arrived home from Ethiopia on leave in 1946, he was gratified that his mother came to meet him at Guildford railway station, before taking the bus with him back to Peaslake. However, he was dismayed when, given his absence of seven years, she said that coming to meet him meant she had 'sacrificed' a day's work! Dorothy was, in her own style, telling him how important it was to her that he had come home, so important that she would neglect her work so as to greet him in person. He did not quite interpret it in that way. The exchange, however, captured in a small incident how seriously Dorothy still took her lobbying activities.

From 1945, she continued to campaign for those she felt neglected or maltreated in the aftermath of the war. The hungry and destitute were a major concern as they had been after the First World War. German refugees from eastern Europe had flooded the zones of Germany controlled by the Americans, British and French, fearing the reprisals of the Russian troops, who (rightly or wrongly) had a reputation for being ruthless, even cruel, to the German populace. Many who fled the Russian Red Army arrived in Berlin, the German capital, which had been separately zoned whilst geographically an island in the 'Russian zone'. It therefore became a magnet for refugees. The majority of those who fled were women and children. Dorothy wrote for the Save the Children Fund magazine to support the case for feeding the hungry, especially the innocent children.[1] She was concerned that the facts of the situation in Germany were being hidden from the British public:

> We believe that if the truth were fairly put, instead of being served up in a *réchauffé* of wartime propaganda, the majority of British people would shrink from imposing torture and death upon thousands of

---

1. Article in *The World's Children*, February 1946.

*Dorothy in 1946, a photograph she chose herself
to go with her 1946 Christmas card*

women and children. Many would also see the importance that, in
the eyes of Germans, the rule of our Democracy should compare
favourably with that of Germany under the Nazis.[1]

She was particularly incensed by those who felt that the Germans should
be 'punished' through depriving them of food. This 'revenge' mentality had
been the huge mistake of 1918–19. As one who had tried to live on meagre
rations as an experiment, she insisted hunger did not help 'clear thinking':

Certainly if I was a German mother condemned to the torture
of helplessly watching my children weaken and droop, I should
find it hard not to hate the government and the democracy that
I believed to be responsible for this situation; and it would be a

---

1. Letter to *The New Statesman and Nation*, published 30 March 1946.

bitter, unquenchable hatred . . . good sense and judgement would tend to give place, under the ordeal of continued hunger, to blind resentment and extremist views.[1]

When so many were starving, Dorothy was appalled, too, that British consumers could refuse bread baked a day beforehand, judging it 'stale' and believing it needed to be thrown away – although she would insist on buying such so-called 'stale' bread and found it perfectly edible. British consumers were rationed, but still had the 2,650 calories required for health every day. She contrasted this with the provision of 1,050 calories for German citizens in the British zone of occupied Germany. Indeed, she also noted that in the French zone, the allowance could fall to 800 calories, the equivalent of the allowance given by the Nazi authorities for concentration camp victims in Belsen. As a consequence, reports showed that German children in 1946 already showed 'retarded or arrested development':

> As a student of food and famine problems ever since 1918, it is horrifying to me to find once more how many people manage to overlook such authoritative reports. . . . Instead they pounce eagerly on the light-hearted verdicts of travellers. . . . or visitors . . . who see no one dropping dead in the streets. Such sceptical observers overlook the elementary fact that people in advanced stages of weakness and disease shun the streets (if they can get there at all).[2]

She was particularly anguished that there was a ban on private individuals sending food parcels or money abroad.[3] The kind of action she had spearheaded in 1919 was in 1945 completely impossible because of government regulations. By October 1946, as a second post-war winter approached, she wrote to MPs and other officials,

> The cost in human suffering of the conditions we tolerate in Germany (and Austria) is unimaginable in this country. Such misery brings hatred and contempt upon ourselves and upon the 'democracy' we represent. What we are active in establishing are unemployment and despair. We must not forget that these are the same causes that brought Hitler into power.[4]

Many of the problems would be eased by the advent of the Marshall Plan which provided American financial aid to the shattered economies in

---

1. Letter to *The Spectator*, published 3 May 1946.
2. Article in *The Manchester Guardian*, published 5 July 1946, p. 314.
3. Letter to *The Spectator*, published 11 October 1946.
4. Dorothy, round-robin letter sent to MPs and others, 11 October 1946.

Europe to rebuild their industries and economic life that, in time, alleviated social deprivation. The Soviet Union and its allies refused the aid, but the western part of Germany did accept appropriate help. The Plan emerged from meetings in June 1947 and was implemented beginning the following year. Dorothy was one of the many voices who had (in the end, successfully) pleaded for the mistakes of 1918 onwards not to be repeated.

Another group of people for whom Dorothy campaigned was the large number of prisoners of war. The allied forces wanted to 'de-Nazify' the soldiers against whom they had fought, but the assessment programme to ascertain which enemy soldier was still a threat (that is, an 'unrepentant Nazi') was farcical, with individuals given interviews of just a few minutes each. Many judgements were made on the flimsiest of pretexts by untrained interviewers. The prisoners were used as labourers by the British government, digging sugar beet and potatoes, which smacked of exploitation. Most of these men wanted only to return home to help their families, but by the end of the summer of 1946, there were still 380,000 remaining in Britain and a further 100,000 in camps in the Middle East. The Repatriation Scheme announced in September 1946 did not satisfy critics such as Dorothy as it would take two years to implement in full. She wrote a long piece entitled 'Friends or Enemies?' for *The Spectator*[1] attacking the slow pace of repatriation and the counter-productive humiliations suffered by the prisoners, noting the plunging morale of the men concerned. The periodical published two letters from prisoners of war in a subsequent issue expressing gratitude that someone had so eloquently publicised their plight.[2]

Dorothy continued to lobby for Germany and the Germans for ten years after the Second World War ended. It led her to issues that might have seemed less mainstream. In 1948–50, she conducted a campaign to protect the forests in Germany.[3] The lack of coal and of fuel in general had led to a wholescale felling of trees, to provide both timber to export and fuel for winter heating, that in turn had led to the destruction of swathes of forest with minimal replanting. This led to soil erosion and problems for water supplies. She also wrote to defend German farmers in Tanganyika.[4] There were also the Germans being expelled from their homes in territory which by the early 1950s was part of Communist Poland.[5] She despaired

---

1. *The Spectator*, 20 December 1946, 667.
2. *The Spectator*, 3 January 1947, p. 14.
3. See for example: *The New Statesman and Nation*, 29 May 1948; *The Daily Telegraph* 16 April 1949; *The Spectator* 24 June 1949 and 15 July 1949.
4. *Contemporary Review*, December 1950.
5. Letter from Dorothy in *The Manchester Guardian*, 16 March 1950.

of the Soviet Union, disappointed that even after Stalin's death in 1953, only Stalin and not 'Stalinism' had 'been debunked'.[1] She saw Soviet policy as dangerous and racist, security issues being used fraudulently to excuse blatant anti-German prejudice. She resigned from the Union of Democratic Control in 1954, an organisation of which she had been a founding member (with Charlie) in 1914, believing that the UDC was influenced by pro-Soviet propaganda:

> I reject the U.D.C. perspective in which the West German Government is seen as a major danger and the Soviet power as pacific and harmless. . . .
>
> Essentially, it is the bane of our national self-righteousness which leads our people – including, alas, many U.D.C. members – to accept the shallow doctrine of Germany's sole responsibility for the World War, and to justify treatment of her as a nation inferior to ourselves – or at any rate to be held down.[2]

One of Dorothy's successful campaigns was for a particular group of refugees: German dentists. The new National Health Service was short of dentists, but the Ministry of Health would not employ Germans as they were judged not to have been trained sufficiently in the syllabus required in 1948 by newly-qualified dentists. Dorothy undertook a background investigation and established that many of the licenced National Health Service (NHS) dentists had themselves not been trained to that standard. In 1921, the British Medical Council had cleared over 6,500 dental technicians (trained simply to extract teeth and make dentures) to practise as fully-fledged dentists. This was because British dental treatment was of low standard in the aftermath of the First World War and removing teeth was considered the quickest, cheapest and most effective approach to dental problems. This was not the case in other nations such as the USA and Germany where the merits of saving as many teeth as possible was stressed. By the Second World War, British dentistry began to 'catch up' and the BMC redesigned their dental training to leave behind the crude 'extraction-first' policy. Whilst this improved British dentistry in the longer term, the dentists already granted registration were not required to improve and enhance their skills.

To Dorothy, the opportunity for the new NHS to employ dentists of German origin, who had had a much more sophisticated training in the 1920s and 1930s than British dentists had been given, was clearly advantageous. Despite most of the refugee dentists having had

1. Dorothy to the editor of *The Manchester Guardian*, 10 May 1956, copy in BFA.
2. Letter from Dorothy, *The New Statesman*, 10 July 1954,

several years of university training in their profession, unlike so many older British dentists, the BMC refused to licence them, claiming they could not show sufficient guarantee of competence.[1] Dorothy began to campaign and lobby with great energy. Eventually, in 1956, the government set up a General Dental Council, separate from the BMC, and this body allowed German dentists to practise in return for attending a 'refresher course'. Her intervention in this matter was clearly crucial as was recalled in 1961:

> In an admirable manner[,] she made herself familiar with the dental curriculum in this country and Germany and was capable of discussing these technically difficult points very well with professional administrators.
>
> The number of memoranda and interviews she succeeded in getting with Government officials including the Minister of the day, Members of Parliament and Peers is beyond belief. The statutory examination which finally settled the matter may partly be ascribed to [her] indefatigable efforts.[2]

Dorothy's defence of the German people, and her refusal to allow others to dismiss all Germans as 'Nazis' or as solely responsible for Europe's twentieth-century wars, did not go unnoticed by those who were striving to improve Germany's image in the post-war world. Soon after her seventh-fifth birthday, the German Embassy in London sent her warm greetings, 'I should like . . . to convey to you my sincere thanks for all the efforts you made during 40 years of your life for a better understanding of our two peoples.'[3] On her eightieth birthday, the ambassador sent her another letter, praising her 'outstanding work for friendship between our two countries and for humanity in general', and it was accompanied by a signed photograph of the German Chancellor, Konrad Adenauer. In her reply, she expressed both gratitude and astonishment. She went on,

---

1. For her full case, see letter (headed 'Shortage of dentists') from Dorothy in *Time and Tide*, 17 June 1950, p. 602.
2. Article by F. S. Salomon in the *Anglo-Continental Dental Society Newsletter*, Spring 1961, copy in BFA.
3. Hans Herwarth von Bittenfeld (German Ambassador) to Dorothy, 29 June 1956, BFA. The ambassador was then resident at 6 Princes Gate in London, in the same terrace that Charlie's parents had occupied a house (No 2) before the First World War and where Dorothy had visited them before her marriage in 1904. Hans Heinrich Herwarth von Bittenfeld (1904–99) was a member of the aristocratic German opposition to Hitler before the Second World War, passing information to the Western allies whilst serving as a German diplomat in Moscow.

It has always been clear to my late husband & to me that the tragedy of a second World War can be traced back to the follies of Versailles. To combat British ignorance regarding Anglo-German relations with all my powers – humble though they were – became to me a call of practical Christianity which has guided my life.[1]

By the age of eighty, Dorothy was somewhat hampered by failing sight and poor hearing. Indeed, even in the decade after the end of the Second World War, Dorothy had begun to feel the passing of the years. Late in 1949, she suffered a blockage in her intestine and an operation seemed essential, something which could well have been dangerous. Writing to David from Nightingale Ward in the Royal Surrey County Hospital, she suggested that, despite the emergency, he did not need to come back from overseas: 'It is best to preserve one's memory of a person as they normally were.' As for herself, she did not 'mind dying'.[2] At sixty-eight at the time of her operation, she had lived longer than her husband and considerably longer than her three sisters. In the event, the blockage disappeared of its own accord and no surgery was required.[3] Her normal routine was re-established – but it could not be indefinitely so.

By 1956, she wrote that 'eye trouble' had 'obliged her to give up the extensive reading which political work requires'.[4] In response, Dorothy realised she had to admit her lobbying days were behind her and in 1956, aged seventy-five, she decided to 'retire' from politics.[5] Her last letter to *The Manchester Guardian* was in support of refugees who had fled Poland. She took part in the demonstration on 22 April 1956 when 12,000 Polish and other exiles walked to the Cenotaph in Whitehall, after a Mass at Brompton Oratory, to protest against the visit of Russian leaders, including Nikita Krushchev.[6] She was moved by the occasion and her letter was full of fury at Communist Russia. Thereafter her voice went missing from the public arena.

She maintained concern for her family in its widest sense and more so as the years took away the last members of her generation of Jebbs. She tried to cheer her late sister Louisa's widower, Roland Wilkins,[7] as he struggled

---

1. Dorothy to Hans Herwarth von Bittenfeld (German Ambassador), 5 March 1961, copy BFA.
2. Dorothy to David, 23 December 1949, BFA.
3. Dorothy to David, 15 September 1957, BFA. '[W]hen I got an obstruction in the intestine; – but after a few weeks in hospital, preparatory to an operation, it disappeared.'
4. Dorothy to the editor of *The Manchester Guardian*, 10 May 1956, copy in BFA.
5. Dorothy to the editor of *The Manchester Guardian*, 10 May 1956, copy in BFA.
6. Nikita Sergeyevich Krushchev (1894–1971), First Secretary of the Communist Party of the Soviet Union 1953–64, Premier of the Soviet Union 1958–64.
7. Roland Field Wilkins (1872–1950), son of a professor of Latin, he became

to adjust to retirement in a hotel in Budleigh Salterton after the Second World War. When she visited him, he asked Dorothy to stay in another hotel as he was 'ashamed' of her unstylish clothes![1] Roland died in 1950 and her other widowed brother-in-law, Beverley Ussher,[2] who had been Emily's husband, died in Ireland in 1956. On 30 May 1953, Victoria de Bunsen, Dorothy's fellow Newnhamite and her favourite amongst Charlie's siblings, died, after three years of widowhood. It was Victoria who had introduced Charlie and Dorothy and she had remained a stalwart friend and sympathetic ally to Dorothy, even though their attitudes to life differed considerably. A month after Victoria's death came the loss of Dorothy's only surviving sibling, Dick, owner of The Lyth.[3] These were accompanied by other deaths amongst her friends and correspondents. It felt as if she were outliving her generation.

Her world was cheered, however, by the arrival of more grandchildren. David had returned from Africa, having met a distant cousin, Mary Buxton, in Kenya at his cousin Clarence's farm. He and Mary were married in December 1950 and went on to have five children, four born during Dorothy's lifetime. David took a job with the British Council and, during the remainder of Dorothy's life, he was posted to places in Europe. The first was Graz in Austria, where Dorothy visited him, and then he had periods in Rome and Munich, as well as a year back in London living in the Erskine Hill house. His nearer location meant that mother and son were able to see each other more regularly. The grandchildren were welcomed, but she was still not a 'natural' with children. In addition, her deafness, despite the NHS hearing aid, made it harder for her to communicate easily. On occasions, Dorothy could be sharp with them. She took an

a career civil servant, mainly in the Treasury where he served as Assistant Paymaster-General 1924–35. It was said in his *Times* obituary that he might have risen higher had he been more tactful and cultivated more harmony with his colleagues. He was an accomplished skater and alpine climber. He had married Louisa Jebb in 1907 and was widowed in 1929. He was particularly incensed in old age that his unmarried daughter, Elizabeth (Betty) (1911–80), who he believed should have devoted herself to looking after him, had become a Roman Catholic and had then been professed as an enclosed Cistercian nun at Stapehill. She was a novice there at the time of the 1939 Register and was professed during the Second World War.

1. Dorothy to David, 8 April 1945 and 15 April 1945, BFA.
2. Beverley Grant Ussher (1867–1956). He had married Emily Jebb in 1898 and was widowed in 1935.
3. She continued to visit The Lyth during the 1950s when able and lobbied her relatives with pictures of undernourished children and letters from refugees produced from her large handbag! Conversation with Lionel and Corinna Jebb, 14 September 2010.

interest and yet did not think to buy them gifts very often.[1] Yet, even if she could not play an archetypal doting grandmother, she certainly loved them very deeply.

In these post-war years, Dorothy remained somewhat shabby in her appearance. Even when she tried to dress up a little, she cut an old-fashioned figure, dressed in a kind of faded elegance from a past era. Just as Charlie had continued to wear starched winged collars to the end of his life, long after most other men had abandoned them for everyday wear, so Dorothy continued to recycle her Edwardian wardrobe. When David, following his engagement to Mary in 1950, took Dorothy to meet his fiancée's parents at the latter's home in Essex, Dorothy on arrival immediately apologised for her clothes. Desperate to find something more formal to wear, she had donned her 'going-away' outfit from her marriage in 1904. Forty-five years on, the brown tussore silk with its golden embroidery had a further outing. Her apology, however, revealed her own sense of how absurd this sartorial choice must have seemed. The outfit was none too clean, but somehow Dorothy was able to sweep in, as if from another era, and no one bothered.[2] She was diffident yet warm towards her hosts and soon all got along happily. Now nearing seventy, she could use her eccentricity to disarm rather than make others uncomfortable. She could laugh at herself.

Dorothy was still very respected in the 1950s, but perhaps she also realised that she still needed to be loved as well. Her mother and her dear sister Eglantyne had long left her. With Charlie's death in 1942, the last established source of unconditional love had been taken from her, as she had struggled to find an equivalent uncomplicated connection with her children, as we explored in an earlier chapter. Dorothy therefore attempted to deepen other relationships, not least with her long-standing (and long-suffering) housekeeper, Florence. Mrs Hawkins' daughter, Victoria, had long grown up and married, but Florence had remained doggedly loyal to 'Mrs Buxton' and had never hinted at 'retiring' from her position. Their relationship had been quite formal and Florence addressed her as 'Ma'am'. Mrs Hawkins took Dorothy a cup of tea at 7a.m. and then at around 9a.m. they discussed the meals to be prepared that day. It was all reminiscent of the domestic routine of a gentry house in the late nineteenth century. At several levels, their lives were deeply entwined and inter-dependent. In the 1950s, Dorothy made some efforts to make the interaction less old-fashioned, but Florence was quietly resistant and did not reciprocate. She would persist with some of the outward formalities to the end of Dorothy's

---

1. Conversation with Mary Buxton, 11 February 2007.
2. Conversation with Mary Buxton, 11 February 2007.

life. It was as if Dorothy was locked into an old 'class relationship' that she had no way of escaping. Therefore, despite Florence remaining loyal to the very end, their relationship was not without ambivalence.

On the one side, Florence was indebted to the Buxtons who had taken her and her daughter to live with them in 1930 when the housekeeper needed employment. The Buxtons gave her a home, as well as a safe place to bring up her daughter. Florence kept the house clean and did all the cooking and much of the household shopping. She did not have to do laundry, which was always sent out, and the garden was Dorothy's own province. The household all helped her with some aspects of housework. David, unusually for a boy in the 1920s, was taught the essentials of cleaning and enjoyed using the earliest form of vacuum cleaner. Charlie was undomesticated, but insisted on contributing by cleaning the shoes of everyone in the house.[1] There were no dinner parties or formal occasions, although sometimes there would be guests around for tea. However, such occasions became less and less frequent as the years went by and Florence had only to cater principally for the immediate family. Hence the duties were substantial, but not overwhelming. For her work, the sum of ten shillings and six pence a week was agreed, which in twenty-first century terms would be about £30. This was not a bad wage for 1930, given that that this was in addition to her accommodation.

However, it never occurred to Dorothy that this sum should be raised. When Dorothy died in 1963, the housekeeper (by now seventy-two years old) was still earning exactly the same wage on the same terms as in 1930.[2] This was in spite of the fact that, by the early 1960s, the purchasing power of the wage had been reduced to one-third of its original level. This lack of thought on the part of Dorothy embarrassed the Buxton family when they found out about it. Dorothy, nevertheless, did have concerns for Florence's future. In a memorandum to her children, she wrote,

> At the very least I would want to make some demonstration of my gratitude to her – which is very great. Thanks to her[,] my public role work has been feasible ever since her arrival in 1930. She has made my home a very happy one in a way which I cannot imagine anyone else could have achieved.[3]

1. David Buxton, autobiographical notes, BFA. Of his father's role, he wrote, 'CRB was *not* domesticated but felt that he must play his part in household chores. So as early as I remember he took up shoe-cleaning which remained his contribution for many years. No-one else ever helped and he did it for all of us, taking considerable pride in his skill.'
2. Conversation with Victoria Houghton, 4 January 2007.
3. Dorothy, memorandum to David and Eglantyne, 18 April 1962, BFA.

In the event, David in particular was helpful to Florence's daughter, Victoria, in securing the old housekeeper a home for her retirement and ensuring financial security. However, the situation illustrated poignantly Dorothy's lack of awareness in one of the closest of her day-to-day relationships. She wanted to reach out to her housekeeper and yet never thought to reward her loyalty in the most obvious way she could have done.

With her daughter Eglantyne, the ambivalence was even more pronounced. Dorothy found a pattern of living that gave them both sufficient space. She did not stop trying to find a common ground. They ate the main meal of the day together and they discussed what they were reading, but the emotional gulf between them remained wide. They simply could not 'understand' one another, but in Dorothy's final years they had ceased to fret about it.

Meanwhile, David and Mary were anxious that Dorothy was not caring for herself properly. Visiting periodically, they could see what those who lived alongside Dorothy did not perhaps notice: that she was becoming thinner little by little. She also had begun to be slightly stooped with an air of physical frailty. The frailty led to her spending some time in a nursing home at one point, where she complained about the poor quality of the food and being woken at 5a.m.![1] Nevertheless, despite the evidence of her increasing weakness, she robustly defended herself against David and Mary's concerned comments. 'As regards myself I cannot refrain from putting up a little defence! – as I do not like the idea of you & Mary writing me off as unreasonable & reckless in matters of health!'

She went on to defend her diet, exercise and her mental attitude. She had, she insisted, taken Mary's advice on vitamins and she would now follow their advice and take a longer rest after lunch on the verandah couch and also go to bed early.[2] Withdrawing from her public lobbying also meant she was less pressured with work commitments. The family letters she did write were, according to one nephew, 'somewhat shaky, but showed no falling-off of her old vivacity and spirit'.[3]

In March 1961, Dorothy celebrated her eightieth birthday with both her children. She had now decided that her last great task was to write a biography of her sister, Eglantyne. She had long toyed with this idea, but, sensing that she had little time left, she announced that this project would be her priority. In January 1962, she used this as the reason for her 'meagre' responses to friends' messages for Christmas and New Year, 'I have no time to lose and must concentrate upon my task.'[4]

1. Dorothy to Annelore, undated except for 'Tuesday', but likely 1957, BFA.
2. Dorothy to David, 15 September 1957, BFA.
3. Arland Ussher to David, 18 April 1963, BFA.
4. Dorothy to various friends (round-robin letter), 24 January 1962, copy in BFA.

Dorothy in April 1963, the day before she died

It was not a task she accomplished or even properly began. By early 1963, her ailments increased and made life difficult for her. She became weaker and at times confused. She did not like to be left alone. Sometimes she even seemed not to realise that Eglantyne was her daughter. She was, however, generous in expressing thanks for all that was done for her.[1] David visited on Sunday 7 April and took the last photograph ever taken of her.[2] The next day, 8 April, early in the morning, she died in bed of a 'sudden cardiac failure' brought on by chronic heart disease aged eighty-two. Her funeral was held on 11 April, which in 1963 was Maundy Thursday in Holy Week, at the local Anglican church in Peaslake where Charlie's had taken place twenty odd years before. She was then buried with Charlie in the Peaslake cemetery, up on the hill. The inscription on his grave stone had used the phrase: 'God hath made of one blood all nations.' For Dorothy, the inscription read: 'To them that love God, all things work together for good.'

The main newspapers, such as *The Times* and *The Manchester Guardian*, ran obituaries, as well as local papers such as the *Surrey Advertiser*, whilst tributes were paid in journals associated with the causes she had espoused.[3] Many personal letters of condolence were received by the family. Whatever ambivalence there was in her personal relationships, in the public domain Dorothy was much admired and revered. Gwen Catchpool whose late husband had spoken at Charlie's funeral, wrote that 'at the last monthly Meeting of Hampstead Friends several people spoke one after another with deep appreciation of her, and a minute was recorded remembering her splendid life'.[4]

Save the Children sent a 'magnificent wreath' for the funeral, whilst the association that linked the German dentists also sent a 'magnificent spray of flowers'.[5] One of the supporters from the dental association wrote that,

> During the 23 years I have known your mother, met with her and corresponded with her, I have learnt to appreciate her as probably the kindest, most merciful and humane person I ever met and I know that hundreds and thousands of people who have cause to thank her for her ceaseless and determined efforts for so many good causes, are unlikely ever to forget her.[6]

---

1. Eglantyne junior, miscellaneous notes, BFA.
2. Herbert Sulzbach to David, 30 April 1963, BFA. David had sent the diplomat a copy of this last photograph.
3. For example, the *Anglo-Continental Dental Society Newsletter*, No 5 (April 1963) and *AJR Information* [Association of Jewish Refugees Newsletter] Vol XVIII, No 5 (May 1963), p. 9.
4. Gwen Catchpool to Eglantyne junior, 23 April 1963, BFA.
5. Eglantyne junior to David, 12 April 1963, BFA.
6. Kenneth Farnham to Eglantyne junior, 10 April [1963], BFA.

Gerhard Puritz, the deputy chairman of the Church Council of the Lutheran parish of St Mary in London wrote that the memory of Dorothy's generosity would remain always in their hearts, as well as their church records.[1] The general secretary of the Association of Jewish Refugees in Great Britain wrote in his letter of sympathy,

> Nobody who met her could fail to be impressed by her devotion to any cause she considered important and justified, and by the interest she took in the personal well-being of the people with whom she came into contact. Our community owes a great debt of gratitude to her, and we shall always remember her with affection.[2]

One poignant letter came from one of the staff at the German Embassy, Herbert Sulzbach,[3] whose life experiences chimed with many of Dorothy's causes. A German Jew from a Frankfurt banking family, he had fought valiantly for four years (mainly on the Western front) in the First World War and during the conflict had come to admire the British 'enemy'. He forged business links in Great Britain after the war wanting to improve Anglo-German relations. Dorothy's was a voice he heard responding on the other side of the divide. When Nazi persecution became a dangerous reality for him, he escaped to Britain from his own country in 1937, leaving behind his assets. He was one of the destitute refugees for whom Dorothy lobbied. In 1940, he was interned as an enemy alien, again suffering an injustice for which Dorothy publicly expressed outrage. He then tried to join the British forces and, again, it was Dorothy who lobbied for men like him to be accepted without suspicion into the anti-Nazi cause. He took on the task of re-educating German prisoners of war, acting as an interpreter, and encouraging peace and reconciliation, causes dear to Dorothy's heart. At the time of Dorothy's death, he was working in the cultural department of the German Embassy. The effect of Dorothy's long years of work for people like him was expressed in his short condolence letter to David, 'It is difficult for me to express the sorrow I feel – the deep sadness at the loss of THE friend in this country, your wonderful mother.'[4] The Embassy's own publication, *The German View*, quoted a comment in an article published some years before in the *Rhein-Nacker Zeitung*, 'A woman like this makes it easier for us Germans to find our way back after criminal

1. Gerhard Puritz to Eglantyne junior, 7 May 1963, BFA.
2. W. Rosenstock to Eglantyne junior, 22 April 1963, BFA.
3. Herbert Sulzbach (1894–1985).
4. Herbert Sulzbach to David, 10 April 1963, BFA.

mistakes. And when we are confronted with a wise and understanding person like her it should make us even more conscious of how grievously our country went astray.'[1]

The year before she died, a biography on Birger Forell (1893–1958) was published. He was a priest of the Church of Sweden, who had been one of Dorothy's main contacts in Nazi Germany as he worked at the Swedish Church in Berlin. For many years he worked tirelessly for refugees and prisoners of war and was one of her main correspondents. The author of the biography quoted Forell's view of Dorothy as a 'modern saint', 'She stands nearer to the angels of Heaven than anyone else I have got to know.'[2]

Dorothy may have at times during her life been a prophet who was unheeded, but she did not die without being honoured.

---

1. *The German View*, Vol IV, No 8 (24 April 1963), quoting from the *Rhein-Neckar Zeitung*, Seite 12, Nr 42, 20 February 1959, copies of both in BFA.
2. Harald von Königswald, *Birger Forell: Leben und Wirken in den jahren 1933–58*, Eckart-Verlag, Witten & Berlin, 1962, p. 108. '"*Sie steht den Engeln im Himmel näher als jeder andere, den ich kennengelernt habe*" schreibt Forell über *sie, und später nennt er sie "eine modern Heilige – aber man darf es nicht laut sagen, sonst wird sie wütend.*"'

Chapter 11
Not yet silenced?

To her contemporaries, as well as to a modern audience, there was much that is uncomfortable about Dorothy Buxton. Her lifestyle presented an immediate challenge to anyone who encountered her. Her frugality and abstemiousness were potentially an affront to the comfort to which most people aspired. She would suggest to those she visited that they might want to donate to a refugee a coat or some shoes she saw in the hallway. Or she would ask quite pointedly for her host to make a financial contribution to feed the starving, producing a graphic photograph or a refugee's desperate letter to increase the pressure. Anyone who wished to maintain their wardrobe undiminished or wanted to eat a good meal without feeling guilty (and that was most people) found this direct reminder of their good fortune unsettling. Some of her relatives were used to her approach and were both firmly on their guard against her tactics and also willing teased her. Others were left perplexed and uncertain how to respond.

One powerful element of her challenge was that Dorothy's commitment to the deprived and the refugee could not be dismissed as 'champagne socialism', where someone advocates reform and redistribution of wealth whilst living their own life in considerable comfort even luxury. From the First World War onwards, Dorothy lived in her domestic life with consistent and rigourous self-sacrifice. She shunned new clothes, superfluous personal effects, fashionable furniture and carpets, elaborate meals with wine or lavish entertaining. She did not use money for taxis when she could walk. She kept a little book where she scrupulously recorded every penny that she spent. She started out in life with privileges and access to wealth, but as an adult she did not spend it on herself. She gave away much of her income and did so anonymously in many cases: much of her personal generosity in sending food and clothes to the destitute went unrecorded. All her work for charity and all her lobbying were done without a salary or wage. She worked conscientiously and with little rest even to the extent of undermining her own health.

This inevitably was a challenge to the way that many other people lived – and many still do live – in the wealthy Western world, exhibiting both wastefulness and over-consumption. The reaction of discomfort subsequently expressed itself through criticism of her. Her detractors would remark that she still regularly travelled throughout Europe (admittedly staying in cheap accommodation or camping), employed a housekeeper to cook and clean and intermittently sent her children to fee-paying schools. Whatever her personal frugality, she did not surrender all the perks of her upper middle-class background. In other words, dismissing her way of life as somehow hypocritical provided an excuse either to ignore the witness of what she did do or else not to take her seriously.

However, this understandable, but simplistic reaction cannot deny the sacrifices that she clearly made. She did share the resources she had – money, accommodation, time – and what she kept for herself was in order to maintain the infrastructure to support her unsalaried work or to give her children education. She cannot be accused of living a selfish life. How many of the twentieth-century socialists and communists could say that they lived without perks and luxuries? Stalin and the Russian communist elite enjoyed them, as indeed did some leading Labour Party politicians in Britain.

Even those who accepted that Dorothy lived the life she advocated would, nevertheless, try to undermine her arguments by noting she was 'difficult' or 'went too far', that her abrupt interactions alienated rather than persuaded others. Her writing and speaking were impassioned, so critics claimed they were 'over the top' and exaggerated; the hidden judgement there being that she would have been more effective if she had been less strident and demanding. To her contemporaries, the gentler appeal of her sister Eglantyne chimed more easily with their views of femininity. Dorothy was too hectoring and blunt. She recognised this trait in herself and it was a major factor in her own downplaying of her role in the public campaigns in which she actually contributed substantially.

Dorothy could be labelled as 'judgemental'. She inhabited an intellectual world where absolutes in standards and principles were deemed admirable. Clarity of thought demanded prescriptive conclusions. Actions were either right or wrong. Most of her contemporaries in her younger days adhered to such an approach. They might disagree with one another, sometimes strongly, but the idea of not having a position would have been seen as weak. In the twenty-first century, the world view has shifted in 'western' countries. Psychological studies have revealed the complexity of human emotions and have even challenged the idea that individuals have complete control over their behaviours. A modern approach would be more likely therefore to be relative and neutral, with an aspiration to see all sides of a situation and making judgements tentative and provisional. In such a context, those with definitive values can be accused of being 'judgemental', whether right or wrong. Dorothy's absolute pronouncements, both on political questions and personal morality, can therefore strike a modern reader as harsh and simplistic. They did so to some of her contemporaries as well. Whereas in her world such an approach was likely to gain attention, in today's world it can lead to irritation or exasperated dismissal.

What should be remembered was that Dorothy was by nature a retiring person, who preferred to work in a garden surrounded by creatures and plants rather than meeting people or socialising. She would like to sit and write on her own, undisturbed by others. She did not lack self-confidence in her views, but she did lack self-assurance in the public arena because she was an introvert. Giving speeches, attending meetings, having conversations were all activities that drained her. She was nervous when she did do these things and, to conquer her reticence, she became forthright and outspoken. People were generally offended by her tone, not the content of what she said, and it was her shyness that was a large factor in her abruptness and social awkwardness. Her seemingly dismissive and absolute judgements could be seen as influenced by her fear of not being heard. In her world, the hesitant and nuanced argument could easily be ignored. A dogmatic utterance in contrast demanded to be taken seriously: whether in agreement or opposition. Dorothy was criticised for not understanding other people, but it could equally be argued that they did not understand her. They could interpret her brusque or inept presentation of opinions as being from motives that were not actually present. Any assessment of her achievements must therefore begin by noting that they were accomplished against the background of a naturally diffident and shy personality. She had strong opinions and was not reticent in expressing them privately or in writing: however, representing them and acting upon them effectively in public was ever a struggle for her.

Her voice in the public arena was also challenged because of her gender. Women did not have access to the vote or the possibility of being an MP until nearly halfway through her life. Women could study at the University of Cambridge in her young days, but they were not allowed to take degrees until she was an old-age pensioner. For Dorothy to put herself in the public arena and organise a major charity in 1919 was a much greater achievement than a similar woman doing the same nearly a century later. She had to overcome contemporary social prejudice against women in public life. Her almost obsessive desire to have accurate facts was partly because she needed to insure herself against casual dismissal by men who were in power and whose conscious and unconscious bias would lead them to ignore her. The accuracy of her contribution was a powerful tool in her bid to be heard.

Her ability to stand up to these pressures stemmed from her unusual childhood which mixed study with adventure, the learning of the school-room with the lessons to be had outside. Aunt Bun and her mother both encouraged her to have self-confidence and an absence of fear, so that she was intrepid in tackling whatever was before her. Only her innate reticence would hold her back, something that her upbringing could not counter. She had only her siblings as other child companions, but one by one they left home and so she developed her own self-reliance on which she drew all her life. It made her unafraid of 'ploughing her own furrow' and a detachment from what others thought of her. It did not bother her in later life if people thought her unkempt or eccentric. She wanted them to be attracted to her ideas, not to her person. In this sense, she was without self-consciousness. This was the factor that countered her shyness and allowed her at times to speak in public and go where it seemed absurd (in contemporary terms) for her to tread. Her mother especially had instilled in her a duty to make a mark on society and use the life she had been given for the public good, as well as private satisfaction. This goal stayed with her and gave her the drive and persistence she displayed throughout her life.

Her major strength was, as mentioned, a desire to have the full facts. Impressions or anecdotes were of little value. She had a scientific mind that wanted to establish accurate readings and measurements and this she transferred to her political endeavours. It was no good, for example, saying that miners in Germany were not being given sufficient food. She wanted to know how many miners, how long they worked, how many calories their rations provided, and whether the rations were being supplied in full and from where. She would travel to make assessments herself if she had insufficiently trustworthy local contacts – or else to establish such contacts for the future. Her Save the Children work began with establishing the facts of the famine, so that no one could contradict her when she made an appeal. Few others had made such an effort to discover precisely what was happening. She contacted people on the spot who were on the frontline working on the problem, who could give her the information on which she could rely. It was this trait which gave her authority and also confidence. A representation from Mrs Buxton was not purely a forceful statement, but usually a catalogue of substantial evidence too. People might disagree with her interpretations and conclusions, but they could rarely contradict the facts she presented.

Her major weakness was a lack of intellectual rigour in her analysis. Jane Harrison had said Dorothy had a 'brilliant mind' when at Newnham College, but Dorothy fell into the trap of using her gifts to argue strongly for a position rather than learning how to assess both sides of an argument and make a considered evaluation. Weighing up a series of options was not her way. She was a campaigner and an advocate rather than a judge. As we have seen when considering her education, she would both at school and university 'wing it' – that is, she would not read comprehensively the various interpretations of a subject, but simply gather the evidence that interested her instinctive opinion. In many ways, her force of argument could swamp her peers and she 'got away with it'. Except that by university days, her fellow students would applaud her rhetoric, but not elect her as a leader. In all these debates, her information would be accurate, but beneath the impassioned presentation, her analysis could lack breadth. This did not mean she was always wrong. In some campaigns, it was not relevant: if children were starving, they needed to be fed. It was a question of 'how?' not of 'why?'. Such a case did not require nuanced understanding and so advocacy rather than fine judgement was what was required.

But when it came to judging political situations, her approach proved more uncertain. In considering the Soviet Union or Nazi Germany, her conclusions were swayed by the ideals to which she was emotionally attached. It was therefore partly a matter of chance whether in the end she was right. She clearly did not appreciate early enough the weakness in the Soviet system and so became for some years misguided in her conclusions because initially she was emotionally drawn to the idea of communism. Her accurate facts were only those she was allowed to gather and which convinced her because she was already sympathetic to the ideal enunciated of an equal and class-free society. The rhetoric of communism for a while obscured the reality of what was being imposed on the peoples of the Soviet Union. Once she understood what was happening to them, she altered her opinion, but it was too late to prevent others regarding her as a naïve commentator.

With Nazi Germany, the clarity of her understanding from the beginning of the regime was prophetic. Her emotions as well as her intellect rebelled against the avowed racism and the use of unfettered force advocated by the Nazis to achieve their internal and external goals. Nazis were open and unapologetic about their ideology and their methods, but many chose to ignore this. Dorothy saw that the concentration camps were the heart of an oppression that could lead to unimaginable horror. She did not specifically predict the Holocaust and the death of six million Jewish people – as well as gipsies, homosexuals and political opponents – but she recognised very early that any regime that has no respect for prisoners was not going to have respect for whole populations in the future. She was a prophet on this issue because her emotional attachment to the German people and the Jewish people ensured she took the Nazi's actions seriously. Just as she had been emotionally attached to the class-free idea of Bolshevism, so others ignored Hitler's methods because they were emotionally seduced by his promises of full employment and nationalistic pride.

Dorothy understood her weakness. As she became older, she became more attached to searching for information and less concerned about political dogma. In a similar way, her religion became a matter of action and not doctrine. She was concerned about those who were forgotten or voiceless or marginalised. Her concern over her analysis as distinct from her information led her to want others to lead campaigns. An example would be her fixation in the late 1930s to persuade the bishops of the Church of England to support her position on Germany. She even asked them to sign a letter that she composed, but which lacked her own signature. She wrote more than one letter to the press for others to sign. This was an indication that she no longer believed that her name would carry weight in itself in the public domain. Her self-appointed role was to persuade others who she believed had power that they must act.

However, she did make a significant contribution in her own name in three specific areas. The first came during the First World War with her own initiative to translate and distribute articles from non-British newspapers. This grew into an enterprise that encompassed a team of many people, but the inspiration and drive began with Dorothy. It was her commitment to ensuring that more than one narrative was presented to people in Britain, that the concept of a 'free press' would not be smothered by the propaganda of a wartime scenario. Her readership was not huge, but it was influential: members of the British government, parliamentarians, party officials, representatives of the Dominions, and figures from the literary and academic worlds. These were part of the opinion-forming, as well as decision-making elite and no one in that world could therefore claim that they did not know of alternative views expressed in enemy countries. One might argue that ultimately the terms of the Versailles Treaty and the post-war settlement did not reflect this understanding and that therefore Dorothy's efforts were ineffective. But this does not mean they were pointless. Maintaining the flame of British 'fair play' and justice was a noble aim in wartime. She stood against the crude and dismissive racism used in the portrayal of people from enemy nations. She stood for the possibilities of eventual peace and reconciliation even in the midst of divisive and bitter conflict. She demonstrated a commitment to accurate and balanced reporting. In some ways, this approach became reflected in the neutral stance that was adopted by BBC radio's World Service in later decades so that even in the depths of future conflicts, its news bulletins became regarded as the epitome of reliability and accuracy in a world of distorted propaganda.

Dorothy's 'Notes from the Foreign Press' operated in a media world of pure print, before the advent of radio and other types of communication, but the values she represented were a significant witness. She deserves credit for her contribution to the history of the press in Britain.

Her second contribution was the foundation of the Save the Children Fund, a campaign that evolved into an enduring charity. It was Dorothy who had the vision for SCF and who then had the energy to drive through its foundation. Her sister Eglantyne followed her and then was very soon at her side. As Eglantyne's inter-personal skills were seen as those more relevant for establishing international relationships and encouraging donors, Dorothy relinquished the leadership to her. Yet, her support for Eglantyne was still crucial in 1919–20. After two years, she slipped aside to concentrate on other campaigns and allowed her sister to lead in creating the permanent charity that has been prominent in caring for children in distress for a hundred years. Dorothy kept her connection to SCF, serving many years on its Council, but her role in its foundation has been obscured, not least because archive material for the first eighteen months of SCF is sparse. Yet from what can be established, it is unlikely Eglantyne would have begun SCF on her own. The initial impetus needed Dorothy. The campaign was an audacious idea and required a fearless passion to rouse the conscience of ordinary people as well as wealthy backers. At the time, Dorothy could never have realised what she was setting in motion. For a woman in 1919 to have such an impact in a society where men assumed they should lead was remarkable. It was Dorothy's courage and refusal to be thwarted that set the whole foundation in motion. Countless children have benefitted in the century since.

Her work for the refugees, for prisoners and those without a voice was her third important act of witness, one that was maintained for many years. This is the hardest to assess in terms of results. For once one refugee was housed and one prisoner released, others took their place in the wave of need. To Dorothy, however, refugees and prisoners were not problems to solve, but people to save. This work began in the First World War and continued to the 1950s before her failing faculties made further work for her difficult. In her years of lobbying, she raised consciousness on refugee issues and helped generate a generosity of spirit towards those forced to flee from their homes that is still relevant. She refused to allow the refugee, the prisoner, the alien to be forgotten. Ministers and government officials could not ignore the tide of facts and figures, questions and representations, that swept into their postbags. Dorothy would not be ignored and she helped resolve ongoing issues from the use by British forces of 'aliens' willing to fight against the Nazis to the ban on German dentists practising in the

NHS. For those concerned, these were not trivial matters, but the heart
of their lives and careers. That someone was willing to represent them and
fight for them was simply life-changing.

After such a record in public service and witness, why has Dorothy
Frances Buxton's name faded from view? She has never been given any
honour or award by the British state. There is no statue of her or blue plaque
on places she lived. Up until this book, no one had written her biography.
Despite her faults and weaknesses and the irritations of her personality in
some eyes, this was a meagre response to her undoubted achievements.

There are perhaps three reasons that might suggest an explanation for this
neglect. First, when she became a recognised name during the First World
War, she was labelled as unpatriotic and a pacifist. To oppose the continuation
of the war and to advocate a negotiated peace seemed to many in 1914–18
a betrayal of their loved ones who were risking their lives on the battlefield.
Of course, that was untrue, as Dorothy was wanting to save their loved ones,
but in the emotional and anguished atmosphere of the times, her espousal of
an anti-war approach made her suspect. She was seen as pro-German rather
than anti-war and to be pro-German was utterly despicable to many people.

Her campaign for the starving children in 1919–20 aroused the conscience
of the nation, but she was still treated with wariness. For some she was still
campaigning for Germans, not only for children. The taint clung to her name.
This was one of the factors that encouraged her to hand the leadership of the
Save the Children Fund to her sister Eglantyne. The latter had been active as
a translator in Dorothy's work publishing articles from the foreign press, but
she had not been prominent. She was able to assume a non-political public
persona untainted with the 'unpatriotic' tag that dogged Dorothy.

In the aftermath of the 1919 Peace Treaty, Dorothy argued that the
Germans had been badly treated and she continued to defend the German
people throughout the 1920s. Even in the 1930s, her hatred of Nazism
was not anti-German. During the 1940s, the fact that many British
people equated Germans with Nazis meant that her campaigns for anti-
Nazi Germans in the UK and against their internment and the bar that
prevented them fighting for the Allied forces put her under suspicion yet
again. Germany was not popular even in the 1950s, yet she still spoke
up for the German people, both collectively and for individuals. Looking
back, her positions were logical and defensible, but they did not chime with
the political atmosphere of the time. She was mainly right and just in her
arguments, but her approach was not in line with the public mood. For a
British citizen to be pro-German at any time between 1914 and her death
in 1963 was not going to bring public acclaim. Dorothy's was not therefore
a name that was cherished and passed on to future generations.

Dorothy's public reputation took a second hit from her espousal of Bolshevism. To many British people, the revolutionary politics of communism represented the violent overthrow of much that they held dear. Even among those who were left-wing in their sympathies, many were protective of democracy, free speech and a free press. Hence, Dorothy's somewhat uncritical embrace of Bolshevik ideals from 1917 heaped yet more suspicion on her. Critics were alarmed that she appeared to judge the Russian revolutionaries on their aspirations and not on their actions. Even though she later repudiated communism, she was still seen as uncomfortably 'left-wing' for much of her public life. Her disinterest in playing any role in the British political class socially added to this sense of danger: she could not be trusted to keep her criticisms within acceptable limits or proportion. She appeared to protest from the side-lines rather than being part of the conversation. Her demeanour and unpredictability might be seen by some to be as dangerous as her views, as it indicated that she was beyond influence and a maverick. Such people may well be respected, but rarely embraced. Dorothy remained an outsider to a political world where official public recognition and praise could be mainly found only inside its boundaries.

Finally, her own diffidence and hiddenness meant that she was reluctant to put herself forward (as distinct from the cause she espoused) in any situation. From the 1920s she withdrew from anything but occasional public speaking. Her name became just that: a name at the bottom of a letter to a newspaper or at the end of a briefing report. She did visit ministers and officials for meetings, but the general public did not see her. Her publications were generally relevant to the time they were published and not long-term classics. She did one radio interview about her sister Eglantyne, but she was not a regular broadcaster. By the time television began to be established among the mass of the population, she had retired from the political fray. Even with Save the Children, she had deliberately downplayed her role in the charity's literature after Eglantyne's death. Inevitably, therefore, her name was revered in some quarters and by many she had helped, but as that generation passed away, the memory of all she achieved faded.

Yet remembering her is not just an historical exercise. The things she stood for and achieved remain pertinent in the twenty-first century. The issue of establishing accurate information and facing the reality of a situation is a relevant goal in an internet age when spin and fake-news can be so pervasive. Her protest against the propaganda of the First World War was to provide another perspective, a source of information that revealed what was happening on the other side of the conflict and also the view from neutral countries. This witness to the need to hear many voices and opinions is not a message for one age only, but something to consider in every era.

Her advocacy for the protection of the child – and by association of all those who are vulnerable – is not just a message for her own time. It has resonated through the decades since and is the reason that the charity she was so instrumental in founding is still at work through the globe a century later. The need she brought to the forefront in the wake of the 1918 Armistice has not been overcome. The continuing toll of conflict and its resultant hardships scars human society. The cry to save the children remains a powerful necessity. She would be humbled that Save the Children still answers to the call she made in 1919, yet she would be depressed to think human society had failed to evolve sufficiently to make such a call redundant.

Finally, her care for the refugee and the alien has been a message that has rarely faded from relevance. Her compassion for those who had to flee their homelands in order to survive and protect their families remained undiminished to the end. Decades after her death, the wave of refugees in Europe and elsewhere continues to be a challenge just as it was after both world wars. Dorothy would be their unwavering advocate.

In these ways, Dorothy Buxton's story is both a chronicle of the early twentieth century in which she lived, but also a voice that has resonance in an era long after her death. She still has something significant to tell us.

Appendix
Charlie's praise for Dorothy

I still feel rather a hankering to give to the world that thing I wrote about you – *in a quite disguised form*, which would be easy by altering names & calling it a Western Idyll or some such title – do you think this a lapse into vulgarisation? I think as a suggestion of what marriage can be in modern days, it could well be advantageous to the world to peruse it! Also I think it is the best thing I have produced, & the desire to produce something visible – when most of one's activity leads to nothing of that kind – weighs with me.

Charlie to Dorothy, 20 March 1918, BFA.

Here we reprint what Charlie's believed was the 'best thing I have produced', but not in 'a disguised form'! Whether this is a lapse 'into vulgarisation' must be left to the judgement of the reader.

DOROTHY JEBB
by Charles Roden Buxton

Rome, 31 Dec 1914

I. It is easier to write of her in absence. I am glad that I have been separated from her through four months of travel and active work. I have been able to see her life as a whole. I have escaped from the tyranny of the moment. It seems possible now to say what I have desired to say – but could not say, because I could not detach myself sufficiently from little things. I have desired to say what I knew and what I felt about this woman, one of the chosen spirits of the world, with whom my life has been linked by a strange and happy chance. I am the only man who can tell the truth about her. If I do not tell it, it will lie buried, with all the other good things that have perished for want of words.

II. I will write it down, if I can, plainly and truly. I do not want any borrowed thoughts. I will not follow the common custom, saying that my love is more good, more wise, more beautiful – so much the better for the world! Not do I want to be led away by borrowed phrases, by what other men have said of other women. These memories seem to offer forms of words to express what I mean. But they are dangerous. The image waves before my eyes, and is infinitely difficult to fix precisely. The words of other men give it a spurious precision. In defining they distort it.

III. Does it seem strange to write of her now, in these months of terror, with a world in flames, and the palace of order which humanity had built for itself, shaken to its base? For me, who have tried to live many of my hours in the world of country and mankind, the breaking down of hopes which belong to the world only drives me back more forcibly than ever upon the personal life which remains untouched, the inner circle which remains unbroken. I must have life and I must have joy, and I will find them there, if I cannot find them elsewhere.

IV. For hours and days, nay for weeks, busied with many things, I have let that deep spring of life and joy flow on neglected and unregarded. I want to repair the waste of those hours and days and weeks. I am glad that something has driven me back to drink at the spring, even though that something be a world in flames.

V. She has gained the power, not easily but by little slow advances, by self-mastery ever increasing, of living in the spiritual world. She has reached something like the position which the saints of Christian or Eastern thought have won through prayer and fasting. To reach it while still living in the practical world of modern England, to strike the right balance, without the self-abandonment which cuts of the saint from the world, is infinitely hard. But she has done it. This atmosphere is good for those who share it. They cannot wholly slumber or plod. The air is not too rarefied to breathe; it is the wine of morning on the Alpine snows. It demands some strenuousness. Yet to breathe it is a priceless privilege. You must think of all the heaviness of the fogs below, continually choking most of us and dragging us back from the way, if you are to appraise at its right value this stimulus of the heights.

VI. If our recognition of the ideal is more than lip-service, we must know, we cannot hide from ourselves, that in the soft, cushioned life, in the familiar grooves of convention, in the sweet taste of meats and drinks, there resides a tremendous power, perpetually battling against the ideal which we say we follow. Who shall save me from this body of death? Thanks be to God, who holds out to us the possibility of victory, through the communion of more powerful and more far-sighted souls. In that communion we can recognise around and within us, an ocean of love, an ocean of good; let us bathe ourselves in it.

VII. As she is at home in the mountain air of the spiritual world, not alien to it, not fearing it, so she is at home in the world of hills and rivers, trees and plants, beasts and birds and creeping things. She takes familiarly to the house that is roofed by blue air and floored by waving grass, as men take to their little houses of bricks and wood. She finds there an infinitely varied society. She knows as little of loneliness as she does of fear. Owls and cuckoos answer her call.

VIII. Yet she does not live in the spiritual world as a spirit, in the nature world as a bird. These worlds do not make the world of men and women an unsubstantial thing to her; she is in it and of it. She shares the weaknesses of the world; she yields to fatigue, and irony, and anger. She sees in our world, too, her true sphere of action. She is the friend of the unbefriended, meeting them on the ground of their own needs, spending herself without stint to help and strengthen them. She would mould this world of ours if she could, nay, break it and recast it. She has equipped herself for it. She has made her brain a keen sword, and kept it sharp. She is a fighter in our human battle-ground, clear in the choice of ends, relentless in the pursuit, not sparing the men and women who wince at the defiance of custom, or the exposure of their own cherished opinions. A champion of God, smiting without hesitation, without fear, without even sober self-retreating.

IX. She is a bringer of discomfort, so men think, and rightly think. If the spiritual world and the nature world are the background of her life, they are nevertheless a background always present. The scent of them hangs about her, and it brings a challenge with it. It is the challenge of the open air to the house with shut windows.

X. I cannot define the beauty of the clean soul. I cannot even define the beauty of the face and body which are the garment of the clean soul. I cannot separate, even in thought, the woman from the form of the woman. Her unflinching eyes, the virginal simplicity of the outline of the face, pure and grave and austere, the straight lithe body, the small but shapely limbs – I see them all as the inevitable expression of the clean soul – perfectly right, far too much loved to be admired.

XI. To think that I should have been singled out for the honour of living ten years with such a woman, and yet should have been so dull, so blind, so slow to see her as she was; that I should have proved myself ungrateful, that I should have failed in forethought and in sympathy even at the moments when she was suffering agony of body and minds!

XII. She has shared my life, from the highest things to the lowest; shared my work and my pleasures. We have adapted ourselves to one another's ways, and formed a home together. She has longed, equally with me, to have children of our own, hers and mine, mine and hers. She has born them to me, in anguish and in peril. My blood has been mingled with hers, my inheritance of gifts and powers has been united to hers, in the creation of lovely forms of children. Yes, my blood has been mingled with hers, irrevocably; perhaps to flow on, and on, into the coming time.

XIII. At times it comes to me with a shock, that I might have missed all this. It was only slowly and with dim eyes that I saw my opportunity. But I did see, surely and clearly at last, the one woman of the world for me, and clung to her and demanded her. Yes, on the bridge over the swirling Thames, and again in the woods of Madingley amid the hyacinthine sea of blue-bells, and once more in the spacious library with the bright fire and the long low arm-chair, I told her I would have her for my comrade, mind and spirit, flesh and blood. Words stuck in my throat, and she thought me cold; she knows I was not, now.

XIV. I was slow to fall in love with her, but I have never been out of love these ten years. I have busied myself with many things, and sometimes for days together I have never thought of her, but when I thought of her I was in love with her. Both of us know today, as we knew ten years ago for the first time, the hard embrace of youth and maid, the embrace that will not part, that cannot be close enough. Now indeed that embrace is the symbol of a hundred, a thousand other ties that have grown up around it in the changing years, grown up around it and made the parting for ever impossible.

XV. She had changed and grown. Her familiar face was not the same after she had born her first child. There was in it the fulfilment of something destined to be, the coming of maturity, the wisdom of the depths and heights. She was changed, too, by the long wave-tossed wandering, the fearless threading of the tangled mazes of thought, which led her to the knowledge of God.

XVI. Have I helped her? Yes – why not claim it? She was living in a smaller world when I found her; her intensity of desire and aspiration beating against narrow limits. There was too little choice of direction; she might have chosen a path that would have proved a by-way, and pursued it as if it had been the grand highway of the world. My sweetest thoughts are when I think that it was I who brought her into a wider place, and showed her untried paths, and a multitude of new faces – blessing them as well as her.

XVII. If anyone should ask, in days to come, how I lived my life with her, whether wisely or no, whether kindly or no, let this be said of me – that at least I saw with ever clearer vision what manner of woman it was that I had found; that I knew the blessedness I had inherited; that while I hailed in her one of the world's saints, yet I did not fall down and worship her, nor place her in a shrine apart, but daringly claimed her as my comrade, and lived with her the life of comrades; that together we created a home; that so seeing, so living, so creating, I drank deep at the wells of happiness; that I demanded of life greater things than other men demand, and was not disappointed.

Bibliography
for use with the footnotes

Anderson   Mosa Anderson, *Noel Buxton: A Life*, George Allen & Unwin, London, 1952

Angell   Norman Angell, *After All*, Hamish Hamilton, London, 1951

BB1   Ben Buxton, 'A real national movement', in *The Friend*, 21 May 1999, pp. 4–5

BB2   Ben Buxton, 'Dorothy Buxton's long crusade for social justice', in *Cambridge: Magazine of the Cambridge Society*, v. 50 (2002) pp. 74–75

Beaumont   Katherine Bentley Beaumont, *Women and the Settlement Movement*, Radcliffe Press, London, 1996

Booth   Charles Booth, *Life and Labour of the People in London, Volume 6*, Macmillan, London, 1902

CC1905   C. Dunkley (editor) *The Official Report of the Church Congress, Held at Weymouth . . . 1905*, Bemrose & Sons, London 1905

CC1906   C. Dunkley (editor) *The Official Report of the Church Congress, Held at Barrow . . . 1906*, Bemrose & Sons, London 1906

CRB1   Charles Roden Buxton, *Electioneering Up-to-Date*, Francis Griffiths, London, 1906

CRB2   Charles Roden Buxton (editor) *The Secret Agreements*, National Labour Press, Manchester, 1918

CRB3   Charles Roden Buxton (editor) *Towards a Lasting Settlement*, George Allen & Unwin, London, 1915

CRB4   Charles Roden Buxton and Noel Buxton, *The War and the Balkans*, George Allen & Unwin, London, 1915

CRB5   Charles Roden Buxton and Dorothy Frances Buxton, *The World after the War*, George Allen & Unwin, London, 1920

CRB6   Charles Roden Buxton, *In a Russian Village*, Labour Publishing Company, London, 1922

DFB1   Dorothy Buxton, *The Challenge of Bolshevism: A New Social Ideal*, George Allen & Unwin, London, 1928

NRB4   Noel Buxton, *Travels and Reflections*, George Allen & Unwin, London, 1929

Clarke   Peter Clarke, *Liberals and Social Democrats*, CUP, Cambridge, 1978

De Bunsen   Victoria de Bunsen, *Charles Roden Buxton: A Memoir*, George Allen & Unwin, London, 1948

Florence   P. Sargent Florence & J R L Anderson (editors) *C K Ogden: A Memoir*, Elek Pemberton, London, 1977

Fry   Michael G. Fry, *Lloyd George and Foreign Policy, Volume 1*, McGill-Queen's University Press, Montreal, 1977

Grey   Edward Grey, Viscount Grey of Fallodon, *Twenty-five Years 1892–1916, Volume 2*, Hodder & Stoughton, London, 1925

Hamilton   Mary Agnes Hamilton, *Remembering My Good Friends*, Jonathan Cape, London, 1944

Hammond   Mary Hammond & Shafquat Towheed, *Publishing in the First World War*, Palgrave Macmillan, Basingstoke, 2007

Harris   Sally Harris, *Out of Control*, University of Hull Press, Hull, 1996

Jones   Raymond A Jones, *Arthur Ponsonby: The Politics of Life*, Christopher Helm, London, 1989

Lockhart   J.G. Lockhart, *Cosmo Gordon Lang*, Hodder & Stoughton, London, 1949

Mahood   Linda Mahood, *Feminism and Voluntary Action*, Palgrave Macmillan, Basingstoke, 2009

Marlor   Duncan Marlor, *Fatal Fortnight*, Frontline Books, London, 2014

Masterman   C.F.G. Masterman, *The Condition of England*, Methuen, London, 1909

MCM   *Morley College Magazine*

Mottram   R.H. Mottram, *Buxton the Liberator*, Hutchinson & Co, London, 1946

Mulley   Clare Mulley, *The Woman who Saved the Children*, Oneworld, Oxford, 2009

Richards   Denis Richards, *Offspring of the Vic*, Routledge, London, 1958

Russell   G.W.E. Russell, *Lady Victoria Buxton*, Longmans, Green and Co, London, 1919

Swartz   Marvin Swartz, *The Union of Democratic Control in British Politics during the First World War*, Clarendon Press, Oxford, 1971

Weaver   Stewart A Weaver, *The Hammonds: A Marriage in History*, Stanford UP, Stanford, CA, 1997

Wilson   Francesca Wilson, *Rebel Daughter of a Country House*, George Allen and Unwin, London, 1967

Woolf3   Leonard Woolf, *Beginning Again: An Autobiography of the Years 1911–1918*, Hogarth Press, London, 1964

Woolf4   Leonard Woolf, *Downhill All the Way: An Autobiography of the Years 1919–1939*, Hogarth Press, London, 1967

Wright   Patrick Wright, *Iron Curtain: From Stage to Cold War*, OUP, Oxford, 2007

Index